Oscar Browning

The Flight to Varennes

Oscar Browning

The Flight to Varennes

ISBN/EAN: 9783337251444

Printed in Europe, USA, Canada, Australia, Japan

Cover: Foto ©ninafisch / pixelio.de

More available books at **www.hansebooks.com**

THE FLIGHT TO VARENNES

And other Historical Essays

BY

OSCAR BROWNING

London
SWAN SONNENSCHEIN & CO.
PATERNOSTER SQUARE
1892

ADVERTISEMENT.

The greater part of these essays have been reprinted from various periodicals, with the kind permission of the Editors.

To

HENRY SIDGWICK

THIS BOOK IS DEDICATED BY

HIS AFFECTIONATE FRIEND

THE AUTHOR.

CONTENTS.

	PAGE
I. THE FLIGHT TO VARENNES	1
II. A CRITICISM ON CARLYLE'S ACCOUNT OF THE FLIGHT TO VARENNES	52
III. THE FOREIGN POLICY OF WILLIAM PITT	77
IV. THE COMMERCIAL TREATY OF 1786	132
V. THE TRIPLE ALLIANCE OF 1788	148
VI. ENGLAND AND FRANCE IN 1793	170
VII. HUGH ELLIOT AT NAPLES	202
VIII. HUGH ELLIOT AT BERLIN	237
IX. QUEEN CAROLINE OF NAPLES	260
X. REPUBLICAN GOVERNMENT	325

I.

THE FLIGHT TO VARENNES.

IT is now many years ago since the late Mr. Croker published in the *Quarterly Review* his well-known account of the journey of King Louis XVI. to Varennes, and of the Comte de Provence, afterwards Louis XVIII. to Brussels.[1] His narrative was founded mainly upon the "Mémoires sur l'Affaire de Varennes," then lately published in Brussels, which contained the relations of Comte Louis de Bouillé, of MM. de Raigecourt and De Damas, and of Captain Deslon, to which was added the evidence of the courier Valory. The apologies of the Marquis de Bouillé, and of the Duc de Choiseul, with the accompanying documents, had been printed the year before. Fourteen years later, Carlyle published his history of the French Revolution. The second volume of this work contains some chapters upon the Flight to Varennes, which are the most exciting portions of the whole work. Carlyle's narrative, which has been accepted as the standard English account of this momentous occurrence, is unfortu-

---

[1] This article was reprinted, with additions, in Mr. Croker's "Essays on the Early Period of the French Revolution," pp. 105, foll. London, 1857.

nately both inaccurate and untrustworthy from beginning to end.[1] Had Carlyle read Croker's article in the *Quarterly Review*, he could not have possibly made the gross mistakes into which he falls. For instance, he reckons the distance from Varennes to Paris at sixty-nine miles, which Croker had already placed accurately at a hundred and fifty; he consequently makes the Royal travellers travel at a snail's pace instead of going as they actually did at a very reasonable rate. He relies implicitly upon the narrative of Choiseul, which Croker had already shown to be an apology for misbehaviour, and consequently untrustworthy. He applies no criticism to the narrative of Bouillé, who was equally anxious to excuse himself, and to throw the blame on others, and he accepts without question the foolish gossip of Madame Campan. He does not even take the pains to read with accuracy the authorities with which he was acquainted. It is not, however, our present purpose to criticise Carlyle, but to gather from the new authorities, which have been published since the appearance of his work, a trustworthy account of one of the most thrilling episodes in all history, whether it be regarded in its incidents or its results. This episode, which is fortunately known in all its details, is far more impressive in its naked truth than it ever could be in the most imaginative fiction.

After the arrest of the Royal family, the chief actors in the flight were sent for trial to Orleans,

---

[1] An examination of Carlyle's narrative in detail is appended to the present essay.

where they underwent a searching examination. A full account of this evidence was published with facsimiles by M. Bimbenet in 1843, and republished by him in 1868. In 1866 M. Ancelon published "La Vérité sur la fuite et l'arrestation de Louis XVI. à Varennes, d'après des documents inédits." This work contains portions of the diary of Madame de Tourzel, who accompanied the Royal family. In the fifth volume of "Revue des Questions Historiques" (1868), M. Victor Fournel submitted the evidence available at that time to a searching analysis.[1] In 1874 the Abbé Gabriel published at Verdun, "Louis XVI., le Marquis de Bouillé et Varennes," the best narrative of the occurrences which had appeared up to that date. Before this, the "Procès verbaux" of the principal towns concerned in the matter, of Châlons, St. Ménehould, Clermont, and Varennes, had been published either separately, or as appendices to other histories. These accounts, written at the very time of the occurrences, are of the highest value as irrefragable evidence. Lastly, the Memoirs of Madame de Tourzel were published *in extenso* in 1883, while the diary and letters of Count Fersen, published in 1877, although dealing but little with the subject, throw unexpected gleams of light on some of its darkest places. Almost every particular of the event is now discoverable, and it only remains for us to combine these scattered lights into a true and consistent narrative.

---

[1] These articles have recently been republished under the title, "L'Evénement de Varennes," with few additions.

The flight to Varennes was not merely a picturesque and thrilling episode in the French Revolution, it was also a great crisis in European history. Europe at this time was trembling at the approach of Jacobinism. The *émigrés* were beseeching every court, not only to deliver their Sovereign from the durance in which he was placed, but to stamp out a fire which endangered their own security. The Comte d'Artois had formed a plan by which France was to be invaded from several sides, from the south by Spain, from the east by Savoy, from the north by the Austrians. The centre of this combination was the Emperor, Leopold II., who had recently succeeded after the death of his brother Joseph. His position was a difficult one. He had found himself on coming to the throne in alliance with Russia, and at war with Turkey. His Belgian provinces were in revolt, his Hungarian provinces were disturbed. Prussia had concluded an alliance with Turkey, and was threatening war against the Emperor, in which she was not unlikely to have the assistance of England and Holland. To move prematurely in defence of France, or to risk a defeat, might have led to the breaking up of the Austrian dominions. Leopold was uncertain of the attitude of the maritime powers towards the Revolution. If Austria exposed her flank, they might assist Prussia in the attack which she was always ready to make upon her rival. But the king once out of Paris and at the head of an army, the situation would be changed. Louis would then become a nucleus round which the forces of order might rally. By his successful escape

from duress he would have won the sympathies of
Europe. To espouse his cause warmly would be the
path both of honour and of safety. A false report
reached Leopold at Padua that the king had been
rescued by Bouillé, and was safe at Luxemburg. He
wrote immediately to his sister, " The king, the
country, France and all other monarchies will owe
their deliverance to your courage, your firmness, and
prudence. Everything that I have is yours, money,
troops, everything, dispose of it freely." He sent
necessary orders to the Low Countries, he called upon
Sardinia, Spain, Switzerland, Prussia, to take
measures for assisting the King of France. Five
days afterwards the terrible truth was known.

Thus, on the success or failure of the flight, the
action of Austria, and through her of Europe, depended.[1] The king was to go to Montmédy, but he
was not to stop there. A camp was to be formed
round the old château of Thonelle in the neighbourhood. Bouillé's faithful German regiments were to
be joined by a number of *émigrés*, but above all
10,000 Austrian troops were to be massed upon the
frontier near Virton, a few miles off. This was the
kernel of the plan. Unless the Emperor sent his
troops, Bouillé could not be certain of the fidelity of
his soldiers, and he could have no excuse for moving
the regiments which were to serve as a guard to
the king's flight. Once out of Paris the king was a
free agent, he would dissolve the assembly, restore
the clergy to their possessions, and, by thus destroy-

---

[1] Albert Sorel in *Revue des Deux Mondes*, May 15, 1886.

ing the basis on which the value of assignats rested, would cause a bankruptcy in France, and deprive his rebellious subjects of their sources of credit.[1] Escape would be the potent engine of a counter revolution.

The flight of the king from Paris had long been planned and discussed, but it did not assume a definite shape until after April 18, 1791. On that day the king and his family, precisely the same party who started for Varennes, determined to go to St. Cloud, in order that they might perform their Easter devotions with a nonjuring priest. The Royal carriages were not allowed to enter the Cour des Princes; the berline, in which the Royal family were seated, was detained two hours and a quarter in the inner court by the national guard. When the Royal family came back to the Palace, and the soldiers pressed round, declaring their fidelity, the queen answered them haughtily, "Yes, we trust you, but you must allow, at present, that we are not free." The king wished at first to go away in the latter part of May. He could not start before, because he was waiting for a fuller assurance of assistance from Spain, who had not as yet joined the other Powers. Money, however, was urgently necessary. The Emperor had been asked, not only to send his troops to the frontier, but to advance 15 millions of francs for the enterprise. This last demand he refused, and it became necessary to obtain supplies from every avail-

---

[1] Klinckowström's "Comte de Fersen," i. 128. Fersen à Breteuil [wrongly headed Breteuil à Fersen], and Breteuil's Answer, i. 130.

able source. The king was allowed by the Assembly 25 millions of francs, paid by monthly instalments. Two millions of this was due in the first week in June; and, considering the constant demands of Bouillé for supplies, the money could not be dispensed with. So, on May 29, the date of departure was fixed for June 12; the two millions would be paid on the 7th or 8th, but a democratic waiting-maid of the Dauphin did not leave her service till the 11th. Before this proposal could have reached Bouillé, he had already begged that the journey might be put off till the 15th or 20th, in order to give time for the arrival of the Austrian troops at Luxemburg.[1] Sunday evening, June 19, was then agreed upon, but, at the last moment, another waiting-maid of the Dauphin, who could not be trusted, caused the delay of another day. There is no reason for supposing that this change of plan made any difference. Bouillé was still at Metz;[2] he had only to alter the orders already given to the troops, and the sole effect produced was, that Choiseul's horses remained two days at Varennes instead of one.

The most active agent in the preparation for the flight was Count Axel Fersen, commander of the Royal Swedish Regiment in the king's service, and an intimate friend of the king and queen. On the afternoon of Monday he paid a last visit to the Royal

[1] Fersen, i. 132.
[2] Bouillé says in his Memoirs that the news of the delay reached him at Longwy, but the facsimile of his order making the necessary change is given by Bimbenet, and is dated Metz, June 15. He did not leave Metz till June 16.

family in the Tuileries. He found them resolved on departure, notwithstanding the prevalent rumour that their plans for flight had been discovered. They were both deeply affected. The king said, in taking leave of them, that he could never forget all that he had done for him. The queen wept bitterly. To avoid suspicion, she drove out with her children to the gardens called Tivoli, and told her daughter while there that she must practise discretion, and not be surprised at anything she might see or hear.[1] Fersen then returned to his own house to make his final preparations: he visited the hotel of Mr. Quentin Craufurd in the Rue de Clichy, then occupied by Craufurd's mistress, Mrs. Sullivan, to see whether the new coach built for the king's journey had arrived from the coach-makers. At eight o'clock, having come home again, he wrote to the queen to alter the arrangements he had made for meeting the two servants who were to accompany the flight. As he took the letter to the Tuileries he found everything quiet. At a quarter to nine, the three body-guards who were to act as outriders to the royal party, came to Fersen for instructions. Once more he came back to his house, sent off a chaise which was to convey the two waiting-maids to Claye, gave his last orders to his coachman, Balthasar Sapel, and then mounted the box of the hackney-coach which was to convey the Royal family to the barrier.[2]

The queen returned from her drive at seven

---

[1] Relation de la Duchesse d'Angoulême, p. 4.
[2] See Fersen's diary in his Life, i. 2.

o'clock. She then submitted herself to one of those elaborate feats of hair-dressing which excite our wonder in the portraits of the time. This process lasted more than an hour, after which she had an interview with the three body-guards, who were to accompany her flight. Passing to her drawing-room, she found the Comte de Provence, who had just taken an affecting leave of his sister Elizabeth. He had come with his wife to supper, according to his custom every evening, from his residence in his palace of the Luxemburg. The supper was served at nine, and lasted nearly two hours. Monsieur and his wife were to leave Paris that night by different roads. They did not know whether they should join the king at Montmédy, or should ever see him again. The brothers, indeed, then met for the last time. Monsieur left the Tuileries never again to enter it, except as Louis XVIII., in 1814. After supper the queen dismissed her servants as soon as possible. She went to bed, or appeared to do so, and the attendant shut the door of the passage leading to her room.

The Dauphin, on returning from Tivoli, had eaten his supper and had been put to bed at nine o'clock. Madame retired an hour later, after having given orders to be called at eight the next morning. About eleven o'clock the queen knocked at the door of her son's room. He was fast asleep, but when she told him he was to go to a fortress, where he would command his regiment, he threw himself out of bed, and cried, " Quick! quick! give me a sword and my boots, and let me be off." He was dressed like a little girl, in a costume which Madame de Tourzel had already provided. His sister, who had been awakened earlier, wore a cheap dress of muslin, which had been bought a few days before for about three-and-sixpence. A piece of it still exists at Orleans, and M. Bimbenet has given a coloured drawing of it. The two children, with their governess and the two waiting-maids, who were to accompany the royal party, met in one of the queen's apartments. The queen looked out into the courtyard, and saw that everything was quiet. The hackney-coach was standing close by the door, in the farthest corner, by which it had been arranged that the Royal family should escape. Fersen, who had made every preparation with skill and rapidity, sat dressed like a coachman on the box. This door led to the apartments of the Duc de Villequier; since he had emigrated to Brussels, it was but little used, and had been left unguarded. The queen solemnly entrusted her children to Madame de Tourzel. They passed through unknown passages to the unlocked door, and then out into the court. Fersen lifted the children into the coach, gave his hand to Madame de Tourzel, and drove off. A short time afterwards the two waiting maids were told by the queen that they were to drive to Claye. They passed down another staircase, left the courtyard of the Tuileries by the passage Marignan, and found a cabriolet waiting for them at the other end of the Pont Royal. There their unknown guide left them. They entered the carriage and drove off to Claye. Fersen, knowing that the rest of his party could not arrive immediately took a turn round the quays, and returned by the

Rue St. Honoré to the Petit Carrousel, where he waited near the house formerly occupied by the Duchesse de Vallière.[1] For at least three-quarters of an hour no one came. Lafayette's carriage, guarded by dragoons, drove up with flashing lights. The Dauphin, alarmed, hid himself in his governess's dress. Lafayette was on his way to the *coucher* of the king. He held him for a long time in conversation, for grave suspicions had been aroused. On that very afternoon the Royal family had doubted whether it was wise to undertake the enterprise, as the news of their intention had got abroad. The guards had been doubled; everybody was on the alert. About half-past eleven Lafayette at last drove away. The king was seen to bed by the servant who had charge of his rooms. The doors of the great gallery were locked by the porter in attendance, and the keys were placed in his mattress, where they were found the next morning undisturbed. As soon as he was alone the king got up and dressed himself for the flight.

The hackney coach had been waiting in the Petit Carrousel three-quarters of an hour. At last a lady was seen approaching it. It was Madame Elizabeth alone. Her attendant had left her as soon as she was in sight of the carriage. Not long after came the king. Madame de Tourzel tells us, that the king said that he had left the Tuileries alone by the great gate, and that his shoe-buckle having become loose,

---

[1] Madame de Tourzel, i. 300, and Journal and Correspondence of Lord Auckland, iii. 512.

he had stopped to arrange it with all the coolness in the world.¹ The party were now all assembled except the queen. They waited for her some little time, perhaps a quarter of an hour, but probably not more than five minutes, and it may have been during this period of time that Lafayette's carriage passed a second time, and that the king recognising him called out, "You wretch," loud enough for Fersen to hear.² The story of the queen losing herself in the Rue de Bac is quite apocryphal, but there are two credible reasons given for a short delay. One, that leaving the palace last, she had unexpectedly found a sentinel on the top of the staircase by which she was to descend, and the other, which she told Fersen on his visit to Paris in February, 1792, that passing the Great Carrousel her conductor did not know where the Little Carrousel was, and at her suggestion, asked one of the horse-guards who was posted near. When she got into the carriage, the king embraced her, and cried, "How glad I am to see you here."

For some reason, Fersen did not drive straight to the barrier of St. Martin. He went down the Rue St. Honoré till he reached the external boulevard, drove along it to the Rue de Clichy, and so on to the barrier. The guard-house was lighted up. Every one was *en fête*. A marriage was being cele-

---

¹ Madame de Tourzel, i. 307. The well-informed narrator in Auckland, iii. 453 (perhaps Quentin Craufurd), says that the king was "followed at some distance by one of the *gardes des corps*."

² Auckland, loc. cit.

brated with dancing and drinking, but the royal party were not recognised. Just beyond the gate they found the berline, a large travelling-carriage, made to hold six people, which had been specially built for them. It was drawn by four strong Norman horses. Fersen's coachman, Balthasar Sapel, was riding one of the horses, M. de Moustier, a tall body-guard, was on the box. M. de Malden, a second body-guard, had already conducted the king or queen, or both of them, from the Tuileries to the Petit Carrousel, and had ridden in a dicky behind the hackney coach. M. de Valory, a third body-guard, was spurring on one of Fersen's horses towards Bondy, in order that the relays might be ready when the travellers arrived. The hackney coach was driven up close to the travelling carriage. The doors of both were open, so that it was possible to step from one to the other. The whole party was transferred, and the hackney coach having served its purpose, was tumbled into a ditch. Fersen mounted the box, and sat by the side of Moustier. He called out to his coachman, "Get along quick, drive as fast as possible." It was now two o'clock in the morning, and the dawn was already breaking in the east. The carriage had been waiting at the barrier for two hours, and valuable time had been lost. Fersen appeared conscious of this. He cracked his whip and called out, "Quick, Balthasar, your horses are out of breath; go faster," and the coachman urged his roadsters, thinking that his master might kill his own horses if he pleased. Sapel says that they reached Bondy in half an hour, 3 leagues or $7\frac{1}{2}$ miles distant. At any rate they went a good pace. Here they found Valory with a new relay of six horses standing ready in the road. Fersen, after begging earnestly to be allowed to accompany the royal party, took an affectionate farewell. Happy would it have been if the king had granted his request. He leaped upon his horse, from which Valory had just dismounted, and rode by a cross road to Le Bourget. He left during the morning for Mons, where he arrived in safety.[1]

It has been commonly said, that the carriage in which the Royal family travelled was a lumbering coach conspicuous by its form and splendour. This is quite erroneous. It was a solid well-built travelling carriage. We possess a full description of it in the bill of Louis, the coachmaker who made it, and with little difficulty every detail of its construction could be recovered.[2] The body was painted black and green, the perch under the carriage and the wheels the customary yellow. Madame de Tourzel tells us that there was nothing remarkable about it,[3] and the minutes of the town council of Ste. Ménehould, which give an account of Drouet's exploit, make precisely the same remark. It attracted no attention in itself, and an older carriage would probably have broken down several times on the road.

At Claye, the next post, the waiting-maids were overtaken, and the whole party proceeded in the full daylight to Meaux. The king was full of spirits.

---

[1] Fersen, i. 2.   [2] Bimbenet, "Pièces justificatives," 144.
[3] Tourzel, i. 311.

At last he said, "I have escaped from that town of Paris where I have drunk so much bitterness; be assured that once in the saddle I shall be very different from what you have seen me up to the present moment." He read out loud the long memoir which he had left behind him to be presented to the assembly. He anticipated the happiness with which he would endow France, the return of his brothers and of his faithful servants, and the possibility of re-establishing the Catholic religion, and repairing the evils of which he had been the unwilling cause. At about eight o'clock he looked at his watch and said, "Lafayette is now in a terrible fix."[1] It has been said that the king

---

[1] Tourzel, i. 312. We give in a table the approximate distances between Paris to Varennes, and the probable time at which the Royal family arrived at each place.

	Miles.	Arrive at.
Paris to Bondy	6	3 a.m.
Bondy to Claye	10	4.30 a.m.
Claye to Meaux	10	6 a.m.
Meaux to La Ferté sous Jouarre	12	7.30 a.m.
La Ferté to Montmirail	20	10 a.m.
Montmirail to Etoges	17	noon.
Etoges to Chantrix	13	2 p.m.
Chantrix to Châlons.	13	5 p.m. {allowing for the break-down.
Châlons to Pont-Sommevesle	14	6.30 p.m.
Pont-Sommevesle to Ste. Ménehould	15	8 p.m.
Ste. Ménehould to Clermont	10	9.30 p.m.
Clermont to Varennes	10	11 p.m.
Total	150 miles	21 hours.

walked up the hills, "enjoying the blessed sunshine," and generally conducting himself imprudently. As a fact there was very little sunshine to be enjoyed, for the day, although the longest in the year, was a dull one.[1] The king only left the berline once during the journey, and then spoke to no one. The travellers were amply supplied with provisions, and took all they needed in the carriage. The children walked up one or two of the long hills, but caused no delay.[2] Between Chantrix and Châlons the horses twice fell down, and broke the harness. This took an hour to repair, but, as far as we know, the carriage stood well. Châlons was reached at about five o'clock in the afternoon, at least two hours late. an hour or more had been lost in leaving Paris, and an hour by the accident. As it was, the royal party had travelled more than seven miles an hour, including stoppages, and that was a very good pace.

Nothing has been more misrepresented than the slowness of the royal journey. Carlyle says that they travelled sixty-nine miles in twenty-two hours, "slower than the slowest dray rate." From Paris to Châlons is at least one hundred and fifty miles, and twenty-three hours is the very utmost that can be allowed for the journey, including all accidents and all stoppages. Twenty-one hours would be nearer the mark. This gives the rate of over seven miles

---

[1] Comte de Provence's Narrative, p. 70. "The sun which had not before appeared during the whole day, now displayed himself." This was quite towards evening.

[2] Tourzel, 310.

an hour for the whole journey, whereas travellers of those days often did not exceed three or four miles, and did not consider themselves aggrieved if they were detained several hours by an accident.[1]

At last the town of Châlons-sur-Marne was safely reached. The king believed that this point once passed all danger was at an end. At the first post along the road a detachment of Bouillé's army would be met, the precursor of many others, who would envelop the king and protect him safely to his frontier fortress. The horses were changed at the Châlons post-house, at the end of the town near the eastern gate; and tradition says that, as they were starting off, the team fell badly and again broke the harness: a presage of evil omen for their success. On they fared, passed the triumphal arch which had greeted Marie Antoinette on her arrival as Dauphine, past the Pilgrimage Church of our Lady of the Thorn with its miraculous well, past the road leading from Rheims, the city of the coronation, till in a deep and and solitary valley they reached the lonely post-house of Pont-Sommevesle, where the promised succour was to be met. Not a soldier was to be seen. Where was Choiseul? Where were the Lauzun hussars? The king felt as if an abyss had opened beneath his feet. The horses were quickly changed, and the berline

---

[1] Fersen, i. 130. The diary of Essex, the architect, read before the Cambridge Antiquarian Society, March 15, 1886, says that he travelled between Calais and Dunkirk, August 20, 1773, with six horses, at the rate of nearly three miles and a half an hour, baiting the horses every six miles.

rattled on; but a heavy weight was on the travellers' hearts, which foreboded a coming calamity.

In the correspondence between Bouillé and the king there had always been talk of an escort. One reason why Bouillé had been made acquainted so early with the king's plans was because his command extended over so large a part of France, and he had so wide a discretion over the movements of troops. Lately, however, his command had been curtailed, and the Minister of War had intimated that troops were not to be moved without his authority. It is a mistake to place the fault of having an escort to the account of the king. Just before the flight we find Bouillé writing to Fersen, that he is to take great care about the security of the road as far as Châlons. Fersen replies, that it is not necessary to take any precautions between Paris and Châlons, that the best course is to take none, and that Bouillé would be wise to place soldiers nowhere on the Paris side of Varennes unless he can thoroughly trust them, for soldiers will create suspicion, which it is their first object to avoid. Still Bouillé is to be credited with the masterly skill, with which he arranged that his troops should be passing through the towns on the king's line of journey, just at the time when they seemed to be preparing for military movements to repulse the Austrians who were approaching the frontier. The means by which this was effected, and the details of the military operations, will require a fuller explanation.

The regiment of Royal Allemand, on which Bouillé could count better than on any other, was posted at Stenay, a little town on the Meuse, ten miles from Montmédy, and about half-way between Sedan and Verdun. On the day of the king's flight about fifty troopers of the Royal Allemand were sent in advance to Mouzay, a village a short distance from Stenay on the road to Dun. At the beginning of June two squadrons of the Lauzun hussars, each 100 strong, had been despatched from Toul to the frontier of the Meuse. A squadron and a half (150 men) were to remain in barracks at Dun, where there was a bridge over the Meuse which the king must pass. The remaining half squadron, fifty strong, were sent to Varennes. But on the pretext of the barracks of Dun being too small, the numbers of soldiers at Varennes were increased to about one hundred. Two other regiments appeared to Bouillé to be trustworthy; the Royal Dragoons, commanded by the Duc de Choiseul, and the Monsieur dragoons, commanded by the Comte de Damas. The bulk of these regiments had been removed by order of the Minister of War, against Bouillé's wish, into Alsace, but the depôts, consisting of some of the best troops, remained behind. These Bouillé ordered to march to Mouzon, a town on the Meuse between Stenay and Sedan. On the way they were to rest two days at Clermont, and to despatch a squadron of forty men to Ste. Ménehould, on the pretext of escorting a treasure. Thus, with the specious appearance of guarding the Meuse fortress, Bouillé contrived to collect troops in the various towns through which the king's flight was to take place.

The two squadrons of dragoons, 290 men and 250

horses, forming one column under the command of Monsieur de Damas, the contingent of Royal dragoons being under the command of Captain d'Andoins, arrived at Clermont on the morning of Monday, June 20. They were quartered in the town, with the exception of forty men, under the command of Captain St. Didier, who were lodged at Auzéville, a village a mile and a half distant. Scarcely had the inhabitants of Clermont recovered from the excitement of their arrival, when forty Lauzun hussars, wearing bear-skins with red caps, halted in the square of the town. Monsieur de Goguelat, an officer possessing the confidence of the king and queen, had been sent by them to Bouillé to help him in making the last arrangements. The choice was unfortunate, because of the blunderers in this affair none was so bad as Goguelat. He disobeyed the most important orders that were given him, and everything left to his discretion was badly done.[1] Goguelat, starting from Montmédy, had reached Varennes on Sunday evening. On Monday morning he took with him forty out of the 100 Lauzun hussars who were quartered at Varennes. Their orders were to pass through Clermont to Ste. Ménehould, to proceed the next morning to Pont-Sommevesle, to await the king's arrival, or, as they were told, to escort an expected treasure. The officer in command of the detachment

---

[1] Yet the king and queen trusted him and forgave him after the failure of the flight. Bouillé specially asked for him, and Fersen writes of him to Bouillé: "C'est un homme sûr, il ne faut que le modérer."—Fersen, i. 129.

was Lieutenant Boudet, but the troops were under the general direction of Goguelat. On arriving at Clermont, Goguelat found Damas and the other officers breakfasting in the Hôtel St. Nicholas. He delivered the verbal order which he had received from Bouillé, that the dragoons were to be saddled the following day at five o'clock in the afternoon. After luncheon, Goguelat rode on to Ste. Ménehould, distant about ten miles. His soldiers were not to be billeted upon the population, but were to lodge in public-houses in the town. He therefore saw no need to inform the municipality of his arrival, or to sound his trumpets on entering as was the usual custom. This caused great irritation. Ste. Ménehould was strongly affected by the patriotic fever. A national guard had been formed there, but it had not been armed. The irregular entry of the troops was resented by the population, and when they left the next morning for Pont-Sommevesle they were hissed.

At daybreak on Tuesday morning Lagache, a quarter-master of the Royal dragoons, was sent by Damas to Ste. Ménehould to prepare a lodging for thirty-three men and horses, who were to escort the so-called treasure on its arrival from Pont-Sommevesle. He found quarters in an inn looking on the great square and on the magnificent Hôtel de Ville built in 1740, not far from the post-house established in 1788, and kept by Drouet.[1] At about nine o'clock, just after the departure of the hussars, a sound of trumpets was heard on the side of the forest road.

---

[1] There is a plan of Ste. Ménehould in M. Ancelon's book.

Captain d'Andoins, who was in command of the troop, being warned by Lagache, took care to sound his trumpets, and to inform the municipality of his arrival. He drew up his soldiers in the great square, reported himself to the mayor and was well received. This completed the chain of Bouillé's guard, which extended in unbroken series from Pont-Sommevesle to Montmédy. What had caused the desertion of the first link in the chain? how was it that the king on arriving at the post-house, where he felt certain of his escort, had found no one to meet him?

The Duke de Choiseul, commander of the Royal dragoons, had been sent by Bouillé from Metz, in order to give the king the last information about the preparations for the flight. Fersen expressed at the time a doubt as to whether he was the best instrument for the purpose.[1] Although devoted to the cause of the king, he was frivolous and hasty, and had not that spirit of calm patience and decision which was needed in the difficult crisis. However, he was very rich and of high rank, was colonel of a distinguished regiment, and was able to furnish from his own stables the relays which were needed for the royal party at Varennes. It was arranged that Choiseul should leave Paris ten hours before the king. At two in the afternoon the queen sent to him her private hairdresser, Léonard. Choiseul took

---

[1] Fersen writes to Bouillé: "Tâchez, s'il est possible, de ne pas envoyer le Duc de Choiseul ici; personne n'est sans doute plus attaché, mais c'est un jeune homme, un brouillon, je crains quelque indiscrétion . . . Renvoyez plutôt Goguelat."—Fersen, i. 136.

Léonard with him in his carriage without telling him where he was going. They slept at Montmirail, left that town at four the next morning, and arrived at the post-house of Pont-Sommevesle soon after eleven. Choiseul found his orderly there with two horses. He went upstairs to put on his uniform. The hussars had not arrived, but they appeared an hour later. Monsieur de Goguelat, who commanded them, found Choiseul still dressing, and delivered to him a large packet of orders, which he had received two days before from Bouillé. Choiseul picketed his horses, and gave bread and wine to the hussars. The orders given by Goguelat to Choiseul were very precise. He was placed in command of all the troops posted along the road, having full liberty to employ force, if he though it best to do so. If he should hear that the king had been arrested at Châlons, he was to attack the town and to attempt a rescue. In this case he was to despatch orders along the line, so that he might be supported. When the king arrived at Pont-Sommevesle, Choiseul was to await his orders. If the king desired to be recognised, the hussars were to escort him with drawn swords to Ste. Méne-hould. If the king wished to remain incognito, he was to allow him to pass quietly, but half-an-hour afterwards was to follow him along the road, and was to post a body of hussars between Ste. Méne-hould and Clermont, who were to remain there for fifteen hours, and intercept every one who came either on horseback or in carriage from the direction of Paris. This would effectually prevent the king being pursued. Further, as soon as he became aware that the king was at hand, Choiseul was to send M. Goguelat to inform the several detachments, or, if this was impossible, he was to carry the news himself. Choiseul did none of the things that were expected of him. By some strange miscalculation, it had been said that the berline was expected to arrive at Pont-Sommevesle at half-past two in the afternoon at latest, supposing that the Royal family left Paris punctually at midnight. This would allow a pace of eight miles an hour, including all stoppages, and without any accidents. A courier, Choiseul says in his defence, was to precede the Royal carriage by an hour; therefore, when three o'clock and four o'clock arrived, and neither courier nor carriage was to be seen, Choiseul began to be very anxious. He tells us that the peasants of a neighbouring village, which are believed to be those of Courtisols, were assembling in a threatening attitude, thinking that the hussars were come to make them pay their rents. At four o'clock, therefore, he sends off Léonard, the hairdresser, in his own post-chaise, telling him to inform the detachments, that he feared the travellers would not pass that day; in short, that the whole scheme had probably collapsed. He asserts that after this he waited another hour, and finally, at about half-past five or a quarter to six, retreated with his hussars slowly on the road to Orbeval. Unfortunately, the account of the Duc de Choiseul, which has been so often followed, is the nature of a personal exculpation, and cannot be received as evidence. Two things we know for certain—that the Royal travellers found the road between Châlons and Pont-

Sommevesle absolutely quiet and deserted; they heard no news of any troops, or of any disturbance among the peasantry; and that if Choiseul had really remained at Pont-Sommevesle till a quarter to six, and then marched slowly towards Orbeval, the berline which arrived at Pont-Sommevesle between six and half-past must inevitably have caught him up. We do not know when Choiseul left Pont-Sommevesle, but we do know that he entirely lost his head.[1]

It is also certain that Choiseul ought in any case to have waited for the courier Valory. Valory had been ordered, in case the king should not reach Bondy before 3.30 a.m., to ride along the road to Montmédy, and to inform the detachments that the enterprise had failed. Choiseul's neglect to wait for Valory in any case, whether preceding the king or not, was quite inexcusable.

Valory, on arriving at Pont-Sommevesle, found the post deserted, and asked no questions of the post-master. He left money to pay for a glass of brandy for each of the post-boys, and had the new horses brought out into the road. He then mounted a fresh steed, and galloped towards Ste. Ménehould. What had happened in that town since the morning? D'Andoins had been there with his thirty-three dragoons since nine o'clock. They were ordered to remain saddled all day, ready to march at any moment. At five in the afternoon D'Andoins walked out on the road to Pont-Sommevesle, but saw no-

---

[1] We know that he was at Neuville-au-Pont at a little before eight.

thing. Shortly afterwards Léonard, the hairdresser, arrived with Choiseul's message, that the treasure would probably not pass that day. The dragoons saw their colonel's carriage pass with his servant, whom they recognised. Lagache, who was probably in the secret of the flight, thought it well to test the loyalty of the dragoons by sounding the assembly. Each trooper left his occupation at the call of duty, and stood in due obedience by his charger. D'Andoins, coming up directly afterwards, rebuked Lagache for the rashness of his conduct in collecting the troopers. He was evidently frightened by the responsibility of facing an irritated democracy, and his chief anxiety was to save his own skin at any cost. He ordered the horses to be unsaddled, in spite of Lagache's remonstrances. Scarcely half an hour after this had been done, Valory galloped up, and twenty minutes later the berline rolled towards the post-house.

The arrival of a large and luxurious travelling-coach would cause excitement at any time in a town like Ste. Ménehould; but the town was not in its ordinary condition. The passing of Goguelat's hussars had exasperated the citizens, and the arrival of the dragoons, an hour after the hussars had left, increased their excitement. At about half-past ten in the morning, the inhabitants began to assemble in knots in the streets, and at mid-day a formal request was made to the mayor to deliver to the National Guards, who had been already enrolled, the 300 muskets which had been sent for their use from Châlons. This was immediately done, and it was arranged that the new force should mount guard every evening at eight o'clock. Valory tells us that Ste. Ménehould was the first town on the road where he saw the National Guards in uniform. When the large travelling-coach arrived with its outriders and post-chaise, although it was not specially remarkable in itself, it naturally attracted attention. The dragoons, unfortunately separated from their horses, drew up in front of the hostelry of the Golden Sun to gaze at it. Some of them saluted the travellers, as a mark of respect, not knowing who they were, and the queen graciously returned their salutation. D'Andoins kept in the background as much as possible, but he had time to whisper to those in the carriage, "Your plans are badly laid; I will go away to avoid suspicion." He also made a sign to Valory to harness quickly, but Valory interpreted this as a wish to speak to him, and their conversation roused the attention of the crowd. Just as the fresh horses were being harnessed, J. B. Drouet, the post-master, arrived from a field which he had been cultivating in the neighbourhood. The name of it, Malassise, still lives in local tradition. He was a young man of twenty-eight, but had served in the Condé dragoons, and had seen the queen at Versailles. He now thought he recognised her. At this moment the king put his head out of the carriage to speak to Valory or to some one else,[1] and Drouet,

---

[1] At one time the king thought of taking M. de Saint-Priest with him. Fersen says, "Il lui faut en voiture quelqu'un qui puisse parler, si cela était nécessaire."—Fersen, i. 128.

by a sudden inspiration, compared the portrait on the assignat, with which Valory had just paid the relays, with the head of the traveller in the berline, He noticed the long aquiline nose, the short-sighted look, the spotted complexion; and when a message from the Town Council came to ask his opinion, he had no doubt that the berline contained the king and his family. Indeed, the recognition of the king appears to have been made simultaneously by many of the loiterers. Alexandre Dumas relates in his "Route de Varennes" that an old inhabitant of Ste. Ménehould told him that, as a boy, whilst standing at the door of the "Poste aux lettres," the postmaster (not Drouet), cried at the sight of the berline, "Voici le roi et sa famille." The suspicion quickly ran from mouth to mouth; it was increased by the action of the brave Lagache, who, determining that one dragoon at least should do his duty and follow his sovereign, clutched his reins in his teeth, and with a pistol in each hand broke through the opposing crowd, firing a shot as he passed. A man tried to stop him as he rode over the little bridge leaning to the wood, but, on Lagache presenting his second pistol at him, he jumped into the river to save himself. Lagache followed the berline towards Clermont, but with the fatality which accompanied every incident in the flight, he went astray in the wood, and did not reach Clermont till eleven in the night, when the king was already at Varennes.[1] After the berline had passed, D'Andoins

---

[1] Lagache afterwards became General Henri in the service of Napoleon I.

tried to mount his dragoons; but they were detained by the townspeople, who showed so firm a countenance, that, when summoned to disarm, he was not sorry to surrender to the order of the mayor.

Drouet always claimed for himself the merit of having recognised the king, and having followed him at his own risk. The minutes of the Town Council of Ste. Ménehould leave no doubt that he was despatched, together with Guillaume, an officer of the municipality, by the orders of the town, and with the general knowledge and consent of the citizens. Drouet once on his road, D'Andoins and his dragoons disarmed. A message arrived from Neuville-au-Pont, a town about three miles from Ste. Ménehould, to say that eighty hussars from Pont-Sommevesle (fear had doubled their number) had passed through the town a little before eight o'clock: by so small a distance had Choiseul missed the berline. Fearing lest the hussars should intercept Drouet and Guillaume, three citizens, Legay, Lepointe, and Collet, volunteered to follow and protect them. However, as they galloped out of the Clermont gate, the National Guard fired upon them. Collet was killed, and Legay was seriously wounded. A cry arose, "To arms, to arms; we are betrayed! All the muskets available at the town hall were distributed to the populace, even to women. The windows were lighted up, and the town was barricaded on the Clermont side. The tocsin was sounded, and bread was baked all night for the National Guards, who were expected to come in.

In the meantime the king was posting through

one of the most pictureque parts of France, towards Clermont. He passed high above the lovely valley of the Biesme, and through the gorge of Les Islettes, one of the five defiles of the Argonne, unconscious of his fate. At Clermont, Damas did not do his duty much better than Choiseul or D'Andoins. His dragoons had been ordered to mount their horses at five o'clock in the afternoon. He conceived the idea of forming a special corps of thirty troopers to form a guard for the king. From five o'clock in the afternoon these thirty men were drawn up close to the posthouse, ready to start at a moment's notice. With the rest of the troops he intended to follow the king's route, and to stop all travellers from Paris. Two hours passed, and the people began to be uneasy. At half-past seven Léonard, that ill-omened bird of passage, drove by with Choiseul's message, which, however, Damas at first disregarded. Night drew on, and Damas's officers begged him to allow the soldiers to retire to their quarters. At nine o'clock he fatally yielded, and, fearing that the enterprise was at an end, ordered the horses to be unsaddled. Half an hour later the berline arrived. Damas was obliged to excuse himself for not having the escort ready. In ten minutes the new horses were harnessed, and the berline rolled on towards the end of its journey. Unfortunately the courier, who rode on the box of the carriage, called out in a loud voice to the postillions, "Route de Varennes." This was overheard by the postillions of the previous stage, who were returning to Ste. Ménehould. On their way home they met Drouet and Guillaume just outside Clermont, and were able to inform them of the direction the berline had taken. Without this knowledge they would have ridden along the straight road to Verdun. It is painful to think of the number of petty incidents which caused the failure of this momentous enterprise. Damas, being prevented by the people of Clermont from following with his troops, sent one of his quartermasters, Remy, and a few soldiers to follow the [king. They missed the turning to Varennes, and, after riding hard for two hours, found themselves close to Verdun, making the very mistake which Drouet was saved from making. Charles Bouillé, the second son of the marquis, and young Raigecourt, who were awaiting the king's arrival at Varennes, being impatient at his delay, sent an orderly for news. He passed the berline and its outriders at a short distance from the town, but he did not speak to them nor they to him, yet he was in possession of that very information about the position of the relays which would have saved the monarchy of France.

The Royal family arrived at the outskirts of Varennes at about eleven o'clock. Varennes is a little town sloping downwards towards the river Aire with one long narrow street.[1] The traveller as he passes down it first reaches an open square, the Place du Château, where the old seignorial castle once stood. A short distance further will bring him to the Hôtel de Ville and to an open space opposite to it. In 1791 this space was occupied by the church

---

[1] There is a plan of Varennes in Ancelon.

of St. Gengoult, since destroyed. The bell tower of the church stands next to the Hôtel de Ville, and was at that time connected with the main building by a low arch. As he passes down the steep and narrow street, he finds on the right-hand side next to the bell-tower a house which was once the Bras d'Or tavern. A little further, on the opposite side, is the house of M. Sauce, in which the royal family passed the night after their capture. A very short distance brings him to the river, and to the narrow bridge which crosses it. On the other side of the bridge is a large square with a church in the centre. Facing the church, at the angle nearest the bridge, is the Hôtel du Grand Monarque, little changed during the last hundred years. It was here that the relays were stabled, and that Charles Bouillé and Raigecourt awaited the arrival of the king. From the door of the Grand Monarque, two roads diverge, one to Verdun, the other to Stenay. It had been arranged with the king that the relays should be posted at the end of the town nearest to Clermont. As Varennes was not on the post road, no horses were kept there, and even driving there with post horses was a matter of favour. This arrangement had been altered by the unlucky Goguelat, who, counting on the arrival of Choiseul, or Valory some time before the king, had decided to leave the relays where they were.

The 21st of June had passed very quietly for the inhabitants of the little town. The next day but one was the Fête-Dieu; and those who could spare the time were engaged in making garlands and ornaments for the procession customary on that day. The hairdresser, Léonard, who had caused much mischief along the road, reached Varennes at half-past nine with his message of despair. He asked for Choiseul's horses to continue his journey. These were denied him, but he procured others. Had he continued on the road to Montmédy, he would have met Bouillé, and perhaps have induced him to advance to see what was the matter, but stricken by the common fatality, he took the road to Verdun. Having done all the mischief he could by his journey on the king's route, he now discontinued it at the very moment when he might have been of use.

The travelling coach stopped at the entrance of the town, where the king had been told that the relays would be found. Nothing was to be seen; every house was in profound repose. The king descended from the carriage and knocked at a door. A voice from within cried, "Go along with you, we don't know what you want." The queen got out in her turn, and resting on the arm of M. de Malden knocked at the door of a large house in the first square. It was inhabited by M. de Préfontaine, a knight of Saint Louis, and agent for the Condé estates in those parts. He was at this time unwell, and knew nothing of what was going on in the town; he could therefore give the queen no information. Whilst Marie Antoinette was in the house, and the two other bodyguards, MM. de Valory and de Moustier, were looking for the relays, four men on horseback galloped by, one of them called out to the postillions, "Go no further; unharness your horses; your passenger is the king."

The body-guards, after examining a wood in the neighbourhood of the town where no horses were likely to be concealed, sauntered down the narrow street, but never once thought of crossing the bridge. When Valory came back to the king, he was met with the words, "François, we are betrayed." Shortly afterwards the queen came back to the carriage, handed to it by M. de Préfontaine. She was received with the same terrible news. The only course left was to proceed further, but the postillions positively refused to stir an inch. The body-guards promised money, The postillions answered that their horses were tired, that their master at Clermont had charged them to go no further than the entrance to Varennes, and that his wife had especially enjoined them under no consideration to make a longer journey, because they were wanted for the hay harvest the next day. It is said that Madame Canitrot, for that was her name, never forgave herself for having thus caused the death of Louis XVI. and Marie Antoinette. At last the body-guards threatened the postillions with their hunting knives; the carriage moved slowly on; but thirty-five minutes had been lost, and it was too late.

Drouet and Guillaume, after passing the berline, had stopped at the tavern of the Bras d'Or on the other side of the archway.[1] The clock had just struck a quarter-past eleven. A few young men of the neighbourhood were engaged in conversation, and were preparing to go home, when they heard

---

[1] The other two horsemen had been sent from Clermont, but they took no part in the arrest of the king.

the rattle of horses' hoofs. They were Paul Leblanc, the brother of the landlord, Jean Leblanc, Joseph Ponsin, Justin George, son of the mayor, who was then in Paris, Thennevin, bailiff of the neighbouring village of Les Islettes, and Delion from Mount Faucon. The door opened, and Drouet entered in haste. "He drew the landlord on one side, and said, "Friend, are you a good patriot?" "Of course I am," he replied. "Well, if that is so, go as quickly as you can and tell all trustworthy people that the king is at the entrance of Varennes, that he is coming down the street, and that he must be arrested. The landlord first recruited the men who were in his parlour; he then went to M. Sauce, who was Procureur of the Commune, called him out of bed, and told him what he had heard. Drouet's first care was to barricade the bridge, which united the two parts of the town, using for that purpose a waggon full of furniture which he accidentally found there. The other seven armed themselves with muskets, and prepared to stop the carriage as it passed from under the archway. They arranged that they should first ask for the travellers' passports, and when they were delivered gain as much time as possible that the people might assemble in force. At this momentous crisis Charles Bouillé and Raigecourt were sitting at their window doing nothing. They heard a little movement in the town, but paid no attention. Sauce sent his little children to give an alarm of fire through the town. The inhabitants hurried together, believing the bad news, and some of the hussars came out of their barracks to see if they could be of use. One of the gates of the archway was shut, the seven patriots were reinforced by three others, making ten in all. The postchaise, with the two chambermaids, was first stopped by the landlord and his brother. Sauce approached and asked the ladies for their passport. They answered that it was in the second carriage. The occupants of the berline replied to their questions that they were on the way to Frankfort. Sauce held up a lantern inside the carriage and gazed at the faces of the travellers. At last the passport was delivered to him. It was signed by Louis himself,[1] but Drouet or Sauce remarked, that it did not bear the countersign of the President of the National Assembly. Sauce added, that it was now too late to verify the passport, that it was dangerous for the travellers to continue their journey during the night, that they must get out of the carriage and wait for daybreak. When the postillions attempted to proceed, they were stopped by the armed men, who cried, " If you go a step farther, we fire." Nothing was left for the Royal family but to get out.

Sauce offered the hospitality of his house. It was only a few steps distant on the left-hand side of the sloping street. It has since been altered, and local tradition states that it has been moved back in order to make the street wider, but its main features still remain unchanged. On the ground-floor there was a grocer's shop, with a strong smell of tallow, which the queen could not put up with. The upper storey

---

[1] There is a facsimile of the passport in Bimbenet, p. 150.

is reached by a narrow corkscrew staircase, which
has apparently remained unaltered till the present
day. On the upper floor are two rooms, one looking
out into the street, the other into a small courtyard.
In the back room, about fifteen feet by twenty, was
collected the majesty of France. The king seated
himself in an armchair in the middle of the room,
the queen asked for some hot water, wine, and clean
sheets, probably all for the children.[1] The Dauphin
and his sister were placed upon a bed and were soon
asleep, the faithful Madame de Tourzel seated by
their side. The body-guards sat on a bench under-
neath the window.[2] It is incredible that the king
should not have been rescued at this moment. Sixty
hussars were in their barracks at a short distance
from the bridge, with their horses harnessed, ready
to start at any moment. A few of them only had
been disturbed by the cry of fire. That they were
useless in the crisis was owing to Goguelat's errors.
By some strange infatuation he had sent their proper
commander, Deslon, off to Bouillé, where he could be
of no use, and had left them in the charge of a young
lieutenant of eighteen, Rohrig, who lost his head and
did nothing. As soon as he found himself in a
difficulty, he crossed the river by a ford and galloped
off to Bouillé. Charles Bouillé and Raigecourt did
the same. By this time the whole population of

---

[1] The story of the king asking for food is a fable. There
were plenty of provisions in the carriage, and a silver-gilt jug
was left behind in Sauce's house by the Royal family on their
departure next day.

[2] These details are from a manuscript account by an eye
witness, given to me by my friend Mr. Curtis, of Venice.

Varennes was on foot. They built barricades at the entrance of all the streets leading to the country. They dragged out two or three pieces of ordnance which were rusting in the stables of the Town-hall, and placed them partly on the bridge, and partly at the entrance of the Clermont Wood.

When these arrangements were complete, at about one o'clock in the morning, Choiseul and his forty hussars, who, after their departure from Pont-Sommevesle, had left the high-road a little before reaching Ste. Ménehould, and had taken five hours to ride from Neuville-au-Pont through the woods, arrived at the entrance of Varennes. They were stopped by the little barricade and the two rusty pieces of cannon, an obstacle which the forty hussars might have brushed aside in a moment. Almost at the same moment a few dragoons, under the command of Damas, came up from Clermont. The two bodies of cavalry passed easily through the barricade, and entered the town. They first halted in the Place du Château, where the Royal family had wasted thirty-five minutes two hours before. Here they met Sauce. He had been to rouse the principal judge, by name Destez, who was acquainted with the king's appearance, and who, he hoped, might recognise him. As he passed by, Sauce took care to speak to the hussars, and to tamper with their allegiance. Choiseul marched straight down the street, not halting at the house in which the Royal family were prisoners, till he reached the convent which served as barracks for the hussars. He found it deserted, and none but the grooms were to be seen. He drew up his soldiers in the courtyard; told them that the king and queen were prisoners in the town, and they must rescue them or die. Harsh guttural cries of "Der König, die Königin!" rose from the men, who were mostly Germans. Then, breaking his squadron into fours, he trotted up the street with drawn swords and halted opposite Sauce's house. Damas, in the meantime, had crossed the bridge, notwithstanding the barricade, had learned at the Hôtel du Grand Monarque, that the two officers in charge of the relays had galloped off to Stenay, and had returned to the narrow street where he found M. de Choiseul. At this moment, very slight firmness on the part of the hussars, or their commander, would have saved the king, but there was the usual hesitation and delay. Goguelat mounted the corkscrew staircase into the petty prison of his sovereign, to ask for orders, as if the king, in such a situation, could have any orders to give.

The travellers had been already recognised. M. Destez had thrown himself at the king's feet; the king had said, "Yes, I am your king; I cannot remain any longer at Paris without death to my family and myself." A dispute ensued between Sauce and Louis as to whether it was better for the country that he should go or stay. The queen could bear it no longer, but cried, "If you recognise him as your king, treat him with more respect." At one moment it seemed as if the gaoler would give way. The king embraced all who were standing round and moved them to tears. This emotion soon passed. Drouet was always at hand to keep the patriots to their purpose. Sauce's house, and even the room where the Royal family were imprisoned, were besieged by a surging crowd. Tradition says that when Louis asserted his firm intention of not going beyond the frontier, a little bandy-legged cripple cried out, "Sire, we do not believe you." For some time Sauce maintained the specious fiction, that the Royal family should set off whither they pleased at daybreak. The queen did her best to touch the heart of Madame Sauce, and Sauce's mother, an old lady of eighty, on coming into the chamber, fell down upon her knees, bursting into tears and kissed the hands of the children.

When Goguelat entered the room, Louis said to him, "Well, when shall we be off?" He answered, "Sire, we await your orders." Damas suggested a plan of carrying off the whole party on seven horses belonging to the hussars, guarded by the remaining thirty-three. Louis feared that a stray ball might kill one of the party. The plan indeed was an insane one. It would be far easier to have cleared the road by a charge and driven off in the berline. At last the fatal decision was taken of waiting for Bouillé. Every moment that elapsed made the king's fate more certain, and yet the royal party seemed to clutch at every pretext for delay. By two o'clock in the morning five thousand peasants from the neighbouring villages had reached Varennes, and an hour later their number had doubled. The barricades were strengthened, and the hussars placed before Sauce's house found themselves between two fires. It is a comfort to discover amongst all this pusillanimity one touch of courage. Goguelat attempted to disperse the crowd which was collecting round the Royal berline; Roland, an officer of the National Guard, seized his horse by the bridle, Goguelat drew his sword and threatened him. Roland fired his pistol, and the ball was flattened against Goguelat's collar-bone. His horse reared and the rider fell slightly wounded. He was taken into the Bras d'Or tavern, where his hurt was attended to. This pistol-shot might have been the signal of a massacre, but the hussars, instead of attacking the crowd, fraternized with them; jars of wine were passed from trooper to trooper. When Remy arrived from Clermont at four o'clock, he found the hussars drinking and calling "Vive la Nation."

The fate of Quartermaster Remy was another of those strange fatalities which brought about the final catastrophe. He had left Clermont shortly after the passage of the berline with the few horsemen whom he could find to accompany him. Unfortunately the main road through Clermont leads to Verdun, whereas the road to Varennes turns off at a sharp angle. Remy and his dragoons galloped on through the night, and when they asked their way found that they were close to Verdun. There was no means of reaching Varennes, except by passing again through Clermont. Had they taken the right road, they would have been with the berline when it reached the fatal arch, and could easily have cut down the few men who were opposing its passage.

Just as the sun broke over the lovely valley of the

Aire, Sauce asked the king to show himself to the crowd from the window, which looked upon the street. Louis saw a dense mass of peasants armed with muskets, scythes, and pitchforks, and some women staggering, half tipsy, among the crowd. As he stood at the window, there was a deep silence, and when he told those who could hear him that he would not leave them, that he was going to Montmédy, but that he would afterwards return to Varennes, there was a thunder of applause, and reiterated cries of " Vive le Roi ! " " Vive la Nation ! " A few cries were heard of " To Paris ! " " To Verdun ! " Whilst the Royal family were anxiously expecting the arrival of Bouillé, the Municipality were declaring, that they had no intention of preventing the king's journey, but that at dawn of day he might go where he pleased. We cannot believe in the honesty of these professions. As early as two o'clock in the morning the Town Council sent a Varennes doctor, named Mangin, to the Assembly, to tell them that the king was in their town and to ask for instructions. Both parties wished to gain time, the king for the arrival of the general who was to rescue him, the town authorities for the collection of an overwhelming force which would drive the king back to Paris.

At five o'clock an officer of hussars broke into the room where the Royal family was assembled, with a bare sword; it was Captain d'Eslon, who had commanded the one hundred hussars at Varennes, but who had been sent off to Bouillé by the blundering Goguelat. Posted at Dun, he had heard at three o'clock in the morning from Lieutenant Rohrig, that two carriages had been stopped at Varennes, containing a man, some women, and children. D'Eslon, who was in the secret of the flight, could have no doubt as to the truth. He left thirty men to guard the bridge over the Meuse, and galloped with the other seventy to Varennes in an hour and a half. He found the bridge barricaded and defended by an experienced officer, M. de Signémont, who was taking part against his sovereign, although he wore on his breast the cross of the order of St. Louis. D'Eslon, being badly supplied with ammunition, did not dare to charge. He asked leave to enter the town, which after some delay was granted. He walked on to Sauce's house, where he found thirty hussars drawn up in the street, commanded by a National Guard, and after half-an-hour's delay he was enabled to see the king. Like all the other officers who had an interview with their sovereign, he asked for orders. The king replied that he was a prisoner, and that he had no orders to give. D'Eslon returned to his hussars and sent a message to Captain Boudet, who was in command of the hussars in barracks at Varennes, to make a charge from inside the town which he would support from outside. Boudet was at this time closely watched by National Guards and the message never reached him. Even now a little dash and enterprise might have set the Royal family free from their embarrassments. There were at Varennes the sixty hussars who had been left there in barracks, the forty hussars who had returned from Pont-Somme-vesle, the small body of dragoons who had come from Clermont with the Comte de Damas, the half-dozen troopers who had followed Quartermaster Remy, and the sixty or seventy hussars under the command of D'Eslon. They made, in all, a body of one hundred and eighty men. Could they have been combined in united action, they would have dispersed the crowd, however close or however fearless.

But the moments, in which decision was possible, were running out. At six o'clock it was full daylight, and the town officials were collected at the town-hall to determine what they should do about the king's departure. At this moment two messengers arrived from Paris, who had been sent to follow the king, and bore the orders of the National Assembly. They were M. Baillon and M. de Romeuf. The latter was aide-de-camp to Lafayette, and was intimately known to the king and the queen. The king and his family were alone, in the small room at the back of the house of which we have spoken above. Baillon was the first to enter, his clothes covered with dust, his face hot with perspiration. He could scarcely give utterance to a few hurried words. Romeuf followed bearing a paper in his hands. The queen, when she saw him, cried, "Sir, is it you? I never would have believed it." It is indeed possible that, had Romeuf been alone, he would have given the Royal family an opportunity of escape. He now handed to the queen the decree of the Assembly, which ordered the king's return to Paris. Louis read it over her shoulder, and said, "There is no longer a king in France." The queen was less calm. "What insolence!" she cried, and seeing that the paper had fallen on the Dauphin's bed, she seized it and threw it on the ground, saying that it should not sully the couch of her son.

After this, the only chance for the king was to gain time for Bouillé to arrive. He asked to speak with the deputies alone. Romeuf was willing to grant this request, but Baillon refused. The people below called out, "Let us compel him to go by force, we will drag him into the carriage by his feet." The king supplicated for a moment's delay; "Could they not wait till eleven o'clock?" A hasty breakfast was served for the Royal family. The two children were still asleep, and the king went to sleep also. As a last resource, one of the waiting-maids (Madame de Neuville) declared herself to be seized with a violent attack of illness. The king refused to desert her, and a doctor was sent for. All these stratagems could not procure more than an hour's delay; the shouts of the impatient mob surged up from the street. The king went once more to the window to quiet them, and then begged to be left alone for a few minutes with his family. The carriages had been harnessed and brought up to Sauce's door. The Royal family slowly and sadly descended the winding staircase. The king walked first, and was followed by Madame de Tourzel and the two children. Choiseul gave his arm to the queen, Damas to Madame Elizabeth. The bodyguards were placed on the box-seat in front, guarded by two grenadiers, with bayonets fixed to their muskets. When the Royal family had entered the carriage, Choiseul, who had been the chief cause of their calamity, closed the door. He tells us that he then experienced an inexpressible pang of anguish, that he felt as if he was surrendering Charles I. to the tender mercies of the Scotch. Worse even than the fate of the Stuart king was the long agony of those six miserable victims, four of whom perished by a slow and torturing death, while one alone survived to bear through life the gloom and sadness of her darkened youth.

It was now half-past seven in the morning, and there was no news of Bouillé. What had caused his delay? Not a quarter of an hour after the king had left, a detachment of Royal Allemand was seen on the outskirts of the town. It was commanded by young Bouillé, and had been posted in a village between Dun and Stenay. Bouillé dashed across the river by a well-known ford, but was stopped by a deep and narrow trench which carried water to a mill. There was a ford higher up by which this obstacle could have been turned, and it is strange that D'Eslon should not have used it when he found his passage stopped by the barricade. The Marquis de Bouillé had passed the greater part of the night in a ditch by the side of the road leading from Dun to Varennes, his horse by his side, the bridle on his arm. Unfortunately before the news of the king's arrest could reach him, he had left this post and retired to Stenay. He therefore heard nothing of the disaster until four or half-past four o'clock. He did not lose an instant in giving his orders, but they were slowly obeyed. Although the regiment had been charged to be in readiness at daybreak, and although the horses had been saddled all night, the soldiers did not assemble till the clock had struck five. Bouillé placed himself at their head, addressed to them a few stirring words announcing the capture of the king, distributed four hundred louis among them, and set off at a quick trot. They reached Varennes between nine and half-past nine in the morning, when the king was already well on the road to Clermont. Even then Bouillé would have charged had there been any hope of success, but, convinced that it was impossible, he turned rein to Stenay and crossed the frontier that night, to die in England nine years afterwards.

The return-journey to Paris must be described in a few lines. Clermont was reached at ten o'clock. Half-way between that town and Varennes, the municipal officers of the town met the cortége, and found the berline escorted by six thousand National Guards. The heat and dust were terrible. At Clermont a new crowd of six thousand was assembled. Sauce returned to Varennes, fearing that the town might be attacked by Bouillé, and his place was taken by the mayor of Clermont. The king arrived at Ste. Ménehould about half-past one. The carriages were stopped at the gate, and the king had to listen to a municipal address. The Royal family lunched at the town-hall. The queen showed herself to the crowd with the Dauphin in her arms; as the king and queen passed through the chapel, where the prisoners heard Mass, they distributed money to the poor unfortunates, whose fate resembled their own. The procession left Ste. Ménehould at three in the afternoon. In the fields beyond the town M. de Dampierre was brutally massacred. He had assisted one of the waiting-maids into her post-chaise, and had followed the carriages on horseback. He was dragged off his horse and murdered. The assassins returned to the Royal carriage, bearing his head in their blood-stained hands. Châlons was not reached till eleven o'clock. Here the travellers lodged in the *préfecture*, a beautiful building of the later years of Louis XV., where Marie Antoinette had slept on her first arrival in France as Dauphiness. An offer was made to the king to arrange for his escape by a secret staircase. He refused, from fear of the danger it might cause to his wife and children. The next day, Thursday, was the Fête-Dieu, the day on which it had been arranged to celebrate a grand Mass in the camp of Montmédy, and to present Bouillé with the bâton of a French marshal. The king would gladly have rested a day at Châlons to recover from his fatigue. But the "patriots," seeing that the sentiment of the town was in his favour, sent to Rheims for an army of roughs. They arrived at ten in the morning, and, breaking into the palace, interrupted the king's Mass as it had reached the Sanctus, and insisted upon his immediate departure. The Royal family had great difficulty in reaching their carriages, and, in their hurry, left a large sum of money behind them.

The route which they now took was not the same as that by which they had previously travelled; it trended to the north, by Epernay, and rejoined the southern road at La Ferté sous Jouarre. There was probably a desire to take the travellers through a district which was known to be strongly opposed to them. Between Châlons and Epernay the queen offered to a poor hungry wretch a piece of " bœuf à la mode," which Fersen had placed in the carriage. A voice cried, " Do not eat it. Do you not see that they wish to poison you ? " The queen immediately partook of it herself, and gave some of it to the Dauphin.[1] At Epernay the keys of the town were presented to the king, accompanied by an insolent speech from the mayor. As they got out of the carriage, a man was heard to say to his neighbour, " Let me conceal myself and fire on the queen, that no one may know where the shot comes from." They dined there, but no one could eat a mouthful.[2] Between Epernay and Dormans, Pétion, Barnave, and Latour-Maubourg, met the Royal party as Commissioners of the National Assembly. Pétion and Barnave took their places in the berline. Latour-Maubourg preferred to travel with the waiting-maids, telling the king that he could depend upon his devotion, but that it was important to gain over the two others. The queen told Fersen, when they met in February, 1792, that Pétion's conduct had been indecent. At Dormans, cries of " Vive la nation et l'assemblée nationale," prevented the travellers from sleeping. The Dauphin dreamed that he was in a forest with wolves, who were attacking the queen, and awoke weeping. There was much discussion in the berline about the policy of the flight, which Madame Elizabeth warmly defended. At Ferté sous Jouarre they were received with respectful attention

---

[1] Fersen, ii. 8.   [2] Tourzel, i. 332.

by the mayor, and enjoyed the only quiet and repose which they met with during the journey. They reached Meaux in the evening. The day had been insupportable from dust and heat, and the angry crowd would not allow the blinds to be drawn down, nor the windows closed. Saturday, June 25, was the last day of this prolonged torment. It lasted thirteen hours, from six in the morning to seven in the evening. During the whole day the travellers were exposed to the glare of a midsummer sun, and to the insults of the mob. At the barrier they were met by a dense crowd of citizens. No one raised his hat or spoke a word. They entered the garden of the Tuileries by the swing bridge, and were protected, as they dismounted, by the care of Lafayette. The faithful body-guards were with difficulty rescued from summary slaughter.

Such is the true story of the flight to Varennes, more touching in its naked simplicity than any device of art could make it. The Royal family had many chances in their favour, and they would have escaped, unless every one of these chances turned against them. If Choiseul had waited a short time longer at Pont-Sommevesle; if he had retired at a foot's pace towards Orbeval; if he had passed through Ste. Ménehould, or had halted at the parting of the ways, instead of losing himself precipitately in pathless woods; if Goguelat had remained behind at the post-house according to orders; if D'Andoins had not unsaddled his dragoons just before the berline arrived; if Lagache had not lost his way in the woods; if Damas had kept his men ready for action : if Charles Bouillé and Raigecourt had not shut themselves up in their bed-room ; if their orderly whom they sent out for news had spoken with the berline when he met it outside Varennes ; if Valory had crossed the bridge to the Grand Monarque; if Goguelat had not altered the position of the relays ; if the hair-dresser Léonard had taken the road to Stenay, instead of losing himself on that to Verdun; if Quartermaster Remy had not made a similar mistake—if any one of these things had turned out differently, the Royal family might have been saved. The accidents we have enumerated were in the hands of fate, the lack of courage and decision was due to other causes. Varennes, indeed, was a precursor of Valmy. As the resistance of the French Sans-culottes to the discipline of Prussian troops led to the retreat of the Allies, and eventually to the conquest of Europe, so now the enthusiasm, the energy, the activity, the resource of ignorant and undisciplined peasants, showed itself superior to all the wealth, the rank, the splendour, and the power, of the Ancien Régime.

II.

THE CRITICISM ON CARLYLE'S ACCOUNT.

AS an appendix to the foregoing account of the Flight to Varennes, it may be useful to subjoin the following criticism of Carlyle's account of the same event, which was originally read as a paper before the Royal Historical Society in 1886.

The arrest of Louis XVI. during his flight from Paris to Montmédy was one of the most important events in the history of the French Revolution, and probably one of the most important in the history of France. It also forms one of the best known and most admired portions of Carlyle's History of the Revolution. It occupies a whole book of the second volume, fifty-four pages of the Library edition. It may therefore be taken as a fair specimen of Carlyle's style, both in its strength and in its weakness. A careful examination of his narrative from a purely prosaic standpoint will throw light on his manner of composition. It may be said that it is ungracious to criticise in the petty details of fact a narrative which has stirred so many hearts by its tragic pathos, and which in its broad outlines is consistent with the truth. But herein lies the whole distinction between the historical poem and the historical novel on the one side, and history proper on the other. Carlyle would have said, if he had been asked, that his one object in writing history was to tell the truth. It is for this reason that he multiplies fact upon fact and detail upon detail, until he has brought the scene vividly before the eyes of the reader. His accuracy can be trusted where he has visited the scenes which he describes, and where he is not carried away by preconceived prejudices or ideas. In history truth is always more tragic and more moving than fiction. If it can be shown that in Carlyle's account of the flight to Varennes, crammed as it is with picturesque details, he has not only failed to read aright the authorities at his disposal, but that he has completely failed to grasp the direction in which truth would reveal itself in the future, he will be held to have forfeited his claim to be a historian of the first rank. If criticism, applied to this episode of Carlyle's book, shows that almost every statement made by him is either false or exaggerated, we may infer that similar criticisms applied to the rest of his work will produce similar results, and that his book has no claim to be considered a serious history of the period to which it refers. In the autumn of last year I was able to carry out a long cherished design of visiting Varennes. I struck the route of the royal family at Châlons, the point where it becomes most interesting. I rode on a tricycle from Châlons to Ste. Ménehould, through Pont Sommevesle, and from Ste. Ménehould to Clermont en Argonne, where I slept. The next day I visited Varennes, lunched at the " Grand Monarque," where the relays were stabled, which the king never made use of, and visited the house in which the Royal family passed the night. I venture to say that no one who has not carefully and minutely studied the topography of Varennes can understand the most important and critical features of the incidents which happened there.

The first chapter of Carlyle's fourth book and second volume contains a graphic but very inaccurate account of the attempt of the king to spend Easter at St. Cloud, and his detention by the populace on April 18, 1791.¹ There is no doubt that it was this event which convinced the king that he was a prisoner, and that so long as he remained in Paris he could not exercise his free will, or even practise his religion according to the demands of his conscience. It was this detention which matured his determination of flight. Indeed, the flight of the king from Paris had long been under discussion. Mirabeau was always in favour of the removal of the Royal family from Paris, but he wished the king to retire in full daylight, in all the pomp of majesty, either to Compiègne, Fontainebleau, Rouen, or Lyons, and thence to issue orders to which no one could impute compulsion. Louis would not take this advice, but was determined to escape to the frontier; and when, in October, 1790, he consulted Bonillé on the subject, that general advised him to choose one of three places—Valenciennes, Besançon, or Montmédy. The king chose the last, from its proximity to Austrian territory and to Luxembourg, as this gave him the opportunity of taking refuge in a friendly country if he were compelled to leave France, and Bouillé a pretext of assembling an army on the frontier to protect the king's flight.

Montmédy being chosen, by what road should it be reached? The shortest road was by Rheims, Réthel, and Stenay; the longer by Châlons, Ste. Ménehould, Clermont, and Varennes. It is generally said that the king would not choose the first because he feared to be recognised at Rheims, the town of his coronation; but from the correspondence of Count Fersen² it may be doubted whether

---

¹ We see by the account of an eyewitness in Klinkowström's *Comte de Fersen*, i. 103, that the Royal family never entered the royal carriage, but only *a berline*, which was not allowed to leave the Cour des Princes.

² Compare Fersen to Bouillé, Fersen, i. 118, and Bouillé to Fersen, i. 121.

the longer route was not preferred by Bouillé himself. The main objection to the longer route was that there were no post-horses at Varennes, and that private relays would have to be sent there.

Not being able to go to Paris, Bouillé sent his son, Count Louis, to arrange details. He never saw the king or queen, but carried on all negotiations with Count Fersen, who had unrestricted access to the queen. Carlyle is quite justified in calling his third chapter after the name of the Swedish nobleman. Although Breteuil is to be credited with the authorship of the plot, Fersen was the most trusted agent of the king and queen, and the correspondence between the Royal family and Bouillé was carried on principally through him. But Carlyle is not justified in attributing so much importance to the queen's arrangements of the clipping of frocks and gowns and the making of a large dressing-case. Montmédy, the frontier town to which the king was to be taken, was composed of a town of 2,000 inhabitants and a lofty citadel. It was a strong place of arms, and could be defended by 700 men. But the king was not to lodge there. If he did, he might be captured. A camp was to be formed in the neighbourhood, and the king was to live in the Château of Thonelle, which was only half a day's journey from the Austrian frontier town of Virton. It is said in Carlyle's defence that, although he might be wrong in details, he seized with unerring grasp the essential features of the story. It is not so in this case. He shows no glimmering of understanding what the king's design really was, and what course he intended to pursue. The emperor, the queen's brother, was to send a force of 10,000 men to the neighbourhood of Luxembourg, which was at once to serve as a pretext for massing troops to protect the king's flight, and to be at the disposal of the king for any purpose he might desire. A civil war was not only inevitable, but it was to be pressed on. One of the king's plans was to restore ecclesiastical property to the clergy, and thus, by taking away the basis on which the *assignats* rested, to cause a national bankruptcy and upset the party of the Revolution.[1] All this would take a considerable time, and during it Louis and Mary Antoinette must appear as king and queen. It was not, therefore, remarkable that preparations should be made for clothes and a dressing-case, or that the queen's diamonds and the king's habit of ceremony should be carried to the frontier by Léonard, the queen's coiffeur. Undoubtedly, many people were initiated into the plot—perhaps too many. But that did not prevent the escape from Paris, and the failure of the enterprise was made more certain by those who knew nothing of it beforehand.

Next to Count Fersen, Carlyle mentions the Duke de Choiseul. "He and Engineer Goguelat are passing and re-passing between Metz and the Tuileries." This is inaccurate as far as Choiseul is concerned. The Duke de Choiseul-Stainville, now aged thirty-one, was colonel of a regiment of royal dragoons, which was stationed at Commercy, a small town on the Meuse. He was summoned from Commercy to Metz at the end of April, and was informed by Bouillé of the king's design. He then returned to Commercy, where he remained till June 8, when he was summoned to Metz, arriving there in the evening of the same day. It was on this occasion that it took young Bouillé seven hours to decipher one of Fersen's letters.[2] Choiseul left Metz at 4 a.m. on June 10, and arrived in twenty-five hours at Paris. He saw the king in the evening of Tuesday, June 12, and remained at Paris till the day of the king's flight. Therefore, he only made one journey from Metz to Paris, and there was no passing or re-passing in his case.

---

[1] Breteuil to Fersen, i. 128. Same to same, i. 131.
[2] Choiseul, Relation du départ de Louis XVI. 38, foll.

We next hear of a "stupendous new coach of the kind named 'berline.'" A berline is merely a large posting carriage, very common in those days, roomy both at the front and the back, and usually holding six people. Carlyle is never tired of making fun of this berline. He dedicates a whole chapter to it. He calls it "a huge leathern vehicle," "a huge Argosy," "an Acapulco ship." "It lumbers along lurchingly with stress at a snail's pace, noted of all the world." Again : " Lumbering along with its mountains of band-boxes and chaise behind, the Korff berline rolls in—a huge Acapulco ship, with its cockboat —having got so far." There is no proof that there was anything remarkable about the carriage at all. A new coach, built by a first-rate maker, is more likely to be light and handy than heavy and lumbering. A berline was quite an ordinary form of carriage. In the "Life of Count Fersen," vol. i. p. 103, there is an account by an eyewitness of the king's attempt to go to St. Cloud. On April 18, 1791, we are told there that the royal carriage could not enter the Cour des Princes from the Carrousel, and the Royal family, with Madame de Tourzel, the very six who fled to Varennes, on the proposal of the queen, entered the only carriage available, "quoiqu'elle ne fut qu'une berline" (although it was only a berline). Also in the *procès-verbal* of what happened at Ste. Ménehould on the evening of June 21, we are expressly told that the Royal family was in a carriage that was by no means remarkable.[1] Madame de Tourzel says (*Mémoires*, i. 311). "Nous voyagions dans une grand berline bien commode mais qui n'avait rien d'extraordinaire comme on s'est plu à le répéter depuis la triste issue de ce malheureux voyage." Besides this, we have a minute account of the

---

[1] "Un carosse non autrement remarquable" in Ancelon, *La vérité sur la fuite et l'arrestation de Louis XVI. à Varennes*, p. 180.

berline in the deposition of Jean Louis, who built it.[1] It cost £240; it was a triumph of elegance and solidity, and, except that it was new and luxurious, it was not very different from any other large posting carriage travelling along the road.

Carlyle says that the berline was sent to Madame Sullivan's, in the Rue de Clichy. Other accounts say that it was deposited at the hotel of Mr. Craufurd, an Englishman residing at Paris. The truth is that Mr. Craufurd, who was well known in diplomatic and other society, was then residing in Brussels, and his house was occupied in the meantime by Mrs. Sullivan, his mistress, whom he afterwards married.[2]

The next paragraph of Carlyle's narrative describes the hackney coach standing "at the corner of the Rue de l'Échelle, hard by the Carrousel and outgate of the Tuileries." A hooded dame with two hooded children is made to issue from the Duc de Villequier's door into the Cour des Princes, and then into the Carrousel and Rue de l'Échelle, and into the hackney coach.

This is entirely erroneous. Madame de Tourzel, it is true, passed out of Villequier's door with Madame and the Dauphin. She there found a hackney coach standing close by. The coachman lifted the children himself into the carriage, gave his hand to Madame de Tourzel, lashed his two horses into a gallop, and drove, not to the Rue de l'Échelle, but to the open place called Petit Carrousel, close by.[3] "Not long after," says Carlyle, "another dame, hooded or shrouded, leaning on a servant, issues in

---

[1] Bimbinet, *Fuite de Louis* XVI., p. 20, and Pièces justicatives, p. 51.

[2] Croker's *Essays on the French Revolution*, p. 125.

[3] Madame de Tourzel (*Mémoires*, i. 306), says that the carriage stopped opposite the house called "Hôtel de Gaillarbois." The account in the Auckland Memoirs, iii. 452, says "near the house which was formerly inhabited by the Duchess de la Vallière."

the same manner." So far from the interval not being long, the children and their governess had to wait in the carriage three-quarters of an hour before any one came; and when Madame Elizabeth did come she was alone, and had no servant with her.[1] Carlyle does not mention the fact that while the children were seated in the coach Lafayette's carriage passed by, escorted by servants carrying torches. He was probably going to the *coucher* of the king, where he stayed, much to the inconvenience of his master, till past eleven o'clock. I may mention that Carlyle speaks of *couchée*, formed after the analogy of *levée*. This is incorrect; the proper form is *coucher*.

Carlyle says that the queen was disturbed on her way by the passage of Lafayette's carriage as it rolled into the Tuileries and entered the Cour des Princes. There is no doubt Lafayette assisted at the king's *coucher* this night, and kept him very late. The children in the hackney coach trembled as they saw him pass. If Carlyle is right, there must have been two visits to the Tuileries—one for the *coucher*, and the other to see that everything was safe. It is more probable that there was only one visit, and that it was on his return from this that Lafayette was met by the queen. In fact, Fersen says that whilst he was waiting in the Petit Carrousel with the hackney coach Lafayette passed twice.[2]

Carlyle repeats the old story that the queen lost her way, and went wandering over the Pont Royal and into the Rue du Bac. This is quite improbable, and is not supported by evidence. At that time a part of the present Place du Carrousel was occupied by a number of buildings separated by narrow streets. It is possible that the queen may have lost her way in some of them, turning to the right instead of the left. But she arrived very

---

[1] Madame de Tourzel's interrogatory, Bimbenet, P. J. 88.
[2] Fersen, i. 2.

shortly after the king. We read in Fersen's diary : " At a quarter past ten in the Cour des Princes. At a quarter past eleven the children go out, conveyed without difficulty: Lafayette passed twice. At a quarter to twelve Madame Elizabeth, then the king, then the queen. Set off at midnight, joined the carriage at the Barrier of St. Martin, reached Bondy at half-past one."[1] Thus the queen, the king, and his sister all reached the carriage within a quarter of an hour, and there could have been no great delay caused by waiting for the queen. It is indeed possible that the same *garde du corps* who conducted the king to the carriage went back and fetched the queen. Madame de Tourzel tells us that when the queen arrived the king said, with inexpressible joy, " Que je suis content de vous voir arrivée ! " They all kissed each other and thought that their dangers were over.

Carlyle describes the queen as conducted by a disguised body-guard, who, having led her to the *fiacre*, jumps up behind as the conductor of the king had done. This could not have been the case. The three body-guards were M. de Maldent, M. de Moustier, and M. de Valory. M. de Maldent conducted the king, M. de Moustier was with the berline at the Barrier of St. Martin, and M. de Valory was hastening on the road to Bondy. It is indeed possible that M. de Maldent may have conducted the queen as well as the king.[2]

Carlyle, following Choiseul, describes Fersen's drive through Paris, and describes it wrong. He makes him go down to the Rue de Grammont, across the boulevard, up the Rue de la Chaussée d'Antin—" the windows, all

---

[1] Fersen, loc. cit.
[2] Madame de Tourzel says (*Mémoires*, i. 307), " Le Roi nous raconta qu'après avoir été débarrassé de MM. Bailly et de la Fayette, il était sorti *seul* par la grande porte des Tuileries avec une grande tranquillité." This is inconsistent with the other accounts.

silent, of No. 42 were Mirabeau's "—to the Rue de Clichy, going, in fact, due north. As the map of Paris then stood, the direction due north at first would probably have been the best way to reach the Porte St. Martin. But, as a matter of fact, Fersen drove due west down the Rue du Faubourg St. Honoré till he arrived at the exterior boulevard, and then to Rue de Clichy. He wished to call at two places, at his own stables in the Rue du Faubourg St. Honoré and at Mr. Craufurd's (Madame Sullivan's) in the Rue de Clichy.

At last they reached the Barrier of St. Martin and found the berline. " This heaven-sent berline he does at length descry drawn up with its six horses, his own German coachman on the box." As a fact, there were only four horses, and the coachman, Balthazar Sapel, was not on the box, but riding on one of the front horses.[1] The man on the box was the body-guard, M. de Moustier. " Two body-guard couriers behind," says Carlyle. Not so, only one. M. de Maldent jumped up behind, and Fersen got on the box by the side of M. de Moustier.

Carlyle is right in saying that M. de Valory was at Bondy with the post-horses ready, but he is wrong about the purchased chaise and the two waiting-maids. They were waiting at Claye, some miles beyond Bondy, and there is no authority for saying that they had bandboxes. Carlyle laughs at the queen for not being able to travel without maids. As a matter of fact, the maids belonged to the children, and as the queen was going to live in a camp for some months, it was only reasonable that she should have trustworthy servants to take care of her two little children. Besides, the presence of the maids did not, as far as we know, cause the slightest danger or embarrassment. " Next," says Carlyle, " Fersen dashes obliquely northwards through the country towards Bou-

---

[1] Deposition of Balthasar Sapel in Bimbenet, p. 59.

gret, and gains Bougret." Where is Bougret? Who would recognise in this name the familiar village of le Bourget, so well known in the war of 1870. " Finds his German coachman there." How could that be, when the German coachman had driven with him as postillion to Bondy? As a fact, Fersen, mounted on his own English horse, which had been ridden to Bondy by Valory, rode by the cross road to le Bourget, and then, according to some accounts, quietly home, after seeing that everything was safe in the Palais Royal and the Hôtel de Ville.[1]

We will leave out the next chapter, entitled "Attitude," and go on to the fifth, which bears the name of " The New Berline." No names are bad enough for this really beautiful travelling carriage—" miserable berline," " huge leathern vehicle "—but we have dealt with this matter before.

Carlyle throughout is very contemptuous about the mounted body-guard couriers, who " rocked aimlessly around and ahead of it, to bewilder, not to guide." This is very unfair. MM. Maldent, Moustier, and Valory were men specially chosen for the service of couriers, as faithful, strong, and courageous, capable of riding for a long time on horseback. They were of mature age, two of them thirty-seven and one forty. They were of good family, had fought against the mob at Versailles on October 5 and 6, and they were of exceptional stature, as we know from the tailor who made their clothes. They were picked out by M. d'Agoult, the man recommended by Bouillé, as the most trustworthy assistant that the king could find to help him. Two of them had distinguished careers after 1791; let us therefore dismiss everything that Carlyle says about them. Valory rode in front the

---

[1] Fersen says in his diary, i. 2: " Moi la traverse au Bourget et parti." His return to Paris is asserted in Weber, ii. 88, but is very doubtful. Fersen arrived at Mons at 6 a.m. on June 22.

whole distance from Paris to Varennes, 150 miles, to order relays. It was customary to do this when posting, as it is still customary in Norway to order horses by a *forbud*. Had there been no courier to order horses the delay of the journey would have been much greater.

"Then," says Carlyle, "It (the berline) lumbers along lurchingly with stress at a snail's pace." The true story of the journey from Bondy to Châlons is imperfectly known. From Châlons to Varennes we know all about the matter. Let us try, therefore, to see at what pace the Royal family did travel. The distance from Paris to Varennes is about 235 or 240 kilometres—that is to say, 150 miles. It is difficult to ascertain precisely at what time the departure from Paris took place. Fersen says he left the Rue de l'Échelle at midnight and reached Bondy at 1.30. Other accounts say that the Barrière St. Martin was not left till it was 2.30 a.m., when it was already daybreak,[1] Bondy was reached in less than half-an-hour, and that when they left Claye it was 3.30, and quite daylight. The Royal family arrived at Châlons at 5 p.m. Twice between Nintré (Chaintrix) and Châlons all the traces broke. This accident, which took more than an hour to repair,[2] Carlyle wrongly places at Étoges. Had the king taken an old berline, as Carlyle suggests, there would probably have been a worse breakdown. From Claye to Châlons is 134 kilometres. If we subtract an hour and a half for the breakdown, we shall find that the party travelled at the average rate of eleven kilometres, or nearly seven miles, an hour, not counting the delays of changing horses and walking up hills. This is not a bad pace, all things considered. Madame de Tourzel declares that Louis only left the carriage once during the journey, and that the children got out twice as the

---

[1] Balthasar Sapel, in Bimbenet, loc. cit.
[2] Madame de Tourzel, *Mémoires*, i. 310.

carriage was ascending hills.¹ As to the "blessed sunshine," which Carlyle describes Louis as enjoying, we know from the account of Monsieur's journey to Mons that the day was a dull one, and that there was no sunshine to enjoy.

"Royalty," says Carlyle, "flying for dear life accomplishes sixty-nine miles in twenty-two hours." This is a statement of almost incredible carelessness. From Paris to Varennes is 150 miles, as Carlyle might have known if he had read Croker's article in the *Quarterly Review*,² published in 1823. The earliest time they could have left Paris was midnight; the latest time they could have arrived at Varennes was at 11 p.m. Therefore in these twenty-three hours they had travelled at the average rate, including all accidents and stoppages, of more than six and a half miles an hour.

Carlyle next introduces us to the Duke de Choiseul. He is standing "in the village of Pont de Sommevelle." There is no village, and it is not called Pont de Sommevelle. Pont Sommevesle is a solitary post-house in a deep valley between two hills. There may in 1791 have been a farm besides the post-house as there is now, but there was no village, and there could not be. Choiseul had left Paris at 2 p.m, and had slept at Montmirail. He left Montmirail at 4 a.m. and arrived at Pont Sommevesle at 11 a.m., doing eighty kilometres in seven hours—that is, travelling at exactly the same pace as the king. "His hussars," says Carlyle, "led by Engineer Goguelat, are here." Not at all. He might have learned from the Duke's own narrative that they did not arrive till an hour afterwards, when Goguelat entered Choiseul's room as he was dressing. Carlyle has a picturesque descrip-

---

¹ Madame de Tourzel, *Mémoires*, i. 310.

² Croker's *Essays on the French Revolution*, p. 119. The article was first published January, 1823.

tion of the troops posted along the line from Châlons to Montmédi, to receive and escort the king. He does not tell us with what splendid military art Bouillé, who was concentrating his troops in his camp near Montmédi, had arranged that they should be passing through these towns just as the king was going by. He is right in saying that this was a danger which had better have been omitted altogether. It is, however, very doubtful if the king was responsible for this. "It was of his Majesty's ordering, this military array and escort," says Carlyle, "a thing solacing the Royal imagination with a look of security and rescue." Yet in a letter written some time towards the end of May, Bouillé says to Fersen, through whom he always communicated to the king and queen, that a detachment of hussars would leave Vitry in a few days to take the king to Châlons, and escort him to the Ste. Ménehould or Clermont, where there will be other detachments; "you take care of the security of the road as far as Châlons."[1] Fersen replied on May 26: "There are no precautions to be taken from here to Châlons; the best of all is to take none. Everything depends on celerity and secrecy, and if you are not very sure of your detachment it would be best not to place any of them, or at least only to place them at Varennes, so as not to excite confusion in the country. The king will pass them quite simply. We cannot assemble the body-guards because we wish to make no disturbances at Châlons."[2] Nothing could be more sensible than these last remarks, and it appears as if the author of the escorts were, not the king, but Bouillé himself. The two narratives from which Carlyle principally drew his account, Bouillé's and Choiseul's, were both apologies. Choiseul was deeply responsible for the failure of the enterprise; Bouillé,

---

[1] Fersen, i. 126.   [2] Fersen, i. 1.

although he had done his utmost, had not succeeded. Both accounts were published after the death of all those who could have corrected them; and the evidence of letters written at the time must be taken to be of superior weight. A little further on, Carlyle gives currency to the statement that the change of the day of the king's departure from the 19th to the 20th had caused confusion. "The day first appointed, which her Majesty, for some necessity or other, saw good to alter." There is no evidence that this change of date produced the slightest inconvenience whatever, except, perhaps, to Bouillé himself. Let us look into the question of dates. Fersen writes on April 28 that the king would be ready to go on at any time after May 15. He could not start before, because he must wait for an answer from Spain. This probably referred to the dispute going on between England and Spain with regard to Nootka Sound. On May 26 the departure was put off till the first week in June, because at that time the King received two millions of his civil list. His reason for desiring these payments was not, as some have declared, his fondness for money, but the absolute necessity of obtaining funds for the enterprise in one way or another. In almost every letter Bouillé presses for money, to form the camp at Montmédy and for extra pay to the troops. The King sent to Bouillé nearly a million francs in *assignats*, and it was necessary under the circumstances to obtain as much as possible from the civil list. A further delay till June 20 was asked for by Bouillé himself, who wished to give time for the Austrian troops promised by the Emperor to assemble on the French frontier. The departure had been fixed for June 12 because a democratic servant of the Dauphin did not leave till June 11. Bouillé then wrote that it was necessary to delay till June 15 or 20. The departure was then fixed for the 19th. On June 13 Fersen writes to Bouillé that the journey was delayed for a day.

servant of the Dauphin cannot be got rid of without compromising the secret, and her service does not come to an end till June 19. As far as can be seen, this change had no bad effect whatever. Bouillé had not left Metz, and the orders already given were altered without difficulty. There was none of the marching and countermarching spoken of by Carlyle.

Carlyle's account of the disturbances between the hussars and the people of Ste. Ménehould is inaccurate and misleading. He seems to think that the marching and countermarching so exasperated the people of that town that they drove the soldiers out with 300 muskets, taken from the town hall. A hundred hussars were quartered at Varennes. On June 19 Goguelat brought an order from Montmédi that forty of these were to leave Varennes on the 20th, and to go to Pont Sommevesle to escort a treasure from that place to Ste. Ménehould. They left Varennes on the morning of the 20th and marched to Clermont, where they found the regiment of dragoons just arrived. After a rest they continued their march to Ste. Ménehould, where they were to sleep. Goguelat neglected to sound his trumpets on entering the town, or to inform the municipality of his arrival. This caused great annoyance, and they were badly received. When they left Ste. Ménehould next morning for Pont Sommevesle they were howled at by the mob, but nothing more. On the other hand, Captain Dandoins, with his dragoons, who, being properly warned, did sound his trumpets and inform the municipality, was received extremely well. There is no reason to suppose that the Lauzun hussars were specially unpopular with the people, nor were they all foreigners as Carlyle states them to be. The 300 muskets were not delivered to the National Guard until mid-day on the 20th, long after the hussars had left the town. This was done with the intention that the new-formed corps should mount guard day by day fifty at a time.[1] In fact we are told that Ste. Ménehould was the only spot on the journey where the royal travellers met National Guards at all.

Carlyle slurs over the fatal mistake of Choiseul in leaving Pont Sommevesle, and the direct disobedience to orders committed by Goguelat in not staying there even after Choiseul had left. It is true that if everything had gone well the berline might have been expected at about half-past two. Fersen told Bouillé so on June 14. "On sera au Pont de Sommevesle le mardi à deux heures au plus tard. Vous pouvez compter sur cela." There had been an hour and a half delay at Chaintrix, and as much again elsewhere. Choiseul says that the peasants of Elbœuf, probably of Courtisols, were surrounding the troops with menaces; that he waited till four o'clock, when he sent on the king's coiffeur, Léonard, in his own carriage, with his servant, Boucher, to Ste. Ménehould, Clermont, Varennes, and Stenay, and told him to announce the delay of the king and his own position at Pont Sommevesle. He is also said to have given Léonard a note in which he wrote that the treasure would not pass that day, and that he himself was going to join Bouillé. Choiseul, Goguelat, and the dragoons mount their horses and ride away from Pont Sommevesle. It was then, Choiseul says, about a quarter to six. The king reached Châlons at five, and was certainly not longer than an hour and a half reaching Pont Sommevesle. He, therefore, arrived three-quarters of an hour after Choiseul's departure, and found the post quite deserted. Carlyle says the hussars rode slowly away. This they could not have done. Had they gone at a walk to Ste. Ménehould, twenty-three kilometres distant, they

---

[1] Carlyle could not have fallen into this error if he had carefully read the narrative of Sieur Lagache, printed in Choiseul, P. J. 128. Choiseul's text is thoroughly loose and untrustworthy.

must have been at least three hours reaching it, and before that time the berline would have caught them up. Besides they might easily have stopped at Orbeval, the next post, but that was found to be deserted like Pont Somrnevesle. They must have ridden at a good pace. Choiseul turned off the road apparently about eighteen or nineteen kilometres from Pont Sommevesle. If the hussars had gone at a foot-pace, the berline would either have caught them up or have been in sight. The fact is, that Choiseul's narrative in these points is completely untrustworthy, as Croker saw when he wrote his article in the *Quarterly*.[1] He probably left the post long before 5.45, and exaggerates the excitement of the peasants.[2]

Carlyle says, "Near now is that Ste. Ménehould which expelled us in the morning with its 300 national *fusils*." This, we have seen, is an entire mistake. The National Guard was not armed with muskets until after the departure of the hussars. Carlyle also speaks of the "distant village of Varennes." Varennes, like Ste. Ménehould and Clermont, was a town with a complete municipal organization. Had it not been, it could not have behaved as it did.

In the next paragraph Carlyle repeats the statement that the berline has travelled under the weightiest dray rate, some three miles an hour. We have seen how false this is. Between Châlons and Ste. Ménehould the Royal family must have gone at a rate of nearly ten miles an hour.

It had been originally calculated that the king, leaving Paris at midnight, would reach Châlons about one o'clock,

---

[1] Croker, p. 131.
[2] Madame de Tourzel says (*Mémoires*, i. 313), that Choiseul " perdit totalement la tête. L'enterprise était au-dessus de ses forces." Fersen had before protested to Bouillé against employing him.

a distance of 161 kilometres, travelling twelve or thirteen kilometres, or between seven and eight miles, an hour. He reached Châlons at five o'clock, four hours later. Of this an hour and a half had been lost by the two accidents, an hour and a half in some mysterious manner in setting off, and an hour more on the road. Certainly at no time except when walking up hills had the berline travelled less than seven miles an hour, sometimes a great deal faster. And this is more than double Carlyle's estimate.

Chapter VI. is entitled "Old Dragoon Drouet." The first paragraph is an eloquent description of a sunset on a hot summer's day—rather out of place for a day in which the sun did not show itself till late in the afternoon. "Unnotable hum of sweet human gossip rises from this village of Ste. Ménehould." A village, forsooth, with 5,000 inhabitants and 300 National Guards! We then have a description of Drouet in loose, flowing nightgown. This is a translation of Choiseul's "robe de chambre," which means, of course, dressing-gown.[1] Carlyle evidently thinks that Drouet, after his dispute with Goguelat in the morning, had been wandering up and down the street all day in more or less of a huff. "Choleric Drouet steps out and steps in with long flowing nightgown." As a matter of fact, he had just returned from cultivating the field near the town, the very name of which is known—"Malassise." An "old dragoon," Carlyle calls him, "still in the prime of life." As a fact, he was born in 1763, and therefore was now twenty-eight years old. It is true that he quarrelled with Goguelat about horsing his post-chaise in the morning—"Engineer" Goguelat, not "Hussar" Goguelat, as Carlyle calls him—but after that he had gone out quietly and worked on his plot of land. "The great sun," says Carlyle, "flames

---

[1] Choiseul, p. 83.

broader towards setting. The yellow blockhead of a courier spurs past the post-house." Not at all. On arriving at the great square, he naturally rides on past the Hôtel de Ville, not knowing that he has to turn suddenly to the right to reach the post-house. Twelve minutes later comes the Korff berline, "with its mountains of bandboxes," existing only in Carlyle's imagination. The salute of the dragoons to the queen and the recognition of the king by Drouet is well described, but it was probably from the *assignat* with which the relays were paid, and not from the new one brought by Guillaume, that Drouet felt certain of his conjecture.

Carlyle repeats the ordinary story of Drouet recognising the king, and pursuing him with Guillaume on his own responsibility. The official *procès-verbal* of the commune of Ste. Ménehould says that the initiative was taken by the municipality, and that it was by their orders that Drouet and his companion set forth. With regard to the last incident in the chapter, there is no doubt that the "rigorous quartermaster," La Gache, went out alone. Why Carlyle says, "few or even none following him," and "Dandoin's trooper or troopers gallops after them," when it is certain that no one followed La Gache and that La Gache was not a trooper but an officer, who afterwards became a distinguished general, I do not know.

We now reach the seventh chapter, the "Night of Spurs." In the second paragraph, Carlyle admits that the berline is now "rushing." It did forty-one kilometres between Ste. Ménehould and Châlons in two hours and a half, which is a very good pace,—about ten miles an hour, including stoppages. The distance from Ste. Ménehould to Varennes, twenty-eight kilometres, was done in three hours, rather slower than the long stretch between Claye and Châlons. So it is now represented as rushing, when it is really going more slowly than when it was said to crawl. Also Carlyle's imagination makes him accept too readily Madame Campan's story about the unknown on horseback who "shrieks earnestly some hoarse whisper inaudible into the back window." In the third paragraph Carlyle has no word of blame for Damas, the commander of the troops at Clermont, because he bases his narrative on the authority of Damas' report, and Damas would not, if he could help it, implicate himself.

As a matter of fact, Damas mismanaged everything. He unsaddled his men half an hour before the king arrived. La Gache, coming from Ste. Ménehould, was half an hour before he could find Damas. He did not give the order to his soldiers until two hours after the king had passed, when he ought to have sent a detachment to follow him to Varennes. He did nothing indeed until after the king was arrested, and then, of course, it was too late. Damas had strict orders, "if the king wished to pass incognito, to allow him to do so, but to follow him at a distance of a mile or so to Varennes." If the fact that his horses were unsaddled prevented him from doing this, he should have made his men mount the moment the carriage had passed, and followed it as soon as possible. As a matter of fact, this culpable delay was used by a relation of his to defend him before the National Assembly as not being in the secret, and he was not ashamed to employ the same argument himself to secure his liberty.

Let us pass on to Varennes—"a little paltry village," Carlyle calls it. It is in reality, a small town with 1,400 inhabitants. Carlyle evidently never saw it nor realized what it was like. It is true that the carriage halted at the hill-top at the south end of the town nearest to Clermont, because the king had been told that the horses would be there. Goguelat, on his way to Pont Sommevesle, had countermanded this arrangement, leaving them in the stables on the other side of the bridge in the lower town, which Carlyle erroneously calls "the upper town." "Hussars likewise did wait," says Carlyle, "but drinking in the taverns." Not so. The hussars were where they ought to have been—in their barracks, commanded, not by the brave D'Eslon, who had been sent off to Bouillé by Goguelat, but by Lieutenant Rohrig, a young man of eighteen. Indeed, we know that up to 11 p.m. the sixty hussars left at Varennes were ready for instant departure.

"Six hours late," says Carlyle. If this were true the berline ought to have arrived at 5 p.m., which would have been sixteen kilometres, or ten miles an hour, all the way from Paris, including all stoppages and relays, As a fact, the berline was expected at about 9 or 9.30 p.m. Young Bouillé, not Louis, but Charles, had not gone to bed. Frightened by the disastrous report of Léonard, the coiffeur, who arrived at 9.30, he had retired to his room with his friend Raigecourt, of whom Carlyle says nothing. The unhappy Léonard, after scattering dismay at Clermont and Varennes, misses the route to Stenay, where he would have met Bouillé at one in the morning, and drives towards Verdun instead. Young Bouillé had orders to wait for the berline till four in the morning.

Carlyle next represents the "tired horses slobbering their meal and water for thirty-five minutes." Tired horses! why they had only gone fourteen kilometres, or eight and a half miles, in an hour and a half. Meal and water! why the whole difficulty lay in the fact that every house was closed, and that there was no place to get lodging or refreshments. Of the queen's descent from the carriage, and her entering the house of M. de Préfontaine, Carlyle does not say a word. The thirty-five minutes are right, but the two horsemen with "jaded trot" are wrong. There were four horsemen—two from Ste. Ménehould and two from Clermont. We are told that they passed "ventre à terre"; and they cried as they passed, "Postillons, arrêtez vous ; vous menez le roi."

Carlyle's description of the "Bras d'Or" is most amusing. He is evidently thinking of a country inn in Annandale. It does not look on to the market-place, but on to a narrow street. There were no drovers there, but four people whose names are well known — Poulot Leblanc, the brother of the innkeeper; Justin Georges, son of the mayor, captain of the guards; Thennevin, Grellier, of Les Islettes; and Delion, from Mont Faucon. This last may have been a drover, but there is nothing to show that he was. It is extremely unlikely that "Boniface Leblanc" wore a white apron. Drouet blocks the bridge as Carlyle describes. They then return to the archway which formerly connected the bell tower, which still exists, with the church of St. Gengoult opposite, now destroyed. Some half-dozen in all, says Carlyle. There were really ten—Drouet, Guillaume, Chevallot, Coquillard, two Leblancs, Georges, Ponsin, Thennevin, and Delion.

The cabriolet is allowed to pass under the archway. The berline is stopped, but I doubt very much whether "two national muskets levelled themselves fore and aft through the coach windows." Passports are not generally demanded in that fashion. It was quite enough to threaten the postilions. As a matter of fact, Sauce (not "Sausse") asked for the passport with official grocer politeness, holding up a lantern, as we know from the *procès-verbal* of Varennes.[1] They get out, but there is no authority for Carlyle's description of the order in which they walked. They did not cross the market-place, for there was no market-place to cross. They go a few steps down a narrow street. Also the demand for refreshments is apocryphal. We are told by an eye-witness that the queen asked for hot water, eggs and wine, and sheets for

---

[1] Bimbenet, P. J. p. 195. Madame de Tourzel says (*Mémoires*, i. 319), "Un officier s'approcha de la voiture du roi, lui dit tout bas qu'il y avait un gué et lui offrit de tenter de le faire passer." The king unfortunately refused.

the bed.[1] The wine probably came from their own travelling carriage.

I must now hurry to an end. "The clattering of the tocsin, he says, spreads over all the Clermontais, spreads throughout the three bishoprics." This is rather loose. Verdun, less than twenty miles from Varennes, was undoubtedly affected, but Toul and Metz were entirely undisturbed. In some forty minutes, Carlyle says, Goguelat and Choiseul arrived with their wearied hussars from Sommevesle. Forty minutes from what? As a fact, they arrived at one o'clock, about an hour and a half after the king's arrest, two hours after his arrival. They then lost a quarter of an hour or twenty minutes at the barricade which had been formed at the entrance of the town, and did not dare to pass it till Damas came up with his handful of dragoons. The account given by Carlyle of the conduct of these hussars is not at all exact. Choiseul leads them down the street past Sauce's house to their barracks. He harangues them in the barrack square, and it is there that they cry, "Der König! Die Konigin!" He then leads them back again to the front of Sauce's house. Damas, on the other hand, with his four or five dragoons, the only men whom he could persuade to follow him from Clermont, crosses the bridge, notwithstanding the barricade, goes to the hôtel "Grand Monarque," finds that the relays had departed, that Bouillé is off to his father, and Raigecourt with him, repasses the bridge and joins Choiseul opposite Sauce's house.

The indecision of the King and his inability to give an order is not inaccurately portrayed, but there is no word of blame for Choiseul and Damas, who did not act without asking for orders. If Damas could cross the bridge with five dragoons, the king might certainly have been cut out with forty hussars.

---

[1] Fouché, in *Despatches of Lord Gower*, p. 374.

In Aubriot's flight we have another touch of exaggerative poetry. "Swimming dark rivers," says Carlyle. All that Aubriot did was to ford the Aire, a very paltry stream, and ride across fields till he reached the road. Similarly, brave Deslons with his hussars, "darted to the river Aire, swam one branch of it, could not the other." As a fact, he crossed the Aire by a perfectly well-known ford, practicable for carriage horses, and sometimes even for foot-passengers; he was stopped by the deep, narrow mill-stream which runs in a loop from one part of the Aire to another. Deslons, the real commander of the hussars at Varennes, should have known the country well enough to turn the mill-stream by crossing the Aire above the spot where it leaves the river.

I have finished a very ungrateful task. I would say, in conclusion, that any one who reads Carlyle's narrative will have before his eyes a very vivid picture of the affair as it occurred in its main outlines. But when he looks minutely into it he will discover that almost every detail is inexact, some of them quite wrong and misleading. This is the danger of the picturesque school of historians. They will be picturesque at any price.

The historian more than anybody else should take to heart the maxim, "Never be certain unless you know." We now know almost every detail of the flight and capture of the king, and I can recall no event more tragic to one who has studied it in all its details. The naked truth is far more impressive and pathetic than Carlyle's fiction.

Whether the rest of Carlyle's "French Revolution" is equally untrustworthy, I cannot say. I took this episode almost at random, because I happened to be interested in it, and because Carlyle's fame is largely based upon it. I was quite surprised as I went on to find how careless and inaccurate it was.

III.
THE FOREIGN POLICY OF WILLIAM PITT.

IT is even now a matter of dispute between serious and responsible statesmen whether England is or is not a Continental Power. It is said that the "silver streak" so effectually separates us from the mainland of Europe, that we may treat the intrigues and combinations of our neighbours with indifference, and work out our own destiny after our own manner. Undoubtedly the possession of an ocean frontier is a great advantage. So long as our fleet is in proper order, we have no need of a large standing army to watch the course of a petty river or an ill-defined barrier of arbitrary landmarks. But since the dawn of our annals England has been at all times profoundly affected by the course of foreign affairs. Our Constitution may have developed itself in unbroken continuity from its earliest germ, imported from an older England on the shores of the North Sea. But our general history cannot be rightly understood unless England is regarded as part of the European State system. Mommsen tells us in his Roman History that the conquest of Britain by Cæsar was rendered necessary by the impossibility of distinguishing our southern coast from the northern coast of Gaul. To say nothing of our relations with Scandinavia, our later Saxon kings were intimately connected with the Norman dukes. The Conquest made us for a time a part of France. The French wars were only put an end to by the Wars of the Roses. Henry VIII. stands by the side of Charles V. and Francis I., as one of the trinity of monarchs whose feuds and friendships decided the fate of Christendom. Elizabeth was the head of all the Protestants of Europe; Cromwell held the keys of Europe at his girdle; William III. was more important as the chief of a European coalition than as king of England, and the same weighty heritage devolved upon the shoulders of the passive Anne. The history of the first two Hanoverian kings cannot be written until the archives of Europe disclose their secrets. George III., born and bred a Briton, found his reign disturbed by two great wars, in the first of which a domestic quarrel gradually assumed the dimensions of a world-wide conflict, while in the second the farmer king was forced into the position of Dutch William. The peaceful supremacy which England enjoyed for nearly forty years after the Settlement of Vienna, was due to the efforts and sacrifices which she had made during the two preceding decades. Nor is it likely that the rule which has prevailed for two thousand years will be altered in our time. Whether we like it or not, we are still part of the complex European system; and, if we are to bear ourselves wisely, it behoves us to study the history of our foreign relations.

Not that these relations are easy to study. Domestic history may be written with tolerable accuracy from contemporary newspapers and Parliamentary debates, but foreign relations are shrouded in mystery. Some of the most important movements do not become public at all. A hundred years must generally elapse before the necessary documents become accessible. Nor is it sufficient to know the secrets of a single country. We cannot grasp the truth until the relations between all the Powers engaged are present to our mind in a general view. Until Sybel wrote his history of the French Revolution, no one suspected to how great an extent the affairs of Poland had lamed the activity of the European coalition. Friedmann has thrown new light on the fate of Anne Boleyn; Noorden is indispensable for our knowledge of the reign of Queen Anne. We are approaching the time when we may be able to form a judgment as to the attitude of England in the most momentous crisis of her history, when, in the collapse of Governments and the shock of Thrones, she alone, of all the countries of Europe, preserved her Constitution and her independence.

Some books which have been recently published make a contribution to this knowledge, which may be accepted with gratitude in default of more abundant light. A volume of the Camden Society reprints the memoranda of Francis, fifth Duke of Leeds, from the originals in the British Museum. The Duke of Leeds was the first Foreign Minister of the younger Pitt. His memoranda range, with considerable breaks, from 1774 to 1796, that is, from the

duke's twenty-fourth year to within three years of
his death. After 1780 they are set down day by day
as the events occurred, and may therefore be accepted
as fairly accurate. They deal perhaps too much with
domestic incidents and with the conflicts of party,
but they contain much that is interesting. There is
a good account of the Shelburne Ministry, which
intervened between the death of Lord Rockingham
and the accession of the coalition to power. The
name of William Pitt constantly occurs. Perhaps
in no memoirs of the time are we admitted with a
fuller intimacy into the conversations of the Cabinet
and the closet of the Sovereign. The form of the
book makes no concessions to popularity; it is sternly,
even repulsively, historical. Lovers of gossip will
find nothing to gratify them except the memoranda
which refer to the Princess of Wales, which have
been partly used by Mr. Fitzgerald. But the careful
reader may discover a good deal to supplement his
knowledge, while scattered papers drawn from other
volumes in the British Museum throw considerable
light on foreign affairs.

The second book is conceived upon a different
plan. Sir James Bland Burges was Under Secretary for Foreign Affairs from 1789 to 1795, a momentous period in the history of the world. He left
behind him a short autobiographical memoir and a
mass of official correspondence. Selections from this
correspondence, edited by a scholar of competent
historical knowledge, would have been invaluable.
Mr. Hutton is mistaken in supposing that the facts
of this period are "already known to students of

modern history." The most important of them are either not known at all, or are matters of ardent controversy. There is abundant proof in the book, that some of the commonest of them are not known to Mr. Hutton. But perhaps the editor is right in thinking that "for ordinary readers, in quest of sensation and novelty," such information "would bear only a faint interest. Not that those readers will find the book very exciting as it stands. Mr. Hutton has aimed at giving a picture of the man, and Sir James Bland Burges cannot by any effort be made an interesting character. His sole claim to distinction is, that for six eventful years he had access to secrets which many people now living would give their ears to know. When will serious historical study have reached such a standard in England, that unrivalled collections of public documents will be treated from some other point of view than that of a vain attempt to beguile the "ordinary reader"? The supplemental volumes of the Wellington Correspondence are a model rarely imitated in this country. Lord Beaconsfield, the sworn enemy of dulness, who warned precocious children against inquiring too narrowly into the authorship of "Junius," or the identification of the "Iron Mask," gave to these bulky volumes his unqualified praise. The three hundred letters of William Pitt, which are said once to have existed in the Auckland papers, would outweigh all the clever gossip of Mr. Storer which is printed in the published correspondence. Mr. Hutton has indeed attempted to give liveliness to his pages by a less legitimate process. He pours the vials of his scorn on diplomatists to whom England owes the deepest obligations, and whose character was never assailed except by those who, being higher in station, were jealous of their abilities and power. At a time when no Cabinet was considered secure without its usual complement of dukes, and when a diplomat in certain Courts was obliged to be a man of rank and fashion, as well as of knowledge and affairs, our interests would have fared badly indeed, if we had not possessed public servants of such trained capacity as William and Morton Eden, Hugh Elliot, and Daniel Hailes. For three of these Mr. Hutton has very hard words, which we may suppose to be the echo of the "boldness and finish" with which their characters are sketched by Mr. Burges. The fourth, the most brilliant of all, he does not mention. Yet Lord Auckland was the trusted friend of Pitt, who wished to marry his daughter. He was probably the only man in England, except Pitt himself, who could have negociated the commercial treaty with France and the East Indian Convention. During a public career of nearly fifty years he was acquainted with every important secret of State. He was equally trusted by men so different as Lord Suffolk and Lord Loughborough, Pitt and Grenville, Vergennes and Van de Spiegel. He left behind him a collection of State papers, the best monument of his career, mutilated, alas! and impaired by the carelessness of posterity, not one line of which need call up a blush on the face of his warmest partisan. Lord Henley was well worthy of the brother who watched tenderly over his education, while the despatches of Hailes are a striking contrast to the frivolous puerilities of the Duke of Dorset. Hailes was one of the very few statesmen in Europe who foresaw the results to which the summoning of the States-General would inevitably lead. Still we are grateful to Mr. Hutton for giving us what he has thought fit to print. Perhaps at some future time the Burges papers will be made to yield more valuable metal. In the meantime let us sum up the solid results which these two volumes present to us.

An interesting page of Sir James Burges's recollections introduces us for the first time to the Duke of Leeds, then Marquis of Carmarthen, as well as to William Pitt and the historian Gibbon. Gibbon was then forty-three years old, Lord Carmarthen twenty-nine, and Pitt twenty-one. They were dining with Mr. Burges in his rooms in the Temple. Mr. Gibbon, then at the zenith of his fame, was in the habit of taking the lead in the conversation in whatever company he might find himself:—

"His conversation was not indeed what Dr. Johnson would have called *talk*. There was no interchange of ideas, for no one had a chance of replying. So fugitive, so variable was his mode of discoursing, which consisted of points, anecdotes, and epigrammatic thrusts, all more or less to the purpose, and all pleasantly said with a French air and manner which gave them great piquancy, but which were withal so desultory and unconnected that, though each separately was extremely amusing, the attention of his auditors sometimes flagged before his own resources were exhausted. Mr. Gibbon, nothing loath, took the conversation in his own hands, and very brilliant and pleasant he was during the dinner and for some time afterwards. He had just concluded, however, one of his best foreign anecdotes, in which he had introduced some of the fashionable levities of political doctrine then prevalent, and, with his customary tap on the lid of his snuff-box, was looking round to receive our tribute of applause, when a deep-toned but clear voice was heard from the bottom of the table, very calmly and civilly impugning the correctness of the narrative, and the propriety of the doctrines of which it had been made the vehicle. The historian, turning a disdainful glance towards the quarter whence the voice proceeded, saw, for the first time, a tall, thin, and rather ungainly-looking young man, who now sat quietly and silently eating some fruit. There was nothing very prepossessing or very formidable in his exterior, but, as the few words he had uttered appeared to have made a considerable impression on the company, Mr. Gibbon, I suppose, thought himself bound to maintain his honour, by suppressing such attempt to dispute his supremacy. He accordingly undertook the defence of the propositions in question, and a very animated debate took place between him and his youthful antagonist, Mr. Pitt, and for some time was conducted with great talent and brilliancy on both sides. At length the genius of the young man prevailed over that of his senior, who, finding himself driven into a corner from which there was no escape, made some excuse for rising from the table, and walked out of the room. I followed him, and, finding that he was looking for his hat, I tried to persuade him to return to his seat. 'By no means,' said he; 'that young gentleman is, I have no doubt, extremely ingenious and agreeable, but I must acknowledge that his style of conversation is not exactly what I am accustomed to, so you must positively excuse me.' And away he went in high dudgeon, notwithstanding that his friend had come to my assistance. When we returned into the dining-room we found Mr. Pitt proceeding very tranquilly with the illustration of the subject from which his opponent had fled, and which he discussed with such ability, strength of argument, and eloquence, that his hearers were filled with profound admiration."

Francis Godolphin Osborne, fifth Duke of Leeds, was born on January 29, 1751. After receiving the ordinary education of an English nobleman, he went, according to the custom of those days, on the grand tour. The narrative of his three years' travels, kept with scrupulous accuracy, is still extant. He saw Louis XV. and his family at Paris, walked about the garden of Ferney with Voltaire, spent a considerable time at Rome and Naples, and visited Kaunitz at Vienna. He learnt languages, dancing, music, and the high school of horsemanship, besides becoming acquainted with the political condition of Europe. He married shortly after his return a lady who afterwards left him to run away with Jack Byron, the father of the poet. Mr. Burges gives a graphic description of him as he appeared at the age of thirty :—

" He appeared then to have united in himself a combination of endowments such as have rarely fallen to the lot of the most favoured individual. Descended from noble ancestry, heir to the dukedom of Leeds, in possession of an ample, independent fortune, and looking forward to the not distant accession to one still more considerable, he had in these respects no excuse to envy any man. And not inferior were the advantages which nature had liberally bestowed upon him. His talents were brilliant and acute, his memory uncommonly retentive, his powers of conception so prompt that he was able at a glance to comprehend whatever was submitted to him, and to decide upon the line of action to be taken; while his ready wit, and his wonderful faculty of expression, whether by speech or by writing, in prose or in verse, charmed and dazzled all with whom he associated. These rare qualities had received the cultivation derivable from an education at Westminster School and at Oxford, followed by several years' residence at foreign Courts. In addition to all this, few men equalled him in personal beauty of face and figure. His countenance was most prepossessing, and seemed to indicate at once the quickness of his intellect and the suavity of his disposition. He had the gallant spirit of a noble gentleman with the manner and address of an accomplished courtier."

Although Lord Carmarthen received strong marks of royal favour at the outset of his career, becoming a member of the king's household and chamberlain to the queen, this did not prevent him from asserting his independence. In spite of a lecture from Lord North, the Marquis took an active part in the meeting, which resulted in the Yorkshire petition, but felt obliged to resign his offices at Court. He told the king that he could no longer give his support to Lord North, Lord George Germaine, and Lord Sandwich. The king said in his nervous manner: "I'm very sorry; I'm very sorry"; but added he was sure that Lord Carmarthen had acted from conviction, and therefore like a man of honour. Notwithstanding this, ten days later he was summarily dismissed from the Lord Lieutenancy of the East Riding. "My surprise," he says, "could scarcely have been greater had it been a warrant of commitment to the Tower." Lord Pembroke and the Duke of Richmond were his companions in misfortune. His lot was then thrown in with the Opposition, and he took an active part in the attack upon Lord North, which led to his resignation. On the accession of the Rockingham Ministry to office, Lord Carmarthen was restored to his Lord Lieutenancy, and there was a talk of putting him into office, or giving him an embassy. These arrangements were put an end to by Lord Rockingham's death, after he had held office only three months.

Lord Shelburne's Ministry was strengthened by the accession of the youthful Pitt, and weakened by the refusal of Fox to serve under him. Although Fox and Shelburne may have differed as to the independence of America, yet there is no doubt that personal feeling was an important element in the quarrel. Fox would have served with Shelburne under a neutral ruler; he would not submit to a subordinate position. With strange inconsistency, he threw himself into the arms of Lord North, who, night after night for many years, had been the object of his assaults in the House of Commons. The coalition was brought about by the shifty and unscrupulous Lord Loughborough, and William Eden was privy to the arrangement. After a second defeat on the terms of peace with France, Lord Shelburne called his friends together at Shelburne House, on Sunday, February 23, and declared his determination to resign. Lord Carmarthen, who had received the high honour of being chosen as the first Ambassador to France after the renewal of intercourse with that country, was unwilling to serve under the new Ministry, and would only do so if the king's service imperatively required it. For more than a month the country remained without a Government. The king used every effort to persuade Pitt to take the seals, but with rare self-command he refused. On February 26, on the king's renewed request, he promised to do what he could to obey his commands, and not till March 26 did he tell his Royal master that he saw no probability of a firm support or of a want of union in the coalition. At last, on April 1, at half-past ten at night, Lord North was sent for to produce his Cabinet. "Are these the persons," said the king, "whom you and the Duke of Portland wish to name?" "To recommend, sir," answered Lord North. But the king insisted on his phrase, and added, with some malice, "There are two other important places to be provided for, Ireland and France, for I can inform you that Lord Temple will not stay, and Lord Carmarthen will not go."

On December 17, Fox's East India Bill was defeated in the House of Lords by a majority of nineteen votes. On the next day, at eleven o'clock at night, Nepean, Lord North's Under-Secretary, was sent for by the king to Buckingham House. The king was alone, and ordered the astonished underling to demand the seals from the two Secretaries of State, and to bring them to him at once. According to Mr. Burges, the two unsuspecting victims were supping at Lord North's, and discussing quietly what should be done after their defeat. Entering the supper-room, and refusing to sit down, after a few minutes of embarassing silence, Nepean stated the object of his mission. Fox refused to believe it, and Nepean had to repeat his message. Lord North then said good-humouredly, " If such be the case, Nepean, you will have very little trouble with me. My seals are in your custody; you have only to take them to the king." Fraser, the Under-Secretary of the Foreign Department, was at the table, and had no difficulty in producing Mr. Fox's seals. Nepean took them to Buckingham House, and the king received them in silence. The next morning Pitt was appointed Prime Minister. Mr. Burges says that the post was first offered to Lord Temple, but for this there is no foundation. On the following evening, Saturday, March 20th, Lord Carmarthen dined at Lord Temple's. The host and his nephew were very glum, and it was evident that something unpleasant had occurred. In fact, Lord Temple had determined to resign because Pitt would not insist upon the king making him a marquis or a duke. This resignation carried dismay into the hearts of the new Ministry, and caused Pitt the only sleepless night which Bishop Tomline remembers him to have spent. After a moment of indecision, Pitt was more resolute than ever to support his Sovereign, who had told him in a letter that he was like a drowning man glad to catch at every twig. Lord Gower was a member of the Administration from the first, and not, as Mr. Burges says, in succession to Lord Camden. On Tuesday Lord Carmarthen was offered and accepted the seals of the Foreign Secretaryship.

His colleague was Lord Sydney, better known as Tommy Townshend, whom Burke sometimes persuaded "to lend him a vote." Mr. Burges tells an amusing story of him :—

"One day, when he did me the honour to take me in his carriage to the House of Lords, he suddenly remarked, 'I can't imagine why they call me Lord Tommy. Can you tell me?' I answered as gravely as possible that I could not. 'It's very strange,' said he. 'Lord Tommy! I should like to know why they call me that. But I'll ask Lord Carmarthen; he'll be most likely to know—don't you think so?' I told him I thought he could not do better, and I could say so honestly, for it happened that it was to Lord Carmarthen that he was indebted for the title that puzzled him."

The first Cabinet Council of the new Ministers was held at Lord Carmarthen's, on December 28. There was much to be done before Parliament met on January 12. A new East India Bill must be drafted and introduced at the very beginning of the session. An Appropriation Act had to be framed, and the Mutiny Acts, which expired on March 25, must be renewed either in the present Parliament or in a new one. The Ministers were in a considerable minority in the House of Commons, but it was known that the country was with them and with the king. By superhuman efforts the India Bill was prepared in time, but the financial difficulties were so great that Pitt "even hinted at giving the thing up." Mr. Burges takes credit for two valuable pieces of advice given by him to the new Ministers. The first was the introduction to Pitt of the design of the sinking fund, which was to be provided for by a succession duty; and the second was the discovery that a Mutiny Bill could be introduced into the House of Lords, thus turning Fox's flank, and compelling him to give in. This second service was strangely forgotten by the Duke of Leeds, who merely remarks: "So strong was the tide without doors against Mr. Fox and his majority, that they thought prudent to pass the Mutiny Bill in compliance with the wishes of the public." On the morning of the very day that Parliament was prorogued, the Lord Chancellor's house was broken open and the Great Seal stolen. Some candlesticks, a sword, and some money were taken at the same time; but it was felt that the theft had in all probability a political significance. However, a new seal was prepared by the following day, and on Thursday evening, March 25, the proclamation for dissolving Parliament was signed and sealed. "Thus," says the Duke of Leeds, "was an end put to one of the most extraordinary Parliaments that had ever existed, and which, from every motive of prudence and sound policy, ought to have been dissolved much sooner."

Lord Carmarthen assumed the seals of the Foreign Office at a momentous period. England had just emerged, with the loss of her American colonies, from a war which had embroiled her with nearly the whole of Europe. France, Spain, and Holland had successively taken the field against her. Her finances were ruined, and her military prestige stood at a very different level from that which it had reached twenty years before, at the end of the Seven Years' War. We were without an ally in Europe. France, governed by Louis XVI. and Vergennes, was in favour of peace and free trade. Her unfortunate Sovereign, who was to reap the ruin which had been sown by others, had no other wish but to develop the commerce, resuscitate the navy, and invigorate the colonies of his country, and to keep, if possible, some shreds of that Indian Empire which, before the epoch of Clive and Hastings, had seemed destined for the French. The alliance between France and Austria, the masterpiece of Kaunitz, formed in 1756 for the humiliation of Frederick the Great, still subsisted, but it was a drag upon the action of both countries, rather than an assistance to their development. Joseph II., after sharing his mother's crown and power for fifteen years, had recently succeeded to independent sovereignty. He was, perhaps, the most dangerous influence in Europe. Full of good intentions, with a keen insight into the evils and deficiencies of his age, he failed in all his undertakings, and stirred up bitterness and rebellion, where he desired nothing but prosperity and goodwill. He dragged Maria Theresa, against her better judgment, into the "Potato" War of the Bavarian succession. His own master since 1780, he issued countless edicts against the abuses of his time, against the nobles, the clergy, the system of orders, and the monasteries, which had no effect but to cause worse confusion. Religious toleration and the abolition of serfdom were the only solid results which he achieved. Learning nothing by experience, he quarrelled with the Dutch by abolishing the Barrier Treaty, opening the Scheldt, and laying claim to Maestricht. At the same time, he tried to effect the exchange of Belgium for Bavaria, and gave Prussia the opportunity of placing herself at the head of a league of German princes directed against the power of Austria. In all these projects Joseph was checked by France. She had no sympathy with his reckless stirring of sleeping dogs. His conduct towards Holland interfered with her most cherished plans, and she forced a reconciliation upon him by the Treaty of Versailles. Desirous to keep on good terms with Frederick the Great, she resented a course of action which would exasperate that sly old fox, while she had every reason to dread the plans of aggrandizement at the expense of Turkey which occupied the closing years of his reign.

Catherine II., who ruled Russia wisely for thirty-four years, was, next to Joseph, the power from whom England had most to fear. Although she had not taken sides against us in the American War, she had formed in the darkest part of it the confederacy of the Armed Neutrality, in which a number of maritime powers were banded to resist our supremacy at sea. Whatever care she might bestow on French philosophers and handsome guardsmen, her cool head always kept the solid interests of Russia in view; and the two Powers at whose expense it could be most conveniently increased, were Poland and Turkey. The first partition of Poland and the Peace of Kutschuk Kainardji had fallen in times when our attention was occupied elsewhere. Frederick the Great, though he kept a watchful eye on every movement in Europe, was occupied in consolidating his Goverment, and wished for no new war. A statesman, therefore, surveying the condition of Europe with the knowledge which we now possess, would have seen that France, with an outward appearance of majesty, was rotten to the core, and was hastening to the catastrophe which was in ten years to overwhelm her. He would have perceived that the peaceful development of French commerce and industry was the true interest of Europe, and the best means of conquering the tumultuous passions which were soon to carry havoc into every portion of the civilized world. He would have seen that the alliance between France and Austria, however much it might have departed from its original intention, was the best check upon the ambition of both, and was a safeguard to the peace of Europe.

The Marquis of Carmarthen, however, and possibly George III., were of a different opinion. In their eyes France was the hereditary enemy of England, and every intrigue and movement in Europe were to be attributed to French influence. They knocked humbly at the door of Russia, who refused to listen to their blandishments, they strained every nerve to excite the suspicions of Kaunitz; and his repeated assurances, that France had no hostile designs, and was incapable of dangerous action, only confirmed their suspicion of mischief. When they failed to move the minister, they approached the Sovereign himself, and Sir Robert Murray Keith was ordered to assure Joseph that we not only had no objection to his opening the navigation of the Scheldt, but that there was no object of his ambition, however extravagant, which we should not be disposed to support, if he would only give up his unnatural alliance with the House of Bourbon. It is a comfort to learn that Pitt was not the author of this policy. Lord Carmarthen found that he could not prevail upon the Cabinet to give that attention to foreign affairs which he thought necessary, and consequently afterwards gave them little trouble on the subject.

"Mr. Pitt, however, for some time applied himself to the correspondence with great assiduity, and during a day I stayed with him at Wimbledon we had a great deal of conversation on the general subject of European politics; this happened in May, and I was very happy to find our ideas were similar on the great object of separating if possible the House of Austria from France, as likewise a degree of desire to form some system on the Continent in order to counterbalance the House of Bourbon, though at the same time the strongest conviction of the necessity of avoiding, if possible, the entering into any engagements likely to embroil us in a new war."

The true Pitt speaks out in the last clause. The objects he had most nearly at heart were peace, retrenchment, and reform. A solvent and united England would be a tower of strength in a bankrupt and distracted Europe.

The alliance which England sought in vain from Russia and Austria was to come from another quarter. Holland was at this time the second maritime power

in Europe, and from the extent of her navy and her
trade, as well as from her assertion and protection
of liberty, was almost worthy to rank among the
Great Powers. Dutch history, which indeed does
not extend over two centuries and a half, exhibits
a remarkable example of the strength and weakness
of Federal Government. The seven provinces were
united by the loosest bond of confederation known
to political science. Holland, the largest province,
set an example of the whole, but even peace and
war were matters of municipal and not of imperial
policy. When a foreign enemy in the shape of France
threatened their independence, the provinces sought
for strength and unity in the protection of a Stadtholder, who had command of the army and the fleet,
and other privileges of a more disputed kind. When
the pressure was removed, the instinct of separation
reasserted itself, the Stadtholder's power was diminished, and each oligarchy of merchants governed
itself with its Pensionary and Greffier, until a new
danger revived the desire of a personal Sovereign.
As France was the Power most dreaded by Holland,
so it was the interest of France to foster the separa-
tist feeling and the power of the oligarchies, while
since the time of William III. the Stadtholder had
looked for the support of England. Thus we see
in Holland an ebb and flow of weaker and stronger
union, one movement depending on France, the other
on England; one supported by the trading oligarchy,
the other by the mass of the people. In the American
war Holland had first been caught by the Armed
Neutrality, and had then been driven into open

hostility against England. At the settlement of Versailles she was the last of the belligerents to make peace, and the treaty which secured the cession of Negapatam to England was not concluded until Pitt was in office. A minister had to be sent to the newly regained friend, and a better choice could not have been made than James Harris, afterwards Lord Malmesbury. He came, like Eden, from the ranks of the Opposition, and, unlike Eden, returned to them again; but Mr. Burges, who has many hard words for the turncoat Eden, has nothing to say against Harris.

When Harris arrived at the Hague about the end of 1784, he found the party of the Stadtholder in the lowest depths of despair. William V., who then held the office, was not the man to retrieve his position; and his best hope lay in the support of his noble-hearted wife, Frederica Wilhelmina, niece of Frederick the Great. It was nevertheless in Holland and under these conditions that the battle between English and French supremacy had to be fought. Holland had at that time a powerful navy and large naval experience. She had shown a talent for colonization. The Dutch East India Company was the principal rival to the English Company. In alliance with Holland, France might hope to win back something of her commerce beyond seas, and to check the undisputed predominance of the British flag. It was the business of Harris to thwart these designs, to depose the Dutch patriots, as they were called, to restore the Stadtholder to his ancient rank, and to base his power on the security of English support. The steps by which Harris effected these objects are most interesting to trace. There was in the English Cabinet at this time a forward party, who were desirous to press the predominance of England on every opportunity, and a party who desired to avoid European complications, and who sought the aggrandizement of their country in economy and peace. Carmarthen and Pitt may be regarded as types of the two attitudes, and their diverging views led to a rupture in 1791. Still, strongly as Pitt desired peace, he knew that it was often best secured by energetic language backed by decided action; and many of his despatches might have been written by the imperious Chatham. Harris soon saw that, to secure Holland, it was useless to attempt the severance of Austria from France. Austria was too strongly opposed to the interests of Holland to join us in an alliance with that country, whilst France was of necessity the firm support of the patriots against whom our policy was directed. Russia was inaccessible; therefore the one Power that remained to us was Prussia, closely cemented with the Stadtholder by family ties, and under the influence of a long-standing jealousy with the House of Austria. Harris proposed a triple alliance between England, Holland, and Prussia, a plan which took three years to realize, but which, when completed, was an earnest of peace, and for some time gave the law to Europe. It is unaccountable that Mr. Hutton (p. 145) attributes this great service to Mr. Ewart, who had little or nothing to do with it; while he turns the Triple Alliance into a quadruple alliance between England, Holland, Prussia, and Turkey. Harris's views were laid before the Cabinet on May 10, 1785. They are contained in a masterly paper, reprinted among the Leeds memoranda (p. 111). It is represented that Austria and France are connected together, Russia is connected with Austria, Spain with France. The consequence of this league will fall especially on England and Prussia; these two courts, therefore, must concert measures for mutual security. We must increase and consolidate the confederacy of princes now taking shape in the Empire : we must separate Russia from the leaguers, preserve Denmark, neutralize Sweden, and, above all, reclaim Holland. The King of Prussia is better able to give us advice, intelligence, and assistance than any prince in Europe. We must enter into definite negociations with him, and settle precisely what amount of aid each Power is to afford to the other. France must on no account have the low countries, and England will do her best to prevent Austria from obtaining Bavaria.

The first result of this policy was, that the King of England joined the League of Princes as Elector of Hanover, a step which called out strong remonstrances from the Ambassadors of Austria and Russia, but which was gratefully acknowledged by Frederick the Great. Lord Cornwallis was sent on a special mission to Berlin, but Frederick refused to take any active step. He was too old to throw himself into an European war. He counselled his niece to make terms with the patriots and to seek the protection of France. The position of the Stadtholder became worse and worse. At the end of 1785 a treaty of alliance was signed between France and Holland. England protested against it, but was not prepared to go to war without the support of Prussia.

On August 17, 1786, Frederick the Great died. The new king was of an excitable and adventurous disposition. He wished for an alliance with England, and was not disposed to overlook any insult to his sister. Count Görz was sent to the Hague, and both parties in Holland began to arm. Harris pressed hard for the active intervention of England; but Pitt, who had just concluded the commercial treaty with France, was more desirous of peace than ever. With the connivance of Carmarthen, Harris wrote a letter to Pitt himself. He pointed out that a most important struggle was taking place in Holland, that the subjection of Holland to France would isolate England in Europe and be a constant menace to our trade, whereas by alliance with Holland we could best hope to establish ourselves in Europe, and to form useful and permanent connections with other Powers. Pitt's answer was more favourable than the conspirators had dared to hope. Carmarthen wrote in exultation, "Now we have raised his attention to the important object in question we must by all means endeavour to keep it up, and not suffer Holland to be sacrificed either to lawn or cambric." The temper of the Cabinet, however, was very cautious. A letter of Carmarthen's to the king, on January 7, 1787, received a snubbing answer, probably at the instigation of Pitt. Months passed, and nothing was done. In May Harris came again to England, and succeeded in getting Pitt to agree to advance £20,000 to the Stadtholder, either as a loan or otherwise. Their resolution was quickened by the intelligence that the French were preparing a camp on the Belgian frontier, at Givet.

This state of tension was suddenly broken by an unexpected step on the part of the lion-hearted Princess. She left Nimeguen, to which she had retired, and joined her husband at the camp which had been formed at Amersfort. From this place she wrote to the Hague to say that she was coming there to place herself at the head of the Stadtholder's party. On the evening of June 28 she was arrested by some free corps near Gouda, and kept for a day in confinement. She was then released and returned to Nimeguen. This insult offered to his sister was sufficient to decide the wavering character of the King of Prussia. He immediately prepared to march troops into Holland. At the same time Eden, who had just concluded the commercial treaty with France, was instructed to use the most energetic language at Paris. Pitt wrote to him, on September 15, that the French must, as things stand, give up their predominant influence in Holland or fight for it. A Cabinet minute of September 19[1] states that there is every reason to suppose that the French will oppose the Prussian troops, and orders the fleet to be armed and the army to be increased. War between France and England was within an ace of breaking out. Indeed, some of the French

---

[1] "Leeds papers," p. 118.

Ministers desired it, as the best escape from domestic troubles. It was prevented by the firmness and decision of Pitt. On the very day of the Cabinet minute the Prussian army entered Holland in three columns. All resistance immediately collapsed. The free corps were broken up; the Stadtholder was restored to the Hague with all the authority which he had ever possessed. The result of this was to place Holland entirely in our hands. Montmorin, who had succeeded Vergennes as Foreign Minister at Versailles, signed a declaration promising to disarm, and declaring that the king had never intended to interfere in the affairs of the United Provinces. Treaties between England and Holland, and England and Prussia, were signed in April, 1788, on the same day. Two months later an alliance was concluded with the King of Prussia at Loo, a diplomatic victory achieved by the energy and versatility of Harris, to the dismay of the French party at the Prussian Court. In this manner was consolidated the Triple Alliance of 1788, a connection which gave England a predominant voice in the Councils of Europe, and made her the arbiter of war and peace, until the settlement was swept away, with many others, in the rising flood of the French Revolution.

Before the conclusion of the Triple Alliance a negociation had taken place with France, which exhibits Pitt's policy in the clearest light. Among the many marvels of Pitt's career—that he should have been Chancellor of the Exchequer at twenty-three, Prime Minister at twenty-four, that he should have been master of his Cabinet from the very outset, that he should have established a strong government in the teeth of a majority of the House of Commons, that with scarcely a single adequate supporter he should have defended himself against the eloquence of Burke, Fox, and Sheridan—none perhaps is greater than that he should have been one of the best informed and the most enlightened economists of his time, a true disciple of Adam Smith. The seven years of study at Cambridge must have been well spent. It was this instructed view of finance which enabled him to conclude the commercial treaty with France in 1786. Such a treaty had been among the arrangements of the Peace of Versailles. The French Government were strong free-traders; they believed that the wealth of a country lay in the products of its soil, and that, as different countries produced different things, it was advantageous for each that its special produce should be freely exchanged with those of all the others. France was anxious to find a market for her wines, oil, and silk; she had no objection to admit English hardware and cotton in return. She even believed, that with no return free access to the English market would be beneficial in itself. The ancestral jealousy of France was too strong to permit these views to find acceptance in England. The term fixed for the conclusion of the treaty expired at the end of 1785. The time was drawing to an end, and nothing had been done. The French had repeatedly demanded the execution of the treaty. A Mr. Crauford had been sent to Paris with the knowledge that nothing was expected of him. The French had put pressure on us by issuing edicts prohibiting the importation of English manufactures, by declaring that the Treaty of Utrecht, which established a certain degree of reciprocity between the two countries, should be allowed to lapse, and finally by concluding an alliance with Holland. This last step roused Pitt to action. The two years which had elapsed since his accession to office had been spent in party conflicts, in legislation for India, in the attempts to retrieve our finances, and in the fruitless effort to establish free trade with Ireland. He wrote to Harris at this time: "The general state of our revenue is improving daily. We are, I believe, in possession of a million surplus beyond our probable annual expenses, and shall, if the same course of prosperity continues, find ourselves very different in the eye of Europe from what we have been for some time." He, therefore, three weeks before the expiration of the allotted period, writes in the name of Carmarthen for an extension of the time. Vergennes replies by granting a delay of six months, which may be extended to twelve. It should be mentioned here that, at least in the earlier portion of Pitt's career, the most important despatches in all departments were composed by him, and were drafted in his handwriting. Even if his style is not always a sufficient proof of authorship in despatches signed by the Secretaries of State, by Carmarthen, Grenville, or Sydney, the original drafts, in his own unmistakable autograph, existing in the Record Office, do not admit of a doubt. A collection of these despatches, costly and laborious though the work might be, would be a most valuable contribution to the history of the time. Pitt, in his pregnant and feverish career, scarcely wrote a line which is not worth printing. Indeed, Carmarthen could no more have conducted a commercial negociation with France than the Duke of Dorset. His mind was saturated with jealousy of that country. The grand tour had made him a *dilettante*, but had taught him no political economy. His private correspondence is full of innuendoes against Eden, not always of the most delicate character, and he and Harris laughed heartily at the notion that the French could ever be honest negociators.

Eden set himself with vigour to the prosecution of his task. He spent all the morning at the Council Board, examining merchants and traders. He reached Paris at the end of March. The French were in favour of free trade; but, in order that this principle might be adopted to any useful extent, it was necessary to abrogate or to modify the Methuen Treaty with Portugal, which still existed. This treaty had been concluded by John Methuen in Portugal in 1701, as the price for securing the accession of Portugal to the Grand Alliance. Its results were probably mischievous to both countries. By stipulating that the wines of Portugal should always be admitted to England at a third less duty than the wines of any other nation, it drove out the clarets which were then commonly drunk, and drenched our ancestors with fiery port. How much of the obesity of the eighteenth-century Englishman is due to this arrangement, and how much of the enforced abstemiousness of our own days? In return for this, Portugal admitted our cottons and linens free of duty. Thus the manufactures of Portugal were crushed, we obtained for our products the petty markets of Lisbon and Oporto rather than the ample fields of France, while the sunny hillsides of the Duero were over-stocked with vines belonging, not to industrious peasant proprietors, but to over-wealthy seigneurs, who ground the peasants down. Vergennes pressed hard for the abrogation of this treaty; and Pitt, in a private letter to Eden, declares himself willing to grant it. But the pedants of the Cabinet, of whom Jenkinson was the chief, held back their too impulsive superiors. The more the French conceded, the more exacting were the terms we asked. Eden was in despair at the task imposed upon him. The French Ministers, however, were thoroughly in earnest. Eventually the treaty was signed in September. The duty on French wines and brandies was reduced to the amount then imposed on the wines of Portugal, which were in their turn diminished by a proportionate sum. The Spitalfields weavers absolutely refused to admit French ribbons to the English markets. On the other hand, English hardwares, woollens, and cottons, and the beautiful productions of Wedgwood, were welcomed in France.

It is difficult to judge of the effect of a treaty which only continued in force for a few years, and those disturbed by the shadow of imminent convulsions. But it stands as a monument of the liberality of the last year of the *ancien régime*, and of the enlightenment and magnanimity of Pitt. Lord Sheffield, who in those days of darkness posed as an authority on economical questions, said that, as far as he could see, the reciprocity was all on one side, that the French had not gained a single advantage, that they had been for once at least taken in, and had exhibited themselves very ignorant and foolish. On the other hand, Rayneval, the French negociator, takes a higher tone. "The balance which will result from the treaty is uncertain; experience alone will show to which side it leans; but, whatever may happen, we shall at least have acquired the inappreciable advantage of insensibly diminishing the national hatred which has hitherto separated France and England; of substituting a legitimate for a fraudulent commerce, and of turning the profits of contraband to the advantage of the State. These considerations are more important than the indiscreet clamours which the fraudulent are certain to indulge in, both in France and England."

We see thus that by May, 1789, when the States-General met at Versailles, the prosperity of England was fixed on a secure basis. Our finances were sound, while those of France were rotten. We were in close alliance with two Powers who could assist us by sea and land, and whose united voice could speak with authority to Europe. France was hampered by her connection with Austria, who was in her turn seeking an alliance of self-aggrandizement with Russia. That these results should have been obtained in five years, after the close of a disastrous war, is due to the genius of Pitt and to the ability of such diplomatists as Harris and Eden. The world was about to break up and pass away, but its falling masses inspired no terrors as they struck us. Just at this time, in August, 1789, Mr. Burges became Under Secretary for Foreign Affairs. His first care was to provide for a better arrangement and preservation of the Foreign Office papers. He writes to his wife :—

" The immense number of despatches which come from and go to Foreign Courts are piled up in large presses, but no note is taken of them, nor is there even an index to them; so that, if anything is wanted, the whole year's accumulation must be rummaged over before it can be found, and frequently material affairs must be forgotten for want of a memorandum."

To remedy this, Mr. Burges proposed " to enter the purport of every despatch in a volume properly prepared for that purpose." Any one who has had occasion to work at the State papers of this period in the English Record Office must long for the exquisite handwriting, the careful marginal *précis*, and the luxurious bindings, of the French archives. His next step was to cross swords with Lord Hawkesbury, and to wrest from his hands the conduct of a commercial treaty with Naples, and the settlement of a dispute with Spain about Honduras. Mr. Hutton attributes Lord Hawkesbury's encroachments to the "indolence of the Duke of Leeds," and his indifference to ordinary business. This we think hardly fair to the Duke. He was an active Foreign Minister—sometimes indeed too active ; but he was entirely unfit to negociate a commercial treaty, whereas Pitt, who was perhaps the fittest man in Europe for the purpose, had committed a large share of the negociations with France to Lord Hawkesbury. Mr. Hutton tells us nothing about the negociations with Naples and Spain, on the ground that "not the slightest interest now attaches" to them. But we should like to know something about the Honduras business, as it might throw light on the conduct of Spain with regard to Nootka Sound, which nearly produced a European war in the following year. Mr. Hutton is also most tantalizing about the rebellion in the Austrian Netherlands. The Burges papers evidently contain a mass of correspondence on this subject from two agents, named Sundersberg and Sontag. Whatever may be the value of public diplomatic correspondence in these days of Bluebooks and Parliamentary questioning, there is no doubt that the international history of a hundred years since can only be written from a close study of diplomatic archives. The private letters addressed to the Under Secretaries are sometimes more valuable for this purpose than the public despatches sent to the Minister. Of this correspondence Mr. Hutton gives us nothing. Still more tantalizing is his reticence about the affair of Nootka Sound, which he says "has been so often and so thoroughly explained that it would be a waste of time to repeat the well-known incidents." Mr. Hutton has the advantage of us. Although in no crisis did the qualities of Pitt shine forth more pre-eminently, we know of no narrative in the English or in any other language which gives a clear account of the essential facts.

Nootka Sound is on the coast of British Columbia, just north of the eightieth parallel of latitude. It was discovered by Captain Cook in 1774, and that accurate observer gave a glowing account of the trade which might be anticipated with the natives, especially in furs. For the purposes of conducting the trade, some English ships were fitted out from China, and, the venture being profitable, other vessels were despatched from England. The Spanish Government, who based their claim to the whole of this coast on a bull of Pope Alexander VI., confirmed by subsequent treaties, fitted out an expedition from Mexico, entered the bay, pulled down the English factory, seized two English ships and their cargoes, and confiscated them as prizes. The news of this outrage arrived in England through the Spanish Government in February, 1790. We had unfortunately no English minister at Madrid, as Lord Auckland had left in the previous year, and his successor had not been appointed. Pitt took the matter into his own hands and acted with the greatest vigour. The despatches written by him, now extant in the Record Office, speak with all the imperious dignity of the son of Chatham. The Spaniards ask that we shall recognise their sovereignty over these coasts. Pitt refuses even to listen to such a demand, until reparation has first been made for the insult to the British flag. When the Spaniards hesitate to submit, Parliament is taken into confidence, the fleet is armed, and the army increased. There now arises a new danger. Spain was closely united with France by the Family Compact of 1761. By this treaty the two Bourbon Powers were bound to assist each other in all enterprises under the most stringent terms. The instrument dates from the last years of the Seven Years' War, when England was at war with France. The first news of it roused Chatham to declare war against Spain and to attack the Spanish colonies in South America. His failure to carry this measure in the Cabinet led to his resignation. Spain now asked for the assistance of France according to treaty, and the French Court, then in the first throes of the Revolution, thought that it might be for their interests to fulfil these engagements. A popular foreign war would be a safe outlet for dangerous spirits at home. The exact means by which this peril was averted is still a mystery. If the Burges papers can solve it, they will be a boon to historians. The most influential person in France at this moment was Mirabeau. He was Chairman of the *Comité diplomatique* of the National Assembly, and he was confidential adviser of the Court. If he could be gained over, peace might be preserved. But Mirabeau had already pronounced himself in favour of war; what influence could be brought to bear upon him?

Just at this time Hugh Elliot had returned from his embassy at Copenhagen. He had been at school with Mirabeau as a boy, and they had always maintained friendly relations with each other. He was now entrusted with a mission to Mirabeau. Mirabeau held no official position. Lord Gower could not communicate with him publicly, and the mission must be secret. Pitt's instructions are not extant, but a letter from him to Elliot is printed by Lord Stanhope and Bishop Tomline. We do not therefore know what arguments he was authorized to use. But we know that his mission was successful. Lord Gower writes to the Duke of Leeds on October 22, that the popular party has signified to him through Mr. Elliot their earnest desire to use their influence with the Court of Madrid, in order to bring it to accede to the just demands of England, and that, if supported by England, they will prefer an English alliance to a Spanish compact. Six days later Mirabeau informs the Court, rather we fear against the facts, that England has no intention of going to war, and that her armaments were inspired rather by the disturbances in the North than by any intention against Spain. Spain, on the other hand, could not fight without France. This danger having been averted, Mr. Fitzherbert, who had been sent to Madrid, was enabled to conclude a convention by which the Spaniards surrendered every point. Thus, twice since his entrance upon office, had Pitt by the energy of his language and conduct saved us from war.

The adjustment of our difficulties with Spain and France was perhaps made a little easier by the effects of the Congress of Reichenbach. Mr. Hutton says of it (p. 442) that "peace was then concluded between Austria and the Porte." This was not exactly the case, because Peace was not arranged between these Powers until the treaty of Szistowa, and then with great difficulty and with imminent danger of a renewal of the war. But it was at Reichenbach that the preliminaries were arranged. The state of Europe was indeed critical. There was still a danger of war between England and Spain, in which France would have been engaged on one side, and Holland on the other. The Emperor was still quarrelling with his Belgian subjects, and, although Joseph II. had been succeeded by Leopold II. in February, 1790, the matters in dispute were of a very delicate nature. Austria and Russia were leagued together for the dismemberment of Turkey, the existence of which was considered then, as now, important to the balance of power in Europe; Prussia, Austria, and Russia were casting longing eyes on the remaining territory of Poland; and behind all this was the spectre of the French Revolution, threatening all thrones and governments with disaster. As the first partition of Poland had been an expedient of Frederick the Great to divert the hunger of Russia from devouring Turkey, so now Prussia looked for a convenient indemnity in the same quarter. Frederick William proposed to add Dantzic and Thorn to his dominions as accretions long desired by his house, while Austria was to give back the Poles a piece of Galicia which she had taken in 1772, and to indemnify herself by a slice of Turkey. When Austria refused to listen to these terms, Prussia threatened war, and had indeed already concluded a treaty with the Porte against Austria, so that two more European wars were in immediate prospect, in addition to the war which was devastating the East, and the civil war in the

Netherlands. The one Power which was disinterestedly anxious for peace was England, and Pitt could therefore speak with decisive effect in the midst of these surging jealousies. The most weighty exponent of his views was Sir Robert Murray Keith, our ambassador at Vienna, and not Mr. Ewart, as Mr. Hutton erroneously states. An interesting summary of the result of these negociations is given in a letter from Mr. Burges to Mr. Fitzherbert, dated August 9, 1790.

Peace upon the base of the preliminaries of Reichenbach was finally concluded between Austria and the Porte at the little Bulgarian village of Szistowa. A graphic and amusing account of the lengthy negociations is to be found in the published correspondence of Sir Robert Murray Keith. Russia, however, still refused to make peace; and an account of the complicated dispute, to which this gave rise is given with considerable fulness both in the Burges Papers, and in the political memoranda of the Duke of Leeds. It was understood at Reichenbach, that Peace between Turkey and the Porte was to be concluded, like that between Austria and the Porte, on the basis of the *status quo*. This would necessitate the restoring of Oczakow to the Turks — a fortress at the mouth of the Dnieper, which had been stormed by the Russians with immense loss of life. Russia refused to restore the fortress, probably more from *amour propre* than from any other cause. The Powers of the Triple Alliance now meditated an armed intervention. England, in conjunction with Holland, was to send a fleet into the Baltic and the

Black Sea; and Prussia was to march an army of 28,000 men on the Russian frontier, ready to invade Livonia, and march upon Riga. These measures were determined upon at Cabinets held on March 21 and 22, 1791; they were approved of by the king, and a messenger, announcing the determination, was despatched to Berlin on March 27. Two days later the matter was brought before Parliament; and, notwithstanding the vehemence of the Opposition, an address to the king in approval was carried by large majorities in both Houses. No sooner was this step taken, than some members of the Cabinet began to doubt whether the country would support them in entering upon a European war. The Duke of Richmond was the first to declare his hesitation, and he was followed by Lord Strafford, and Lord Grenville; while the Duke of Leeds, Lord Chancellor Thurlow, and Pitt, were unshaken in their determination. On Thursday Pitt had a long conversation with the Duke of Leeds. He told him that several of the Government majority had voted against them; that the feeling of the Opposition was rising. The Duke said, that if there were any change of policy he would resign. Pitt replied, that he felt not only for the Duke, but with him; but dwelt on the consequences which breaking up the Government would bring upon the country and the king. The rest of the Cabinet were sent for. Lord Strafford declared that he had not slept all night, but declared himself against action, in which he was followed by the Duke of Richmond and Lord Grenville. The Duke of Leeds does full justice to the uprightness and consistency of Lord Grenville's conduct during the business. Lord Camden was neutral. At the close of the conversation, the Duke became convinced that a change of policy was inevitable.

The Cabinet met again on the evening of the same day, and of this the Duke of Leeds gives a graphic account:—

"I went to the Cabinet in the evening; Lord Chatham and Mr. Pitt were not come; the rest of the members were present; the Chancellor and Lord Camden in conference on one side of the chimney, the Duke of Richmond and Lord Strafford on the other, Lord Grenville walking up and down the room. I went up to the chimney, and stirring the fire, observed that, as it was probably the last time I should have to do the honours of that room, I thought it particularly incumbent upon me to have a good fire for my company. This produced a considerable effect. The Duke of Richmond and Lord Strafford exclaimed, 'Good God, what d'ye mean?' I answered, from what had passed at our late meetings I took for granted it would be determined at the present to act in a manner directly contrary to what we had communicated as our system to Prussia, in which case I should think myself obliged to *make my bow*. A short silence ensued."

After this the Duke retired with the Duke of Richmond into his own room, and returning to the Cabinet found Mr. Pitt and Lord Chatham arrived. In the discussion which ensued, the Duke, Mr. Pitt, and Lord Chatham, were opposed to the Duke of Richmond, Lord Strafford, and Lord Grenville. Lord Camden said nothing, and the Lord Chancellor went to sleep. At length a despatch was agreed to, which, with some modifications, the Duke of Leeds consented to sign. It was dated the first of April, and advocated a temporary delay. The Cabinet did not meet again for ten days. In the mean time, the opposition of the country to the war had become more pronounced, and Pitt was in receipt of other information, which made him less averse to accept a compromise. Was Oczakow, after all, of such importance that it was worth while to go to war about it? Lord Auckland was at the time minister at the Hague. He was the most trusted, and probably the most able of the English diplomatists of his generation, and all the threads of European diplomacy passed through his hands. He had all along been opposed to our going to war with Russia. The co-operation of Holland was necessary for this purpose, and it was doubtful whether the Dutch desired war. Kinbergen, a Dutch admiral, was well acquainted with the coasts of the Black Sea, and he declared that Oczakow was of little moment compared with Sebastopol. Pitt, after carefully weighing the question, concluded that he might give way upon this point; and Mr. Fawkener was sent to St. Petersburg to propose to Catherine that she should restore Oczakow, but that the fortifications should be destroyed. This was accepted, and Oczakow has passed out of the domain of ordinary human knowledge.

On April 15 the Cabinet met again. Pitt, according to the custom of that day, had drafted despatches for Berlin, which the Duke of Leeds was expected to sign. The Cabinet Council opened with a lively discussion. The Duke of Richmond expressed some doubt as to whether the messenger, who brought the determination of delay, could have arrived in time to stop the previously arranged ultimatum from being despatched to St. Petersburg. The Lord Chancellor (who was for war) said he hoped not, and thought that there was a fortunate east wind, which would prevent the second messenger arriving in time.

" The Duke seemed nettled at this answer, and replied, ' I suppose then you wish to read Homer, my lord ? ' ' What the devil,' retorted the Chancellor, ' has Homer to do with the business ? ' ' Only,' replied the Duke, ' I suppose your lordship may want to have sufficient leisure to read Homer in comfort, which, from your situation, you have not at present ? ' After a little more snarling on one part, and a great deal of grumbling on the other, the dialogue concluded. The Duke of Richmond then asked me if I recollected the day the second messenger went away. I told him he set out on Friday, April 1. Pitt could not help saying, ' Now, do own, Duke, that you enjoy the date on this occasion.' I told him I really answered the Duke, *tout bonnement*, and was sure the date was accurate, however since he mentioned it I could not say I was particularly sorry at such a step being taken on such a day."

The upshot was, that the Duke of Leeds refused to sign despatches which he did not approve of, and the King gave permission to Lord Grenville to sign the despatches of the Foreign Office. Six days later, the Duke formally resigned. Cabinets are Cabinets after all ; and it is some comfort to find that the Cabinets of George III. were not more united than those of

Victoria. Thus ended the question of the Russian armament. The most serious part of it was our sudden abandonment of Prussia. By this we broke up the Triple Alliance, and prepared the way for the desertion of the coalition by Prussia in 1795.

The Treaty of Jassy between Russia and the Porte was not concluded till January, 1792, and by that time the intervention of the European Powers in the affairs of France had become an accomplished act. The arrangement of Pilnitz was made in August, 1791. Mr. Burges gives an entirely erroneous account of this Convention, which is unfortunately accepted by Mr. Hutton. He describes it as pointing towards a dismemberment of France for the benefit of Austria and Prussia; whereas the essence of the instrument lay in the condition, that it was to be inoperative unless all the Powers of Europe should accede to it. "Alors et dans ce cas," said the Emperor of Austria, referring to the words of this exception, "it is to me the law and the prophets." It did, however, lead to war, which was declared by France against Austria on April 20, 1792. Equally unsupported by any evidence known to us, is the statement of Mr. Burges, that the dominant idea of the English Ministry was to excite a counter-revolution in France, under the erroneous impression that the national feeling was decidedly in favour of the restoration of the Bourbons. This statement is made with reference to a letter of Mr. Burges of the date, December 28, 1790; whereas, the *déchéance* of the king was not proclaimed till after August 10, 1792. Nothing is more certain than that the attitude of England towards the Revolution was one of scrupulous neutrality until the late autumn of 1792; that the final outbreak of the war in 1793 was almost accidental, and that we were on the point of opening diplomatic relations with the French Provisional Government after the dethronement of the king.

Before, however, we speak of these matters, it is necessary to refer to a curious circumstance, of which an erroneous account has hitherto been given by English historians, and which is described in somewhat different language both by Mr. Burges and the Duke of Leeds. We mean the proposed coalition between Pitt and Fox in the summer of 1792. The account generally received is taken from Lord Malmesbury's Correspondence, and is to the effect, that Pitt actually contemplated a union between himself and the Opposition, and that it fell through in consequence of the unwillingness of the king to admit Fox to his Councils. This story is positively contradicted by the Memoranda of the Duke of Leeds, which may be taken as trustworthy, since they were written down immediately after the events, without any idea of publication, and they are implicitly supported by the evidence of Mr. Burges. Mr. Burges's account is given in a letter to his wife, dated October 14, 1794, more than two years after the event which it describes.

"I have learnt a very curious anecdote of the Duke of Leeds, which does great credit to his modesty and good sense. Before the present ministerial arrangement took place, and when the negociation for that purpose was depending, many difficulties, as you will readily believe, arose as to the manner in which it was to be adjusted. The Duke having heard of this, and conceiving that a favourable opportunity was thereby afforded to him of again coming into power, devised a plan which he submitted to his Cabinet Council, consisting of the Duchess, Dr. Jackson, Sir Ralph Woodford, Mr. Aust, and Mr. Glover, and which was approved of by them. In consequence of this he drove down to Windsor and requested an audience of the king. After the proper preliminaries, and professions of zeal and attachment, he told his Majesty that it appeared to him that however desirable the depending coalition of parties might be, he was satisfied it could not be effected unless some means could be found to reconcile the jarring pretensions of Mr. Pitt and the Duke of Portland, the latter of whom, having formerly been Prime Minister, and expelled by the former, could never submit to the degrading circumstance of coming into administration while Mr. Pitt continued First Lord of the Treasury. To obviate this barrier, and to render everything easy, the Duke said he had determined to come forward and to propose to his Majesty that he should be named First Lord of the Treasury (in plain English, Prime Minister); that then Mr. Pitt might continue Chancellor of the Exchequer (in plain English, his deputy), in which case he would be answerable to his Majesty that the Duke of Portland would accept of the Secretaryship of State, as from his (the Duke of Leeds) being the senior Duke, no impediments from etiquette would stand in his way. His Grace assured the king that he had no other reason for making this proposal but the most sincere wish to save his Majesty from embarrassment and to serve his country, etc., etc. My information does not go so far as to enable me to state with clearness the answer which was given to all this; nor do I know certainly what passed till about five minutes after the audience was over. When the Duke had made his bow he came out upon the terrace; immediately the king did the like. The Duke joined his suite, and before they had advanced many paces Mr. Pitt came up. He had hardly taken off his hat to make his bow before the king called out to him, 'I am sorry I have bad news for you; but you are out.' 'Out, sir!' exclaimed Mr. Pitt, with much surprise. 'Yes,' replied the king, 'I am sorry to tell you that you are out; you are no longer First Lord of the Treasury; but do you know who succeeds you?' 'I really do not, sir,' replied Mr. Pitt. 'That's very strange,' said the king. 'I should have supposed you might at least have been able to form some idea of who it is. Look about you, and try if you can discover him. Mr. Pitt accordingly did so, and then assured his Majesty he had not been able to find him out. 'Why,' said the king, 'if you can't guess I will tell you; it is the Duke of Leeds, here, who has this moment offered himself to succeed you as First Lord of the Treasury in order to prevent confusion. I am sure you will agree with me that such an arrangement will be very desirable, as you know the Duke so well, and must have so high an opinion of him.' I leave you to figure to yourself what his Grace's feelings and countenance were on this occasion. The consequence, however, was a fit of his stomachic complaint, and his being entirely left out of the arrangement. You may depend upon the whole of this being literally true; for my authorities are indisputable, as you will know when I tell you that they are George Brooks and Lady Holdernesse."

It is a very pretty story, but it has the misfortune of being in its most striking features absolutely untrue, and it is a warning against using the recollections of memoir writers as serious history.

The true account is given in the Memoranda of

the Duke of Leeds. The object of the coalition was not to include Pitt and the Duke of Portland, but Pitt and Fox in the same Ministry. The matter was first opened to the Duke by the circle of flatterers who surrounded him. A meeting took place between the Duke of Leeds and the Duke of Portland. The Duke of Portland was under the impression, that Pitt had no objection himself to act with Fox in the most cordial manner. It was arranged that the Duke of Leeds should communicate personally with the king. The Duke went to the Terrace at Windsor on Sunday evening, August 12. "It was extremely crowded. The king was standing in a circle, talking to Mr. Pitt and Mr. Dundas, the former appearing exceedingly grave. He afterwards, however, resumed his usual cheerfulness, and laughed with the Duchess and me in the old style. The king was very gracious to us." Two days later the Duke went to the Terrace again. He walked for some time with the king, and on asking for a conference the king took him through the castle to the library in the Queen's Lodge, where they talked for half an hour. The Duke narrated his interview with the Duke of Portland with reference to the admission of Fox to the Cabinet, and mentioned the interview which had taken place between Lord Loughborough and Mr. Dundas. To the Duke's great surprise the king answered, that he had not heard anything on the subject for a long time. That Mr. Pitt had some months ago mentioned something like an opening on the part of the Duke of Portland and his friends, to which the king had answered, 'Anything complimentary to them, but no power." The king asked who was proposed to be First Lord of the Treasury. The Duke answered that he could not tell, but that it was meant that some one should be in that situation who was upon terms of friendship and confidence with both parties. The king replied that it would be very awkward for Pitt, after having been so long at the head of that Board, to descend to an inferior situation at it, and that whoever was the First Lord must either be a cipher or Mr. Pitt must appear as a *commis*.

About a week later, the Duke had an interview with Mr. Pitt. He listened attentively to everything that the Duke had to say, and then answered, that there had been no thought of any alteration in the Government; that circumstances did not call for it, nor did the people wish it; and that no new arrangement, either by a change or coalition, had ever been in contemplation. He added that the interviews between Dundas and Lord Loughborough, at some of which he had himself been present, had not in view any change of Administration, and that if anything could be devised to make an union with Fox more difficult than it had been for many years, it was precisely the conduct he had held towards the close of the last Session. Pitt also said, that the king had mentioned to him the conversation the Duke had held with him at Windsor and the following day at St. James's. The Duke was evidently taken aback at the sudden downfall of his hopes; only one conclusion was possible from the reflection which he makes on the circumstances, that Lord Loughborough had given an entirely false account of what had passed between himself and Dundas. That lawyer, was, in fact, so eager for the office which he ultimately obtained, that he stuck at nothing to gain his end. Historians have hitherto believed the story of Lord Loughborough as related by Lord Malmesbury. They will henceforth have to follow the more prosaic but unimpeachable narrative of the Leeds Memoranda. It is probable that the Duke of Leeds and the Duke of Portland, each deceived by his own toadies, were "smelling at the same nosegay." Each thought that he was the one individual who, by his position and peculiar gifts, could combine the jarring antagonisms of Pitt and Fox into an harmonious unity.

It is a great misfortune that neither the Leeds Memoranda nor the Burges Papers throw any light on the most important question of the whole of this period—the outbreak of the war with France. In the conversation with Pitt above mentioned it is tantalizing to read, " He turned the conversation for some time to the affairs of France. I brought him back, however, to the subject of our conference." We would rather have one line about Pitt's views as to our relations of France just after the cataclysm of the tenth of August, than ten about back-stairs intrigues for the shuffling of ministries. The recall of Lord Gower from Paris after the tenth of August was inevitable. He had been accredited to a monarch, and that monarch had been deposed. It was impossible that he should remain at Paris, nor, as an aristocrat and a personal friend of the royal prisoner, would his life have been safe. The French Government expected his departure, and were not offended at it. The position of Chauvelin in England was different. Nominally commissioned by the king, he was known to possess in some degree the confidence of his new masters, and how was he to take his leave? If the Provisional Government sent him letters of recall, would the King of England receive them, and, if he was refused an audience, would it not be likely to lead to the very war which both countries were anxious to avert? Chauvelin had been sent to England as the nominal head of a mission, of which Talleyrand was the informing spirit, to conclude if possible an alliance with this country, to borrow three millions of money, and to offer St. Domingo in return. These objects were as important in the new state of things as they had been before. Indeed, as the tide of European insurrection rose, it was most desirable that France should not increase the number of her enemies. Chauvelin therefore remained in a dubious position, snubbed alternately by Grenville and by his own Government, afraid to move forwards or backwards for fear of making bad worse. He had no relations with the Opposition. Talleyrand, with marvellous insight, had seen at once the suicidal folly of any step in that direction. So matters remained through the recess of 1792. In the autumn the relations of the two Governments became more strained. The unexpected repulse of the allied armies, the conquest of Belgium which followed closely upon the Battle of Jemappes, which united the Netherlands to France and seemed to threaten Holland, made the peril more urgent for the English Government. This feeling of insecurity was increased by the decree of November 19, which, passed in hot haste in an afternoon's debate, though it referred only to countries already invaded by French arms, sounded like an appeal to all nations to throw off their allegiance to their legitimate rulers.

This decree, repeated in stronger terms a month later, and the opening of the Scheldt, together with the invasion of Nice and Savoy, and the execution of the king, have generally been regarded as the causes of the revolutionary war. An examination of English and French State papers does not support this conclusion. The invasion of Nice and Savoy, although it was enumerated by Pitt in 1800 as one of the grievances which led to war, finds no place in the correspondence of the time. The decree of November 19 was abundantly explained by Chauvelin; and indeed no one, who reads in the *Moniteur* the debate which preceded it, could attach to it the importance which our Ministry were at first inclined to give it. The opening of the Scheldt was a serious violation of treaties, and, if it had been carried into action, would undoubtedly have put an end to peaceful relations. But there was a great difference between declaring the Scheldt open because "a river which had its source in a free country should never be enslaved through any portion of its course," and the using it as a menace to English commerce. There is, indeed, the strongest proof, that we should not have gone to war upon this pretext. The Dutch, who were the parties most interested, were not disposed to insist upon it. We had ourselves offered the navigation of the Scheldt some years before to Joseph II., under far more dangerous circumstances, as the price of his surrender of the French Alliance. We have authentic records of conversations of Pitt with Maret, in which the position was practically surrendered. The execution of the king was seized by the Ministry as a good opportunity for making the war popular, but not as a *casus belli*. None of these reasons are sufficient to account for the catastrophe. The fate of peace and war lay elsewhere— in the security of Holland. We were bound to that country by the closest ties of honour and interest, and its destiny could not be a matter of indifference to us.

The difficulty of keeping peace lay in the divisions of the two Cabinets of London and Paris. In the English Cabinet there was certainly a war party, to which the king gave his support. Pitt was prepared to make any sacrifice for peace, Grenville probably swerved slowly to the side of war. In Paris, Dumouriez and Le Brun were in favour of peace with England; the Jacobins, for their own purposes, wished for an extension of the war. It is painful to think what accidents prevented an understanding. Pitt, in a conversation with Maret, afterwards Duke of Bassano, had pressed for the recall of Chauvelin and the mission of another agent to treat informally with the English Court. Barthélémy, the negociator of the peace of Basle, the ablest diplomatist in the French service except Talleyrand who was not available, was designated for the post. Le Brun had actually drawn up the instrument recalling Chauvelin. The Provisional Government rejected it, as derogatory to the honour of France, it is believed, by a very small majority. Similarly Fox urged on Parliament the recognition of the French Republic, and the despatch of an envoy to Paris. Instructions for this purpose were drawn up and are still extant, Mr. Lindsay having been chosen for this service. Chauvelin was not recalled, Lindsay was not sent, and both nations drifted into war. One more chance was allowed us. The dismissal of Chauvelin from this country, on the ground that he was a suspected alien, was a high-handed insult, and tantamount to a declaration of war. It was, as Chauvelin said, 'un coup de canon.' Yet at the very moment when he was dismissed by us, he had been recalled by the French Government, and Maret, a *persona grata* to Pitt, had been appointed in his room. The courier recalling Chauvelin met him at Blackheath; Maret and Chauvelin passed each other in the night at Montreuil, and had no conversation, not recognising each other's liveries. On such slight events do the fate of empires hang!

February 1793 marks a new era in the career of Pitt and in the foreign policy of England. The fabric which he had laboriously erected, of peace abroad and financial stability at home, was swept away for ever. Sir Robert Murray Keith, on leaving Szistowa in 1791, congratulated himself that he had crowned a long diplomatic career by placing the peace of Europe on a secure basis for at least a generation. We must not be surprised if Englishmen did not at first realize the nature of the struggle into which they had entered. It was some little time before the conflict began in grim earnest. We looked for a speedy victory over the undisciplined hordes of the *sans-culottes*. We were soon undeceived. The French armies were animated by a spirit which had not yet been taken into account by professors of the art of war. A career opened to ability called into being the genius which it rewarded. The coalition was distracted with conflicting interests. The caricatures of Gillray depict but too faithfully the excesses of the English army in Flanders. The loss of the 37th Regiment in consequence of a drunken debauch, as told by Burges, is but a type of the whole campaign. The Duke of York was recalled; Holland was conquered by Pichegru; Prussia, complaining that her subsidies were not regularly paid by England, retired from the coalition at the peace of Basle, thus avenging our desertion of her in 1791. The Duke of Leeds, now a member of the Opposition, tells us of the efforts made to "treat with any Government in France, under whatever form, which should appear capable of maintaining the accustomed relations of peace and amity with other countries," efforts which resulted in the fruitless mission of Lord Malmesbury.

Here our present materials fail us. The secret history of the next ten years has yet to be written. When the wealth of our archives becomes current coin, we shall be better able to judge whether Pitt should have made peace with France in 1800;

whether he did right in resigning in 1801; whether England was fully justified in breaking off the peace of Amiens and engaging in the deadly struggle in which Pitt was forced to yield, when the courier, booted and spurred, rattled down the streets of Bath, and, bringing the news of Austerlitz, struck his face with the ashen pallor which it never lost, and his heart with the icy chill which froze it in an early death.

IV.

THE TREATY OF COMMERCE BETWEEN ENGLAND AND FRANCE IN 1786.

THE following essays deal more in detail with the Commercial Treaty with France of 1786, and with the Triple Alliance of 1788, described in the preceding essay. They are based in great measure upon unpublished documents.

The eighteenth article of the Treaty of Versailles between England and France contained a provision that commissioners should be appointed on either side to draw up new arrangements of commerce between the two nations on the basis of reciprocity and of mutual convenience, and that these arrangements should be completed within the space of two years, dating from January 1, 1784. The insertion of this article had not been effected without difficulty. The views of France and England as to foreign trade were divergent. The French were what in modern language would be called free traders. Vergennes and his advisers had learnt from the physiocrats that the wealth of a country consists not so much in the amount of gold and silver which happens to be within its borders at any particular time, as in the natural products of the country itself. The English ministers were to a great extent under the dominion of the mercantile system, which taught that the balance for or against the wealth of one country compared with another lay in the larger amount of cash which one of the countries possessed. Thus, in arranging the conditions of peace, while the French ministers wished for a fresh treaty of commerce with England, the English ministers only desired the renewal of the treaty of commerce of 1713, made at the Peace of Utrecht. This treaty, which never came into complete effect, placed France and England reciprocally on the footing of the most favoured nation, but it was deeply affected by the Methuen treaty between England and Portugal, which gave Portugal a special position towards England superior to that of any nation, however favoured.

The Peace of Versailles was made by Lord Shelburne, with Pitt as his Chancellor of the Exchequer; but when the coalition ministry came into power under the Duke of Portland, Fox was less favourable to the demands of France. It was only by the persistence of the French minister that the insertion of clause 18 was obtained, and the English ministry intended that it should, if possible, remain a dead letter. The divergence of views was still further shown in the declaration and counter-declaration of the two Governments with regard to the clause. The English declaration pointed to a revision of existing treaties, the French counter-declaration to the drawing up of an entirely new treaty.

England showed no anxiety to complete her share of the bargain. The Treaty of Utrecht had been complained of as admitting French linens too readily to England. They amounted to three times as much as the English wool exported to France. The years previous to the peace had witnessed a large development of manufactures in England. Hargreaves had completed his spinning jenny in 1765; Arkwright's first spinning mule worked by water-power dates from 1769; Crompton completed his spinning mule in 1779. There was a natural desire to find a sale for these manufactures in France.

In March 1784 Mr. Craufurd was nominated English commissioner, and Gerard de Rayneval French commissioner. Craufurd, however, stayed in England, making inquiries into smuggling, which was then very prevalent, especially in tea and brandy. The Count d'Adhémar, French ambassador in England, pressed for Craufurd's departure, and he eventually went to Paris at the end of September 1784. Up to January 1785 nothing had been done, and Adhémar remonstrated with the British Government. Lord Carmarthen, the Foreign Secretary, who, indeed, understood but little of these matters, replied that they had no need of new arrangements, but that they were quite satisfied with the Treaty of Utrecht. Adhémar, replying with great warmth, threatened to abandon the arrangements of Utrecht if the new treaty were not speedily concluded. Barthélemy, writing from England on April 19, 1785, complains that England imports raw cotton from France and re-exports it manufactured, and was also the means of passing into France Indian and Chinese products which were prohibited in England. In order to put pressure upon England to fulfil the engagements which she was so reluctant to conclude, edicts were issued by the French Government in July 1785 forbidding the importation of a number of British manufactures, thus contravening their own principle of free trade. Only raw material was allowed to be imported from England, and shopkeepers were not allowed to exhibit advertisements of "marchandises d'Angleterre."

This strong measure stirred up the English to action. The Duke of Dorset, the ambassador at Paris, reports to Carmarthen that the manner of Vergennes towards him, which was at first cordial, has materially changed. Vergennes is vexed because the English have done nothing about the treaty of commerce. He expresses a wish that steps should be taken to establish a more friendly intercourse between the two countries. The treaty of commerce, signed at Utrecht between France and England in 1713, had contained ten articles, the ninth and the tenth of which were not to be valid unless ratified by the English Parliament. Their effect would have been to have re-established the tariff of 1664, placing France in the position of the most favoured nation, and doing away with the privileges which the Methuen treaty had given to Portugal in 1703. The Bill to give effect to these articles had been rejected by a small majority, and France was now desirous that these two articles should be put into force. Craufurd explained that England could not admit these articles as a basis for negotiation, upon which Rayneval said that the French were desirous of reciprocity, and that if the English did not approve of this simple principle, they must suggest some other arrangements. " Nous vous offrons tout," he said ; " c'est à vous à juger si cela vous convient, et si vous êtes disposés à admettre la réciprocité. Si vous la jugez inadmissible, c'est à vous à indiquer les exceptions."

On October 6, Hailes, who was Chargé d'Affaires at Paris in the Duke of Dorset's place, writes that he had mentioned the treaty of commerce to Vergennes. He was in very ill humour in consequence of our delay. He complained that no answer had been returned to Rayneval's proposals ; he would offer a proportionate reduction of duties upon any article of equal magnitude we might prefer to name provided we would receive French wines and brandies upon the same footing with those of other countries. Carmarthen replied on October 27 that he was willing to consider propositions for admitting French wines and brandies on favourable terms to England if the French would make similar changes with regard to English products. But he added, " You must protect us from the wrath of the Portuguese."

It is necessary in this place to give some account of the Methuen treaty, which so long stopped the way to an amicable arrangement between France and England. The Methuen treaty dates from the war of the Spanish succession, and was concluded for the purpose of attaching Portugal to the Grand Alliance. By it Portuguese wines were to be introduced into England at one-third less than the duty on French wines, and in return all wool except English was excluded from Portuguese markets. Both parties exulted over the treaty as a victory, but in reality it was a disaster for both. From 1675 to 1696 France had sent an average of 15,000 tuns of wine to England, Portugal only 300 tuns. In 1712 England imported 1,161,908 pipes of Portuguese wine and 16,053 pipes of French wine. Intercourse with France was prevented. It would have been better to have had free trade with France in wool than an exclusive command of the Portuguese market. Bordeaux and Burgundy were the natural exports of France to England. The Methuen treaty prevented English statesmen from making advantageous commercial arrangements with France. On the other hand, the wine trade benefited the Portuguese nobles, but not the common people. The production of grapes drove out that of meat and bread, and Portugal became dependent upon foreign countries for its food supply. Competition also spoilt the profits of the wine trade, and great fortunes were undermined. The habit of drinking port instead of claret did no good to our ancestors in the last century, while the Portuguese peasant, driven from his holding by a feudal superior, was not able to recoup himself by manufactures which the monopoly of England prevented from being established. The English exports to Portugal were much larger than the Portuguese exports to England, and the balance of trade did not offer an encouraging prospect to France.

On October 24 Vergennes announced to Hailes that he should consider the Treaty of Utrecht at an end at the close of the year, and it became known that France, despairing of English friendship, was beginning to negotiate with Holland. The fear of a Franco-Dutch alliance stimulated the English ministry. Craufurd at last sent a reply to Rayneval. He asked what were the articles which France wished should enter England, and promised that England would give similar information, as England was extremely desirous to enter into friendly relations. The news now arrived that France had actually signed a treaty with Holland. This roused into action the mastermind of the Cabinet. Pitt saw that further delay would be dangerous. On December 9, writing in Carmarthen's name, he asked for a further extension of the time, which was just expiring, in order to arrange a commercial system founded on the law of mutual and reciprocal advantage, a system which might form a solid and permanent connection between the trading part of the two countries. Vergennes replied by granting six months' delay, which might be extended to twelve. William Eden, afterwards Lord Auckland, was sent by Pitt for the especial purpose of negotiating the treaty, while France was represented by Gerard de Rayneval.

There is no doubt that it was due to the initiative of Pitt, that any steps were taken to meet the wishes of the French. He showed great discrimination in selecting William Eden as a negotiator. Eden had formerly been attached to the Opposition, and was an intimate friend of Lord North and Lord Loughborough. But he possessed a clear head and great industry, and probably no better instrument could have been selected for the work. In January 1786 Eden tells his brother Morton that he is spending all the morning at the council board examining merchants and manufacturers. At the same time the treaty had many enemies, both in England and in France. Fox said that our commercial prosperity had never been so great as when our relations with France were most strained. Adhémar and Barthélemy, the representatives of France in England, were both opposed to the treaty. They were keenly alive to the suspicious conduct of the English Government towards France; they did not see that these feelings were not shared by Pitt. Adhémar warned his country against *Anglomanie*. Even the success of Pitt in transferring the duty upon wine from the customs to the excise, which was done to prevent contraband, and to check the manufacture of British wines, did not open their eyes to his sincerity. A negotiation was set on foot, which has been little noticed by English writers, for transferring the great inventors Watt and Boulton from England to France. This was very nearly carried out, and it is difficult to say what effect such a transference might have had on the comparative development of French and English commerce.

At last, on March 30, 1786, Eden arrived in Paris. He saw the minister Vergennes on the following day. He was introduced to the Royal Family and to M. de Rayneval. To him Eden communicated some minutes of a treaty, which on April 17 took the form of a project agreed upon by the two negotiators. The chief points of it were as follows: 1. The object of the treaty is to secure friendship and good-will, and an entire liberty of navigation and commerce between France and England and their respective dominions. The hindrances to trade at present existing only tend to encourage contraband. 2. Each nation is to be placed in the position of the most favoured nation as far as is compatible with existing treaties, or with treaties which may be made in future. 3. Any alteration of tariff in the way of abolition is only to take place twelve months after the conclusion of the treaty. Any reduction of tariff is to be made gradually. 4. The present treaty is not to affect existing treaties between France and England, and especially the Treaty of Utrecht, 1713. 5. The treaty is to continue in force for ten years. 6. Mutual arrangements are to be made on the basis of reciprocity for the benefit of his Majesty's subjects. Pitt criticised this project in a letter dated April 20. He objected to the liberty of future modification given in the first article, because it would enable either Power to evade the treaty at pleasure, and to render it useless. He also suggested an alteration in the terms of the eighth article, which was intended to apply to Ireland.

On May 5 Pitt proposed in the Commons, and carried his motion with regard to the excise of wine mentioned above. He said in his speech that although the consumption of wine had increased, the legal importation of it had diminished in the last thirty-six years. That on the supposition that the importation of wine was the same now as it was thirty-six years before, the revenue was losing to the amount of 280,000*l.* a year. This proposition had once caused the overthrow of Sir Robert Walpole, but it might now be carried without danger. To remove the duty on wine from the customs to the excise would, by checking smuggling and discouraging the manufacture of English wine, stimulate the importation of foreign wines, and improve the revenue. On May 10 Pitt made to Eden a still more detailed criticism on the project agreed upon by him and Rayneval. He remarks, in the first place, that the treaty would be of very little use unless it were accompanied by a revocation of the French edicts prohibiting the importation of English manufactures. Secondly, there must be a more complete safeguard that the terms agreed upon by the treaty will not be arbitrarily altered. It is obvious that Pitt did not entirely trust the French on these points. He thinks that if these matters can be satisfactorily arranged, it will be best to make a definite treaty at once. In this case he is willing to waive the Methuen treaty, and to receive French wines and brandies on the terms of the most favoured nation, or even to make an abatement below the lowest rate of duty at present existing. In return for this England must demand the admission of her hardware and earthenware at moderate duties. France formerly sent to England 10,000 or 12,000 tuns of wine; why should she not do so again? France might, under these altered circumstances, send us many wines of a worse growth than claret. The chief point on which there might be a doubt in the English ministry is waiving the Methuen treaty. But considering the present state of our Portugal trade, the dependence in which Portugal must always be upon English markets, and the great advantages to be received from France, in return for what England should give, Pitt is inclined to think that this point ought not to be in the way of the treaty if in other respects desirable. We see in this letter that Pitt is far in advance of his age. The policy which he was prepared to adopt in 1786 was not accepted in England till 1831 or even till 1860. France pressed hard for the abrogation of the Methuen treaty, but King George and the subordinate ministers were too much prejudiced to yield.

We learn the views of the French ministry on the subject by a paper laid before the *Conseil d'État* on May 21. The preamble states that England makes more liberal offers than could have been expected: ought the French to accept them? Let us lay down certain economical principles: 1. The more things a nation produces which it does not require for its own use, the more it should desire to export them. 2. The cultivation of the soil is the solid foundation of prosperity. The exportation of natural products should be encouraged, so as to develop the cultivation. 3. The interest of the cultivators of the soil should always be preferred to that of manufacturers. 4. It is a mistake to aim at making all nations produce the same articles. It is also wise to encourage competition with foreign nations, because it stimulates your own production. 5. Manufactures should be protected, in those cases where the price is 10 per cent. above contraband prices. 6. The interest of the consumer should be preferred to that of the manufacturer and the merchant.

We see in these abstract principles the influence of that physiocratic school, then powerful in France, which regarded the produce of the soil as the only source of wealth. The French Government had so strong a belief in these dogmas, that they were ready to make considerable sacrifices for their maintenance. The French paper proceeds to apply these principles to practice. France, it says, has a large superfluity of products, and therefore it is the interest of France to send their products in exchange for English products. France would send to England her wines, brandies, vinegars, and salt, the produce of the soil which England cannot rival, while England would supply in return cloth, linen, silk, and fashions. The supply of English manufactures would stimulate competition in France, and an over-supply of any commodity could easily be transferred from France to Spain. What reduction of duties, then, is France to ask for? French wines now pay £99 a tun duty, those of Portugal £46, those of Spain, Germany, and Hungary £50. The legitimate importation of Bordeaux wine is from 400 to 500 tuns; the amount smuggled by way of Jersey and Boulogne about 400 tuns. This does not include either Burgundies or champagnes. Ireland consumes from 1,500 to 2,000 tuns. Formerly 8,000 tuns a year was a moderate importation into England. The Methuen treaty is not strictly observed. By it French wines need only pay a third more than Portuguese wines, whereas in fact they pay double. French brandies and vinegars are at a similar disadvantage as compared with Portuguese. At present 400 tuns of wine at £100 a tun duty produce only £40,000 revenue, whereas 8,000 tuns at £50 would produce £400,000 revenue. If the Methuen treaty were strictly observed, French wines should be admitted to England at £67 a tun. If this were done,

French cloths and cambrics should also be admitted free. Brandies and vinegars were not mentioned in the Methuen treaty, and therefore the duties upon them might be subject to any reduction the English Government might wish.

The paper proceeds to argue that no great danger is to be apprehended from the competition of English cottons and woollens. Fine English woollen cloths, it maintains, are not superior to French, but are cheaper; the best showing a difference of 14 or 15 per cent. This is not from the cheaper price of labour, which is dearer in England, nor from the price of wool, because France and England both import wool from Spain. It comes from the taxes which are laid upon wool in France, and the monopoly of its production. Both these causes could be removed by legislation, and the competition of England would stimulate the French manufacturers to greater exertions. More difficulty would be found from the competition of lower-priced woollens. The English cottons are 20 per cent. cheaper than the French, which is the result of English machinery.

The memoir then concludes with the following propositions: 1. France has an interest in procuring facilities for the importation into England of its wines, vinegars, and brandies, and should make sacrifices to obtain it. 2. The principal offer it can make in return is the admission of English hardware. 3. France also requires admission for artificial flowers, perfumery, fashions, plate glass, and soap, and for these it may admit English cottons in exchange. 4. France may admit English woollens in exchange for its own woollens or other articles. 5. France should ask for its wines to be on the same footing with those of Portugal. If a larger duty is imposed upon them, it should be less than the third provided for by the Methuen treaty. These principles are subject to modification, but a system of prohibition is essentially vicious and vexations. At any rate, France will have the satisfaction of offering an example of enlightenment and magnanimity which England will do well to imitate. This paper was drawn up in evident ignorance of Pitt's personal willingness to waive the Methuen treaty.

As the project of treaty agreed upon by Eden and Rayneval had now been criticised on both sides, and had not proved satisfactory, it was determined to proceed by a different method. On June 3 Eden presented a declaration from the King of England, the counter-declaration of the King of France being dated June 16. The declaration consists of four articles: 1. The navigation and the commerce of the two countries are to be placed upon the footing of the most favoured nation, except where special privileges have been granted to a particular power. 2. Besides this general principle, arrangements are at once to be made for establishing specific duties. 3. Each party is to have the right of reviewing the arrangement after ten years. 4. All the stipulations of the Treaty of Utrecht not annulled by the present treaty are to continue in full force. The counter-declaration also consists of four articles, which are nearly identical with those of the English declaration. They do not insist on the abrogation of the Methuen treaty, a concession which was not obtained without great difficulty. The chief difference between them lies in the tone of the preamble, France rather emphasizing the abolition of all duties, England laying stress on France being placed on an equality with other nations.

After this step had been taken there was a long pause. Eden went regularly to Versailles, and announced in answer to inquiries that he was still without instructions from his court. In the meantime the terms to be conceded by England were in the hands of Jenkinson, afterwards successively created Lord Hawkesbury and Lord Liverpool. He was determined, as Lord Carmarthen said, to see how far the French were in earnest. He lacked the broad and generous ideas of Pitt, and confined himself to driving the best bargain for the country. The result of his calculations is contained in a despatch from Carmarthen to Eden dated July 18, 1786. The Methuen treaty is to be continued, but the duty on French wines is to be reduced from £96 5s. 3d. a tun to £61 6s. 4d., that is just one-third more than is paid by the wines of Portugal. Brandies and vinegars were to be placed on the footing of the most favoured nation, and their superior quality would give them an advantage. In return for this it is hoped that France will admit the hardware, the woollen and worsted of England on moderate terms. French linens are reduced to the level of those of Holland and Flanders, and French cambrics and lawns are to be admitted on a duty of 12 or 15 per cent. In return for this England expects a reciprocity in the matter of cottons. Silks, for which Rayneval had earnestly pleaded, are to be absolutely prohibited. George Rose and the more cautious financiers of the day were afraid of a rising of the Spitalfields weavers. Amicable arrangements are to be made with reference to plate glass, porcelain, and fashions. It will be seen that these terms were harder than Pitt was at first inclined to offer. French wines, brandies, and vinegars were not placed on the footing which they occupied at the beginning of the eighteenth century, and French silks were altogether excluded.

Eden wrote to Pitt that his heart sunk within him when he read these instructions; it was not till the third reading that he began to pluck up courage. Rayneval's reply to these new instructions was dated on August 10. He said that as England was not inclined to admit the principle of free trade, France would proceed on the basis of reciprocity; at the same time it was most essential that the Methuen treaty should be to some extent modified. The duties proposed on wine, brandy and vinegar were too large : £61 a tun would act as a prohibition to anything like national consumption. Before the treaty with Portugal the duties were only £10 a tun for both countries. France was ready to accept the proposals about hardware, and would admit these goods on a reciprocal duty of 10 per cent. As England absolutely refused French silks, they would not insist upon that point, but would arrange for the reciprocal admission of gauzes and silk lace. The necessity for reducing the duty on wines, brandies, and vinegars was again enforced by Rayneval three days later. Vergennes urged that French wines should be admitted on the same footing as those of Portugal. Rayneval suggested in the same letter that silks might be allowed to enter on either side at a duty of 12 per cent. These efforts were unavailing. The Spitalfields weavers refused in the most peremptory way to admit French silks even in the form of ribbons. Jenkinson, created Lord Hawkesbury on August 21, persuaded his colleagues to maintain the differential duties of the Methuen treaty. The other difficulties, however, were gradually smoothed away, and on September 26 the treaty was signed at Versailles.

The treaty consists of forty-seven articles. A very short account of its principal features will suffice. The first article provides that there shall be a reciprocal and entirely perfect liberty of navigation and commerce between the subjects of the two countries, as is agreed upon in the following articles. The second article allows a year's notice to the subjects of either crown for removing their persons or their effects in case of the breaking out of war, a provision which was not respected by Napoleon at the rupture of the Peace of Amiens. The sixth article is concerned with the new tariff which is drawn up on the lines which have already been described. These duties are not to be altered but by mutual consent. Both sovereigns reserve the right of countervailing, by additional duties, the internal duties actually imposed on the manufactures, or the export duties which are charged on the raw materials of certain specified articles. Some of the later articles are concerned with the more general questions of international law: article 22 carefully defines contraband; articles 24 to 28 regulate the manner in which the visitation of ships is to be conducted in time of war; article 29 provides that the flag does not cover the merchandise, and that the property found on the enemy's ships is fair prize unless it have been embarked before the declaration of war. Other articles refer to the adjudication of prizes, and by article 46 the duration of the treaty is limited to twelve years.

The outbreak of the French Revolution so shortly afterwards makes it difficult to calculate the exact effect of the treaty. There is little doubt that it proved to be more favourable to France than to ourselves. The taste of the English in wine was not materially changed, as it has been by the commercial treaty of our own day; whereas English hardware and linen found an immediate sale in France; at the same time the Portuguese did not like the treaty, and were afraid of its result. Lord Sheffield, a political economist of some repute, and the friend and host of Gibbon, writes a criticism of the treaty to Eden on October 4, which seems to be well founded. He says that it is extravagant to pronounce an opinion on forty-seven articles, a very small part of which is known to him, but that as far as he can judge from what he knows the reciprocity is all on one side, and he cannot discover a single advantage the French have gained. He thinks that the French have been for once at least taken in, and have exhibited themselves very ignorant and foolish. The French, he believes, will gain nothing by the importation of cambrics; the reduction of the duty on brandy is not enough to prevent smuggling; and the failure to procure the admission of French silk is attributed to the ignorance and folly of the people, and the timidity of the ministers. An anonymous Glasgow manufacturer, quoted in "Lord Auckland's Life" (vol. i. p. 516), accused the French of infatuation in admitting the four great English staples, woollen, iron, pottery, and cotton; and he does not believe that French brandies, wines, cambrics, and millinery will find the market which is expected for them. On the other hand, the hopes of the French negotiators are expressed in a higher tone. Rayneval writes to Barthélemy on the conclusion of the treaty, "The balance which will result from the treaty is uncertain; experience alone will show to which side it leans; but whatever may happen, we shall at least have acquired the unappreciable advantage of insensibly diminishing the natural hatred which has hitherto separated France and England, of instituting a legitimate for a fraudulent commerce, and of turning the profits of contraband to the advantage of the State. These considerations are more important than the indiscreet clamours which the fraudulent are certain to permit themselves, both in France and England."

V.

THE TRIPLE ALLIANCE OF 1788.

WILLIAM PITT the younger became prime minister in December 1783, just at the moment when a satisfactory peace had concluded a long and disastrous war. The struggle with the American colonies had left England without allies in Europe. The cause of the revolted patriots had been supported first by France, then by Spain, and lastly by Holland, while the armed neutrality of 1780, originated by Russia, perhaps, at the instigation of Frederick the Great, had been joined by most of the European powers. This was a direct defiance of the naval supremacy of England, made at a time when the strength of the country was scarcely sufficient to support its claims. When peace was concluded, England swept the field of Europe to find an ally.

Russia, governed by Catherine II., a vigorous and enlightened sovereign, was mainly interested in extending her dominions, either to the south at the expense of Turkey, to the north-west at the expense of Sweden, or to the west at the expense of Poland. Catherine found a natural ally in Joseph II. of Austria, a prince who, like herself, penetrated with the ideal views of French philosophers, believed that mankind was to be reformed by edicts, and civilization hastened by the imperious orders of an absolute will. Besides a desire to depress the influence of the nobility and the Church, which was shared by many enlightened statesmen of that age, Joseph was anxious to round off the scattered dominions of Austria by exchanging the Netherlands for Bavaria, a project to which he clung with remarkable tenacity. This was, undoubtedly, a wise and statesman-like design. Austria had never been able to consolidate her medley of provinces into a well-defined kingdom. Joseph was quite alive to the danger of being driven out of Germany by the growth of Prussia, and succeeding history has justified his prescience. If Bavaria were added to Austria, the Emperor would be left in his German possessions, the danger of a third German power to hold the balance between the two great rivals would be less, and the kingdom of Burgundy would have anticipated the kingdom of Belgium by fifty years. The plan, however good in itself, could not fail to rouse the jealousy of France, who preferred to see the flat plains of the Netherlands lie open to her as a ready prey, and who dreaded the development of commercial activity in Antwerp. The very excellence of the scheme made it hateful to Frederick, that sly and cynical observer of all political movements. To prevent it he called into existence the League of Princes.

Besides this great design wider projects were continually springing up in Joseph's seething brain. Conscious of his own rectitude and of the benefits of his rule, he cared little for other considerations. He showed as reckless a disregard of vested rights, of the sentiment of nationalities or populations, of the accepted public law of Europe, as Frederick had when he invaded Silesia, or as Napoleon was to show when he compensated plundered monarchs by the spoil of monarchs whom he was yet to plunder. A clear-sighted statesman would have seen that Austria and Russia were at this time the main dangers to the peace of Europe. Their common interests drew them together as Napoleon and Alexander were drawn together in the raft on the river Niemen. But it was the common interest of Europe to watch them narrowly and to cross their ambitious plans. Frederick the Great had insulted Catherine as a woman, and although they had much in common as sovereigns, Catherine never forgot or forgave the insult. The reports of our ambassador at St. Petersburg are full of evidence of her ill-feeling towards him, and tell us how she rejoiced at his death. The diplomacy of Europe had no secrets for Frederick, yet he confined himself to the interests of his country. He was ready to divide Poland with Russia in order to increase his own dominions and to lure Russia from conquest in the East. He had seen through the character of Joseph II. in his first interview with him; and while he probably foresaw that ultimate failure of the Emperor's plans which Joseph desired might be written on his grave, he did not think it worth while to oppose him actively until the Bavarian exchange appeared imminent.

While such was the condition of Russia, Austria, and Prussia, France was at this time governed by one of the most peaceful and benevolent sovereigns who ever swayed her sceptre, and by a well-meaning and straightforward minister. History will at some time do justice to the qualities of Louis XVI. and to the industrious honesty of Vergennes. It is true that they had been misled into taking the part of America against us, an action fatal in its results to the French monarchy. But they were now sincerely desirous of peace and of the development of French commerce. In fact, the condition of France was desperate. In five years the great Revolution was to burst forth which destroyed constitution, priests, nobles, and king. Little aware of the chasm on which their power was built, the rulers of France still knew that the country required peace, and that material prosperity should be their first care. The French navy had suffered severely during the war, French colonies had been taken by the English and not restored at the peace. An Indian empire, which France regarded with pride and hope as a nucleus of wealth and honour, was destroyed, and the kernel of a British empire planted in its stead. Could a statesman have foreseen what no statesman could then fathom, the utter rottenness of French government and society, he would have left her to her own devices, feeling sure that she could not endanger the peace of Europe. It might have been wiser perhaps to have assisted her to develop her strength, in order that she might the better cope with those devastating forces which a few years later menaced the civilized world.

It was natural that Louis and Vergennes should attach great importance to the French alliance with Holland. The Dutch had fought by their side against the English; they were close neighbours; they were the second maritime power of Europe; they had the instinct of successful trade, and especially of trade with the East. France and Holland could each give something which the other lacked. United they would present the appearance of a maritime commercial power backed by the prestige of a military nation which had once been great. The other ally of France was Austria, joined to France by treaty for nearly thirty years and now joined by marriage. This alliance, which dates from the beginning of the Seven Years' War, was the masterpiece of Kaunitz. It reconciled powers which the tradition of Europe had regarded as hereditary enemies, to oppose them to Prussia, who had ventured to beard the majesty of the Empire. It was not likely that Kaunitz would, so long as he was minister, consent to the undoing of a work which he regarded as the glory of his life. Nor was it probable that Marie Antoinette, who had great political influence, would allow a rupture with her tenderest associations. Yet the Franco-Austrian alliance was of little use to France; it damaged the Court in the eyes of the people and it did not protect or save it in the hour of danger. It was a drag rather than otherwise on the designs of Joseph. His plans for the exchange of Bavaria, for opening the Scheldt, were directly opposed to French interests, and his restless and unquiet ambition must have been a constant source of anxiety to his peaceful allies. The interests of France and Austria were as naturally opposed to each other as those of Austria and Russia were united. Thus we see France continually expostulating with the Emperor, employing in turn a more or less decided tone, never sympathetic and often hostile. Joseph was not without suspicion of the internal weakness of France. He cared little for the cumbrous paraphernalia and deep-seated abuses of the *ancien régime*, while the good sense and good government of Englishmen appealed powerfully to his sympathies.

It follows from this review of the condition of Europe in 1784 that, with the exception of Prussia, there was no power which England had less reason to fear than France. If a French and English alliance was outside the range of practical politics, yet a benevolent neutrality was practical and desirable; on the other hand, Austria and Russia were the true disturbers of the peace of Europe. The one thing which kept the ambition of Joseph within bounds was his close connection with France; yet we find that during the first year of Pitt's accession to office the whole of our suspicion is directed against France; not a movement takes place which we do not attribute to her sinister designs. In vain Catherine and Kaunitz assure us that we are mistaken; their denial of French conspiracy only suggests doubts of their own sincerity towards us. Not only this, but it is repeated again and again that the main object of British diplomacy should be to dissolve the unnatural alliance between France and Austria. If space permitted, I could multiply instances of this unreasonable suspicion drawn from the Foreign Office papers in the Record Office: one will suffice. On September 7, 1784, Lord Carmarthen writes to Sir. R. Murray Keith, ambassador at Vienna, that in his opinion nothing is to be expected from Kaunitz, and that Keith is to seek an interview with Joseph himself. He proceeds: "Were it possible by any means to obtain the confidence of the Emperor on the general state of European politics, much surely might be done. Some assurances of eventual assistance, communicated with caution and observed with secresy, might gratify the natural reserve of his character at the same time they flatter his ambition; *and let the latter passion be as prevalent in his mind as the most bitter of his enemies wishes to represent it, I can scarcely conceive a length to which it would carry him in the pursuit of which it would not be our interest to second his views on condition of effectually rendering the House of Austria what she ought to be, the formidable rival of the House of Bourbon.*" This extraordinary statement from an English minister was written just after Joseph had declared the Scheldt open to navigation in defiance of treaties and to the amazement and indignation of the rest of Europe.

In this juncture of affairs a course of diplomatic action was begun which changed Holland from the attitude of a doubtful friend, or even of an enemy, to a close ally, and which built up the fabric of an alliance between these two maritime powers and Prussia, which for a short time gave the law to Europe and checked the ever-swelling ambition of Austria and Russia just as they seemed to have the objects of their desire within their grasp. As soon as peace was signed between England and Holland it became necessary that ministers should be exchanged between the two Courts. Sir James Harris, afterwards created Lord Malmesbury, was chosen for this post by Fox and the Duke of Portland, and after their dismissal from power the appointment was confirmed by Pitt and Lord Carmarthen. Sir James Harris accepted the post with the full approbation of his former friends. He was a bright, versatile, and witty man; he had served with distinction both in Spain and Russia, and he was to continue in employments which have handed down his name as one of the most brilliant and successful of English diplomatists.

In order to make his course of action clear, it will be necessary to give some account of the condition of Holland at this time. The seven provinces formed a union of the loosest kind. The province of Holland had the pre-eminence, and in times of danger the other provinces were ready to concede to her a prerogative vote. But there was nothing in the Dutch constitution to make this necessary, nor did occasion for it often occur. Each State was free to act as it pleased. Confederate governments are only held together by some definite power being reserved for the central authority. In most cases the care of posts and telegraphs, of carriage, of the higher justice, and of peace and war, is surrendered by the subordinate States. In Holland no constitution of this kind existed. It was possible for the separate States to enter into alliances entirely independent of the rest. Liberty and diversity of action were valued before unity and efficiency. The States were generally under a government of an aristocracy of merchants; the main object of their rulers was to preserve their own power and to make as much money as possible by trade. They found that an alliance with France served both these purposes; France supported them against the English, who were their great rivals in commerce, aided their pretensions to Eastern trade, and by judicious influence kept the provinces back from too close a union. The party who wished for the maintenance of this loose confederacy and of the French alliance called themselves the Patriots, as being depositories of the best traditions of Dutch freedom. Opposed to these was the party of the Stadtholder, a name once given to the viceroy of the king of Spain, and since the revolution to an officer chosen by each separate province and invested with the command of the army and the fleet. Since the days of William the Silent the Stadtholderate had been hereditary in the House of Orange, although for long periods the office had been altogether suspended. The Patriots were strongest in the province of Holland, and especially in the town of Amsterdam. The party of the Prince, as it was called, rested on the attachment of the nobles, the common people, and the provinces of Zealand and Guelderland. As the Patriots were devoted to France, so were the Prince's party to England. But at this time the English party was weak and of no reputation. William V. of Orange was a man of feeble character, not likely to regain what he had lost nor to keep what he had gained. But his high-spirited wife made up for his deficiencies. Frederica Wilhelmina of Prussia, niece of Frederick the Great, had a stout heart to defend the interests of her family, and blue pleading eyes which Harris sometimes confessed to be dangerous.

When Harris arrived in Holland, the affairs of the country were in a serious crisis. The Emperor Joseph had, as we have seen, determined to open the river Scheldt to commerce, a course to which the Dutch were strongly opposed. He had also demanded the cession of the town of Maestricht, to which he imagined that he had some claim. Harris tells Carmarthen in his first despatch (December 7, 1784) that France is determining to support the country against the Emperor's claims—had offered one of her best generals and had given leave to raise troops in France. Besides verbal orders, Harris had received two other papers for his guidance, one a memorandum dated in October, the other formal instructions dated November 21. In the first of these he was told what attitude he was to adopt towards the different parties in the Republic. To the Patriots he was to give general assurances of friendship and goodwill from England, but lament their present attitude towards this country. The more moderate men among the Republicans he was to warn that French influence would be fatal to their constitution and liberties, and their Republic would become little better than a province in the hands of France. The real friends of England, and those entitled to our confidence, he was to recommend to cultivate friendship with the King of Prussia, who ought, in conjunction with England, to be the ally of the United Provinces. They were to be pressed also to co-operate with England in destroying the alliance between France and Austria. In his regular instructions Sir James Harris was ordered to assure the Prince of Orange of our esteem, to find out who are friends to England, to urge the country to return to its ancient connection with us, to notice any treaty with the Court of France, to see what assistance Holland is likely to receive from France or Prussia in her dispute with the Emperor. To these were added two secret instructions. Our ambassador was to discover if there were any who, while supporting the person or the office of the Stadtholder, were still anxious for the French alliance, and to sound well-disposed persons as to the chance of surmounting the present strength of the Patriot party. In no case was the name or authority of the King of England to be placed in jeopardy.

Harris arrived at the Hague, December 6, 1784. His first impressions are very dismal. He says in a private letter, preserved in the British Museum, that there is no chance of doing any good, or any occasion for doing more harm than they are doing themselves. His mission, therefore, will be one of little action. The Prince of Orange told him that his happy days were over, and that he looked forward to nothing for himself and his children except misery and disgrace. He finds that the English party is composed of a set of men dejected, oppressed, and divided amongst themselves. Something might be done with a good leader, but the Prince of Orange was unfit for the post. The princess might do something by inducing the emperor to restore the power of the Stadtholder at the price of opening the Scheldt. If this cannot be done, it is better that Holland should sink into a state of entire insignificance. In the meantime the emperor pressed his claims with vigour. Two Austrian ships were ordered to proceed down the Scheldt and to reply if they were fired upon. Joseph demanded a large compensation from the Dutch for the relinquishment of his supposed rights to the town of Maestricht. This produced a schism between the views of France and Prussia. While the French Court urged the Dutch to submit to the emperor's claims, perhaps from desire to avoid a war, Prussia urged them to resist. Frederick was still more eager to withstand the ambition of Joseph from the news of the contemplated Bavarian exchange, which now became public. These events assisted the views of England in Holland. The peasants, called upon by the Patriots to fight against the Emperor, decked themselves with Orange colours and declared for the Stadtholder. Had the Prince of Orange been less sluggish, the crisis might have been turned to greater advantage. Harris certainly loses no opportunity of effecting his object. He urges Ewart, our representative at Berlin, to take action with the King of Prussia through Herzberg or Görz, on the ground that, as the ministers at home are engrossed with the House of Commons, any good that is ever done on the Continent must be effected by the king's ministers abroad and not by those about his person. He proposes an alliance between England, Prussia, and Holland to check that between France, Austria, and Russia. Frederick suggests in answer that England should in the electorate of Hanover join the Fürstenbund, a suggestion which was readily adopted.

During the spring and summer of 1785 Harris was in England, and was able to communicate with the ministers in person. He found them evidently friendly to an alliance with Prussia, but Frederick was too old and cautious to accept the offer. During his absence the French carried on a mediation between the Dutch and the Emperor, which eventually resulted in their paying the Emperor a large sum of money, which the French, in great part, contributed as a loan. Harris used all the arts of obstruction which the Dutch constitution admitted of to prevent a *rapprochement* between France and Holland, but in vain. Harris, on returning to the Hague, found the Prince of Orange absent. He saw a great deal of the princess, and urged her to use all her influence with her uncle, the King of Prussia; but she could get nothing out of him, and on September 15 the Prince and Princess of Orange left the Hague, the princess for Friesland, the prince for Breda. The night before their departure Harris had a long and affecting interview with the princess. She felt that she was leaving the Hague never to return; in a few days the prince would be deprived of every remnant of authority. She scarcely regretted the altered prospects of her children; they were too young to know ambition, and would, she trusted, be happier in a private station. M. de Maillebois, the French general, had suggested that she should give up the Prince and be Stadtholder in his place. This, which her uncle Frederick would have approved of, she rejected with disdain, and declared that she would never desert her husband. "I may," she said, "wish at times that the Prince possessed many qualities which he has not, and that he could be divested of several he has; but these feelings I conceal in my own heart, and they neither have nor ever shall influence my conduct. I am bound to share his fate, let it be what it may, and I trust in God to be enabled to meet it with firmness and resignation." The princess arrived in Friesland the following day, and landed amidst the acclamations of the people, who crowded on the shore to receive her.

There were at this time two parties in the English Cabinet, one in favour of a spirited foreign policy, the other of peace and retrenchment. Whilst Carmarthen was engaged in the useless attempt to detach Austria from France, Pitt was giving the strength of his mind to the improvement of our finances. He writes to Harris in October 1785: "The general state of our revenue is improving daily. We are, I believe, already in possession of a million surplus beyond all our probable annual expenses, and shall, if the same course of prosperity continues, find ourselves very different in the eyes of Europe from what we have been for some time." The end of 1785 was marked by the signature of the treaty of alliance between Holland and France. England protested against it, but was not prepared to go to war without the active support of Prussia. During the first months of 1786 France was gaining influence in the States, and the Stadtholder was subject to renewed insults and attacks. The province of Zealand remained true to England. By the mouth of her pensionary Vandespiegel she offered to detach herself from the rest of the confederation and join England, if England would accept the offer; but that, of course, could not be done without the risk of war. The Cabinet went so far as to promise the Prince of Orange material support if he would place himself at the head of his party. Vandespiegel was to give his best assistance on his side. A strong memorial was presented to the States-General, informing them that England was anxious for the maintenance of the ancient constitution of Holland and that she was aware of the overbearing ambition of France. Just as events were in the highest condition of tension they received a new turn by the death of Frederick the Great. Lord Dalrymple writes from Berlin that on August 15 he fell into a kind of lethargy, from which he woke the next day and was able to dictate to his secretaries. The same torpor came on again, but at night he was able to speak distinctly. At midnight he was given over, and early in the morning of the 17th the closed gates of the palace announced that the king was dead.

The new king was of a very different character. Lord Dalrymple describes him as being a very poor specimen of a king—tall, but undignified and ungraceful; honest, courageous, and sensible, but not refined or elevated in his ideas. His morality was far from good, and he was seriously in debt. At the same time he was well disposed towards England, and wished his daughter to marry the Prince of Wales. Prince Henri, on the other hand, Frederick's brother, was in favour of a French alliance. The first step of the new king was to send Count Görz to the Hague. He avowed to Harris his master's strong desire for an alliance with England, but this had no effect on the conduct of the States of Holland. They favoured the development of free corps throughout the country— an armed mob, as Harris calls them—and the prince, feeling his life insecure, by the advice of Harris, surrounded himself with a guard. In September the States of Holland suspended the Stadtholder from his functions and rescinded the Act of 1766, which gave him the power of military nominations. The Patriots held a meeting at the French ambassador's, where they discussed the propriety of declaring the Stadtholder an enemy of the Republic, depriving him of his office and declaring it no longer hereditary in his family. To add to the distress of Harris, England refused to accept Count Görz's proposal of a joint intervention; and the King of Prussia, finding action in favour of his sister harder than he had expected, recalled his ambassador and rebuked him for exceeding his instructions. Harris was reduced to a condition of despair. However erroneous were his ideas about the danger of French ambition, he must deserve credit for the instinct which convinced him that a most important battle was being fought out in Holland, that the subjection of that country to France would isolate England in Europe and be a constant menace to our trade, whereas by alliance with Holland we could best hope to establish ourselves in Europe and form useful and permanent connections with other powers. As a last resource he wrote to Pitt himself, who had just concluded a commercial treaty with France. Pitt naturally dreaded anything which would plunge England into a war, and shrank from expenditure on objects which were not calculated to increase or develop the material resources of the country. Harris, in his letter to Pitt of November 28, gives a retrospect of his mission, points out the danger of the political direction of Holland belonging to the French, and asks that such measures may be taken that the friends which he has succeeded in gaining for England may not be abandoned by him. Pitt replies with great caution, but in language which was more satisfactory than Harris or Carmarthen expected. The latter says, in exultation, "Now we have raised his attention to the important object in question, we must by all means endeavour to keep it up and not suffer Holland to be sacrificed either to lawn or cambric." After another correspondence Harris was requested to state his views for information of the Cabinet, and did so in a full despatch. He showed that the republic might still be saved if England would provide funds. Months pass, and no step is taken. On May 1, 1787, he writes a more serious remonstrance. He details the efforts he has made to create an English and Stadtholderian party since his arrival in the country. He points out emphatically that foreign assistance is necessary, and that some great power must be found who may not only think it worth while to afford pecuniary supplies, but who may consider themselves as sufficiently interested in preserving the republic from becoming a French province to declare that if France should invade it the step will not be regarded with indifference. England is the only power that can take this position. May he come to London to confer with the Cabinet in person? His orders of recall were despatched on May 8, and on the same day he informs his Government that the French are forming a camp of 30,000 men at Givet, and are preparing to interfere in force.

We have a full record of a Cabinet dinner at which Harris was present, held at Lord Chancellor Thurlow's on May 23. The Chancellor, the Duke of Richmond, and Lord Stafford were in favour of intervention. Pitt was more cautious; if we did anything, we must be ready for war. Harris urged that France did not desire to fight *for* Holland, but *with* Holland against England; that she had neither an army, revenue, nor ministry; and that England would never find a more favourable moment for taking a high and becoming line. Pitt in reply lamented any interruption to the growth of affluence and prosperity in the country, and asked whether this was not increasing so fast as not to make her equal to resist any force France could collect for some years hence. The next day Pitt went minutely into the whole matter with Harris, and on the 25th a Cabinet minute was presented to the king advising pecuniary assistance to the Stadtholder to the amount of £20,000, advanced as loan or otherwise.

On the evening of the day following Harris's return to the Hague he met five of the Stadtholder's friends in a private room in the Old Palace. Each of them came by a different route, muffled up in his cloak. Sir James told them the result of his journey to England. He said (1) that the King of England granted the pecuniary assistance asked for, (2) that in case of an invasion from France England must be left to act for herself without giving a direct promise, but (3) if it were necessary for them to seek an asylum one would always be given them in England. A plan of action was agreed upon and M. Nagel communicated what had passed to the Court of the Prince at Nimeguen. Nagel returned, saying that the plan of action was adopted by the prince and princess, and that the prince would put himself at the head of Van der Hop's army at Amersfort. This army was soon joined by English officers who volunteered for service, and every day grew in numbers. An event now occurred which changed the whole situation of affairs. The Princess of Orange suddenly left Nimeguen and went to the camp at Amersfort. Soon after her arrival, on June 23, she sent a messenger to inform her friends who had met with such secrecy in the Old Palace that she was determined to come herself to the Hague and to place herself at the head of the Stadtholder's party. The prince had given his consent and letters to the States-General and the States of Holland empowering her to act and negotiate as circumstances might demand. "She asked for our advice," Harris says, "and we could not refuse our consent, but warned her of the danger she might incur." On June 25 an express arrived, ordering a room to be prepared for her in the palace on the 28th. However on the evening of that day she was stopped in the neighbourhood of Gouda by some free corps and carried under a strong guard to Schonhoven. She wrote an indignant letter to protest against her detention, and there was great danger of an outbreak at the Hague. The streets were patrolled by horse and foot soldiers, who dispersed the people. The States of Holland passed a resolution approving of her capture. On the morning of June 30 she was released and returned to Nimeguen. I cannot find whether Harris suggested this bold step or not, but it is difficult to believe that she would have acted without his advice, and we may, I think, regard this new departure as part of the *plan of action* suggested by her partisans.

The princess wrote to her brother urging him to avenge the insult offered to her. He prepared immediately to march troops into Holland. The English Cabinet made desperate efforts to prevent the French from interfering. No doubt France was pledged by treaty to support Holland in case of attack, and could not back out of her engagement without dishonour. But Montmorin, who had succeeded Vergennes, was not only sincerely desirous of peace but could not afford to go to war. There exists in the Record Office a despatch dated July 27, 1787, which, from the erasures and the sentences contributed in autograph by the different ministers, shows the care with which it was drafted. We then contemplated mediation, but mediation to restore the Stadtholder. Meanwhile negotiations were going on with the Court of Potsdam, where there was a strong French party opposing the alliance with England. A letter from Pitt to Eden, dated September 14, 1787, is most warlike in tone, and says that the French must, as things stand, give up their predominant influence in Holland or they must *fight for it*. A war between France and England was on the point of breaking out. Montmorin declared that there was a strong party in the French Cabinet in favour of intervention, and that many regarded a foreign war as the best remedy for the internal calamities which were advancing with fatal rapidity. A war between France and England in 1787, whatever its result, would certainly have changed the destinies of Europe. War in Holland was so imminent in August that Harris burned his cyphers and sent his important papers to England, as the troops levied by Holland were coming very near to the Hague. A convention between England and Prussia provided for a joint intervention in favour of the Stadtholder. Before this England prepared a fleet for the defence of Zealand and sent an English general to Germany to levy troops. The Cabinet minute for arming the fleet is dated September 15; a haughty message is sent to the French Government and a note to the Courts of Europe. On the same day the Prussian army entered Holland in three columns. All resistance immediately collapsed. The free corps were broken up; the States of Holland agreed to bring back the Stadtholder to the Hague with all the authority given to him in 1747 and 1766. Harris wrote that he can scarcely believe in the reality of what has occurred; he had no conception of a success so rapid and so complete. It was now too late for France to intervene; if the French ambassador came to the Hague, he must enter it with orange-coloured ribands or not at all. Five days later the prince returned to his capital. A mile from the town the horses were taken from his carriage, and when he arrived at the palace he was borne on the shoulders of the mob. He was invested with every privilege that had been taken from him. He ascribes his restoration solely to the friendship and support of England. Within a week he was joined by his noble-hearted wife, who was received with the same enthusiasm and promised every satisfaction. The States of Holland were induced to repudiate the intervention or mediation of France. On October 2 Mr. Grenville, who had been sent on a special mission to Paris, was able to write that France had laid aside all thought of active interference and that he considered the Dutch business to be at an end. On October 28 Montmorin was forced to sign a most humiliating declaration of disarmament, coupled with the statement that the intention of the king was not and never had been to interfere in the affairs of the United Provinces. It may be doubted whether it was sound policy to weaken by this unnecessary degradation a power which was too weak already to withstand the revolutionary flood which was soon to overwhelm Europe.

It would be tedious and unnecessary to follow the details of the negotiation of the treaty between England and Holland. Vandespiegel, the warm friend of England and pensionary of Zealand, was now made Grand Pensionary of Holland. The Dutch were renowned for haggling about minute points, and the most difficult matter to arrange was the possession of Negapatam, a town on the Coromandel coast with a good harbour, which had been ceded to England at the peace. It however remained in the hands of England, and the definite treaty between England and Holland was signed on April 15, 1788. A treaty between Holland and Prussia was signed at Berlin on the same day and at the same hour. The treaty was communicated to the Court of Versailles, and was naturally not received with satisfaction. France declared that she did not intend to allow the treaty to pass unchallenged. She required an explanation of its tendency, and was not satisfied with it when given.

The treaty between England and Prussia still remained to be concluded. The King of Prussia was to stay with his sister, at Loo, on June 11, and Harris was invited to meet him there. In view of this important negotiation he was summoned to England to receive direct instructions from the Ministry. He was the bearer of an autograph letter from George III. to the princess saying how much he should desire an alliance with her brother in his capacity as king, similar to that which already existed between them in his capacity as elector. The king mentioned the peace of Europe, and especially a settlement of the dispute between Russia and Turkey, as an object of the alliance. The history of the negotiation is curious and romantic. There was a strong French party at the Prussian Court, and the king, weak and vacillating, did not know how to make up his mind. The princess told Harris that her brother was afraid of him, from his supposed leanings to Austria, and that he had a most difficult part to play; at the same time she promised her whole support. Among the king's attendants was a Colonel Stein, brother of the famous minister, who was reported to be in the interest of France and opposed to the English alliance. Harris had determined to see the king alone, and gave a hundred ducats to the servant who stood at the king's door, promising as much more if he would exclude Stein till the next morning. The bribe was successful, as Stein twice presented himself and was not allowed to enter.

Harris saw the king at seven in the morning on June 12. He went over everything which had passed between the two Courts since the signing of the convention of October 2, explaining anything which seemed to show a reluctance to contract an alliance with Prussia. The king said that he had always desired to see the Courts united, and that he did not see why this should not immediately be done. Harris offered the option of immediately signing a provisional treaty or postponing it for the purpose of concluding a general treaty on a broader basis, to which other powers might be invited to accede. The king asked for some hours of calm consideration. The rest of the day was passed in every kind of amusement, and it was not till after midnight, while the brilliant company were dancing, that the king asked Harris to walk with him behind the pavilion, in which the ball was being held, and told him that he had decided to conclude a provisional alliance at once, with an act of guarantee for Holland, and to consult other powers as to forming a more extensive connection in the future. Harris and Alvensleben had no secretaries. They spent the rest of the night in drawing up the treaty with the secret articles. At nine o'clock the next morning Harris was summoned to the king's closet; he had already seen the draft, and had only a trifling alteration to propose. The treaty was formally signed by Alvensleben and Harris, in the presence of Vandespiegel, and entitled the provisional treaty of Loo. Harris had triumphantly removed the king from the

French influence which surrounded him, and left him in a state of complete devotion to the interests of England and under a full conviction of the fairness of our conduct towards him. This is one of the few instances where a minister has made a treaty directly with a foreign sovereign without the intervention of that sovereign's responsible advisers.

Thus was concluded the triple alliance of 1788—a very important event in the history of Europe, which, lost in the folds of the French Revolution, which broke out in the succeeding year, has received less attention than it deserves. For a time the three allied powers gave the law to Europe. It made peace between Austria and Turkey at Sistowa, between Russia and Poland at Werelä, and between Russia and the Porte at Jassy; it secured the Netherlands to Austria, and causing the dispute about Nootka Sound, prevented a war between Spain and England. So far it tended to quell the disorders of Europe, to curb the ambition of some powers, the revolutionary movements of others. It was powerless to conjure the terrible doom which hung over the devoted head of France. The whole course of its influence bears traces of the calm and majestic mind of Pitt. Still the advocates of non-intervention may have something to say on the other side. It bound England closely with Holland, and thus was the final cause of the war with France in 1793. A careful study of the evidence shows us that the quarrel between France and England in that year, which led to a twenty-two years' struggle, was not caused by the opening of the Scheldt, by the conquest of Belgium, by the decree of November 19, or by the execution of Louis XVI., but by the threatening attitude of France towards Holland. The moment France menaced the independence of Holland the *casus foederis* arose. Again, it led us to contemplate the so-called Russian armament of 1791, and the breach of faith with Prussia, of which public opinion in England compelled us then to be guilty, paved the way for the desertion of the coalition by Prussia in 1792, when she concluded the separate peace of Bâle. The peace of Bâle, whether or not it was an example to be imitated by other powers, laid Germany open to the attacks of Napoleon and kept the north of Europe quiet while its neighbours were being pillaged and revolutionised. Thus the triple alliance of 1788, although it is now almost forgotten by historians, may be regarded as the final cause of some of the most momentous events which have influenced the history of England.

VI.

ENGLAND AND FRANCE IN 1793.

PROBABLY no event in the history of England during the last hundred years is so important as the outbreak of war with France in 1793. It led, by a chain of almost necessary consequence, to our long struggle against Napoleon I. It added millions to our debt, it caused the distress and discontent which paved the way for the Reform Bill of 1832, its results placed England at the head of the European system. From a narrower point of view, it formed a turning point in the career of Pitt. Up to that time he had pursued a policy of peace, retrenchment, and reform. The most enlightened minister of his age, he promised fair to anticipate by fifty years some of the most important changes which our own age has witnessed. From that period, he was the minister of war, extravagance and coercion. His name was a synonym for blood, violence, and treachery, not only upon the Continent, but among English Liberals. The war then kindled was not extinguished until it had killed him in its course. His friends saw the "Austerlitz look" on the blanched countenance of their dying chief. Passing a map of Europe in his last days, he said, "Roll up that map, we shall not want it any more."

The character of our conduct in that crisis has long been disputed amongst politicians. War was opposed in 1793 by Fox and the Liberal party who followed him, and he lost no opportunity of urging the desirability of peace. However, when he became Foreign Minister after the death of Pitt, he did not make peace. In 1853, after the death of the Duke of Wellington, the question was argued by Richard Cobden. In his pamphlet, "1793 and 1853," he tries to show that our war with France was neither necessary nor just. His arguments are those of a partisan, and the authorities which he recommends to his reverend correspondent, and on which he probably relied himself, are such ordinary books as the *Annual Register*, the *Pictorial History of England*, Alison's *History of Europe*, and the *Parliamentary Debates*. The present writer has had the opportunity of reading nearly all the dispatches in the English Record Office and the French Foreign Office which bear upon the subject; and his aim is to present as clear and impartial an account of the origin of the war as can be done in the limited space at his disposal.

It is now admitted on all hands that the war was none of our seeking. It was declared by the French Government, and would, perhaps, not have been declared by us. It may be urged that there was such a fundamental antagonism between the principles of the French Revolution and those of the English Government that the outbreak of war was merely a question of time. But we were a grave and serious nation, dealing with a crowd of heated anarchists, unused to govern, intemperate of language. Neither their words nor their actions could be interpreted by ordinary rules. Had we exhausted every precaution ; were we guilty of no false step which we might have foreseen would lead us into the path along which we have no desire to move ?

From the first outbreak of the Revolution the policy of the English Ministry had been to preserve a strict neutrality. Although the contrary has often been maintained, there should be no doubt of it since the publication of the *History of the Politics of Great Britain and France in* 1800. This work, written by Herbert Marsh, the celebrated Professor of Divinity and the translator of Mosheim, is an exhaustive examination of the conduct of the English Government in its relations with France at this period. He proves, as far as could be proved from the materials within his reach : (1) that the British Government knew nothing of the Conference of Pilnitz, and that when requested in 1791 to join a coalition against France it absolutely refused to do so; (2) that we behaved with extreme friendliness to France in the affairs of San Domingo; (3) that we were one of the first to recognise the new French Constitution of 1791 ; (4) that in January, 1792, we took measures for reducing our armaments by sea and land ; (5) that when France had declared war against Austria on April 20, 1792, the British Government took every pains to assert its neutrality ; (6) that the proclamation of May 21 against seditious writings was a mere act of internal policy, and was not directed against the French.

Evidences of this position might be easily multiplied to any extent. On September 20, 1791, Lord Grenville writes from Weymouth that M. de Biutinaye, an emissary of the French *émigré* princes, is to be told "that his Majesty's resolution extends not only to the taking no part either in supporting or opposing the measures which other powers may adopt, but also to the not influencing in any manner their determination in that respect." "Sir R. Keith has been authorised to explain to the Emperor [of Germany] his Majesty's determination to take no part in the business of France unless any new circumstances should arise which might have an influence on the interests of his own subjects. This is all that has passed, and the princes ought to know it." Nor was the disposition of the French Government to us of a less friendly character. Chauvelin's instructions as Minister to England are dated April 19, 1792. He was the ostensible head of the French mission, but the moving spirit of it was Talleyrand, the famous Bishop of Autun, who could not be formally commissioned to the English court because no member of the Assemblée Nationale of 1789 was allowed to hold public office. He is charged to use every argument to keep England out of the new coalition, and to persuade her to enter into a defensive alliance with France for the mutual guarantee of each other's possessions. England might persuade Austria and Prussia to withdraw from the league. If Spain took part against France, France and England with South America might join against her. A defensive alliance might include a ratification of the Treaty of Commerce of 1787. But above all he was to try to obtain a loan of three or four millions in England, if possible, with the guarantee of the English Government. In return for the guarantee he was to offer the cession of the isle of Tobago, almost entirely inhabited by English, of course with the consent of the inhabitants. The English Government were to be told that for their object there was no time like the present.

On August 4, 1792, Lord Gower writes to Lord Grenville that the Royal family, especially the queen, are in great danger, and he demands instructions for his conduct. Lord Grenville replies on August 9, the very eve of the attack on the Tuileries and the last day of liberty for the monarchy of France, that no instructions could be of any service to their Majesties in the present crisis, that we have been strictly neutral during the last five years, that if we could do any good matters might be different. "The king's feelings might lead him to depart from the line he has chosen. But any measure of the kind could only commit the king's name in a business in which he has hitherto kept himself unengaged without any reasonable hope of its producing a good effect; on the contrary, interference might do harm. We are not indifferent to the fate of their most Christian Majesties. Express our sentiments of regard, friendship, and goodwill, but make no declaration."

We see that up to the 10th of August, the British Government preserved an attitude of scrupulous neutrality. From that day the face of affairs was changed. The king was a prisoner in the Temple, the Royal authority was in abeyance. The Government were compelled either to recall their ambassador or to recognise the validity of the Provisional Committee. In recalling Lord Gower they followed the example of other European nations. Indeed the massacres of September followed closely upon August 10, and the life of an intimate friend of the Royal family would scarcely have been secure. The Duke of Dorset, Lord Gower's predecessor, had been forced to leave Paris because a letter written to the Comte d'Artois, congratulating the Count on his safe escape from Paris, had been found upon one of the Duke's servants. Mr. Cobden makes a great matter of this recall of Lord Gower, and says that after the deposition of Louis Philippe in 1848 our minister continued to be accredited to the French Republic. Such, however, were not the views held either in France or England at the time. On August 28, Chauvelin wrote to Lebrun that the recall of Lord Gower need not affect the neutrality of England: " Ce rappel tient uniquement à ces raisons d'étiquette et de bienséance." Lebrun, on August 29, in his instructions to M. Noel, whom he was sending to England, says that notwithstanding the views of George III., who was rightly believed to be anxious for war, the cabinet is composed of enlightened men, and that Dundas's note recalling Lord Gower was very moderate.

The events of August 10 might well impress the English Government, when we consider the effect they produced upon Chauvelin himself. No sooner had he heard of what had occurred than he writes to

Lord Grenville that criminal and disastrous events have taken place in Paris, that the security of the National Assembly has been violated, that men of violent passions have led the multitude astray. He begs the King of England to use all his influence to prevent the armies of the enemy from invading French territory, giving occasion for new excesses, and compromising still further the liberty, the safety, and even the existence of the king and of his family. No sooner has Chauvelin sent this despatch than he discovers his mistake. A cabinet council is called to deliberate upon his letter. Chauvelin receives new intelligence from Paris. He calls Mr. Secretary Dundas and begs that the dispatch may be returned to him and may be considered as *non avenue*. Dundas writes to one of the clerks of the Foreign Office: " Mr. Aust will not allow any copies of the paper delivered this day by M. Chauvelin to get out of the office, and will inform (by circulating this note) H.M.'s confidential servants who attended the cabinet this day that M. Chauvelin having in the most earnest manner requested the paper to be returned to him, Mr. Dundas, after consulting with Mr. Pitt, thought the reasons stated impossible to be resisted." The paper was therefore returned to Chauvelin, but a copy had been taken of it which is now in the Record Office. Although Lord Gower was recalled from Paris, Chauvelin still remained in London, and it has often been asked why he did so. It has been said that although he was disowned by Ministers he knew himself to be on very good terms with the Opposition, and that he stayed in England that he might be a centre of intrigue. His dispatches give little countenance to this idea, while they supply a natural reason for delay in presenting his letters of recall. When war between France and England became imminent, Chauvelin held some communication with the Opposition by means of Sheridan, who visited him secretly. But whilst there was a hope of peace or even of alliance between the two countries, his great object was to avoid all suspicion of the kind.

There is in the French Foreign Office a dispatch dated May 23, 1792, signed by Chauvelin, but evidently composed by Talleyrand, which if read and pondered by Lebrun, should have deterred him for ever from such intrigues. Talleyrand writes complaining of the indiscretion of French journalists, that the terms *Ministry* and *Opposition* have a very different sense in England to that which is attributed to them abroad. "In reading French papers one would believe that the king and the partisans of privilege and of Royal prerogative were on one side, and the friends of the people on the other, working incessantly, the one for authority, the other for liberty. If this were the case, a revolution might be probable enough. But in fact the mass of the nation is generally indifferent to all these political discussions which make such a noise amongst ourselves. Agriculture, art, manufacture, and commerce, the rise and fall of the funds, these are the main objects of attention, the debates of Parliament only interest the people in a secondary degree. The Opposition is generally regarded as an ingredient as necessary to the constitution as the Ministry itself, but that is all, and whenever they are seen at war with each other, whatever may be the opinion which is formed of their measures, the nation feels sure of liberty. Nor is the Ministry itself as instinctively attached to the king or as zealous for the Royal prerogative as is generally believed in France. Composed of different elements, it contains germs of disagreement which incline it at one time to the side of the monarchy at another to that of the people." He concludes a long dispatch by saying that they must treat with the Ministry alone, and must try to gain their confidence, and that is only to be done by showing the most firm determination to do nothing which may encourage dissension.

These weighty words ought to dispose of the opinion that Chauvelin's object in remaining in England was to intrigue with the Opposition. His real fear was lest his letters of recall should be refused by the Court, and so the rupture be brought about which he and his employers were most anxious to prevent. He writes to Lebrun on August 31 : " It would be natural to recall me as the English have recalled Lord Gower, and I should be glad to go ; but let me make the following observation. Lord Gower's recall is due only to the motive of *delicatesse monarchique*. We have no such reason ; we wish to preserve the best intelligence with England. Besides, Mr. Lindsay (the secretary of legation) remains. It might be difficult for you to draw up my letters of recall, or for me to present them. How very bad it would be if I were refused an audience ! what a triumph for our enemies ! All the friends we have in England are agreed upon this point." Indeed the Provisional Government sent a new emissary to England in the person of M. Noel, who has made a greater reputation as a writer of school-books than as a diplomatist. They at first intended to supersede Chauvelin, and as a *ci-devant* marquis they always regarded him with suspicion. On September 6, however, they definitely tell him that he may stay, yet warn him that he must be prepared to act cordially with the different persons charged with special missions whom the Government are likely to send to London. Some of them were undoubtedly intended as spies, others were got out of the way that they might escape the fate of their brother aristocrats in the prisons.

During the autumn things remained tolerably quiet. The king was at Weymouth from August 17 to the end of September. The centre of disturbance was in the Ministry itself. The king had not given the Ministers his entire confidence. The French Revolution offended every principle and prejudice of his nature. Although we have no positive proof, we have many indications that the king was eager either to join the coalition or to take decisive steps for repressing the disorder in France, and seating his Royal cousin firmly on the throne. The king was supported in the Ministry by Lord Thurlow, the chancellor, whom Pitt was obliged to get rid of, and Lord Hawkesbury, the father of a hopeful son who had just entered Parliament, and who afterwards became Lord Liverpool. Pitt depended upon his brother, Lord Chatham, First Lord of the Admiralty, a person of gentlemanly bearing, moderate abilities, and sententious wisdom, and the two Secretaries of State, Lord Grenville and Mr. Dundas. Lord Camden, the Duke of Richmond, and Lord Stafford formed a middle party, who oscillated between the two extremes. We shall see that Pitt was ready all along to make any sacrifice for the preservation of peace with France. Grenville seems to have gradually drifted to the side of the king, who, as events progressed, became still more eager for war.

The French Embassy had some hope that a coalition ministry would be formed which would be more favourable to their cause. The summer of 1792 was occupied by correspondence, interviews and conversations, all bearing on the possibility of including Pitt and Fox in the same cabinet, and providing the country with a ministry resting on a broad foundation. The true history of these intrigues has yet to be written. The account generally given of them is that Pitt was not unwilling to receive some of the whig party, but that the scheme shattered upon the obstinacy and impracticability of Fox. There is in the British Museum (Add. MSS. 27,918) a secret political diary of the Duke of Leeds, which gives a minute account of these transactions, and one of different complexion from that which is derived from Lord Malmesbury's diary. According to Lord Malmesbury, Pitt was eager for the coalition. There was a certain difficulty about Fox, "*perhaps* it would not be quite easy to give Fox the Foreign Department *immediately*, but that in a few months he might certainly have it." "Pitt did not come with the king's command to propose a coalition, but that he would be responsible that it would please the king *and the queen*, and that the only difficulty at all likely to arise was about Fox, and that difficulty entirely owing to Fox's conduct in Parliament during the last four months." The only authority for these opinions of Pitt is Lord Loughborough, the very man whose restless desire for office and unscrupulous ambition was urging the Duke of Portland to sacrifice Fox. It is certain that the idea of a coalition was mentioned to Pitt and the king in June, but the Duke of Leeds' diary shows that neither of them seriously entertained the idea, and that Fox was perfectly justified in believing it to be impossible. On Tuesday, August 14, the Duke of Leeds, who had been Foreign Minister in Pitt's Cabinet, who expected to be made Prime Minister, with Pitt and Fox serving under him as secretaries, had an interview with the king at Windsor. The Duke expounded his plans, advocating as well as he could the cause of Mr. Fox. "Whether it had any effect I am ignorant, for his Majesty did not, I believe, mention Mr. Fox's name more than once, if even that, during the whole conversation. I mentioned the several interviews which had passed between Lord Loughborough and Mr. Dundas, at one at least of which Mr. Pitt had been present, and which had been mentioned in the newspapers as affording sufficient reason to suppose his Majesty's servants not indisposed to our arrangement, and I took for granted his Majesty was informed of everything that had passed down to the present time. To my great surprise the king answered that he had not heard anything upon the subject for a long time; that Mr. Pitt had, indeed, some months ago mentioned something like an opening on the part of the Duke of Portland and his friends, to which his Majesty had answered, '*Anything complimentary to them*, but no *power*.'" The Duke of Leeds pertinently remarks upon this, "The first part of this brief but curious answer explains the circumstance of the offer of the Garter to the Duke of Portland, and of the Marquisate of Rockingham to Lord Fitzwilliam; and the latter proves but too clearly the great difficulty, if not impossibility, of succeeding in the proposed arrangement." The Duke of Leeds, unabashed by this repulse, went on to suggest that, although Pitt could not remain at the head of the Treasury, he could still be Chancellor of the Exchequer as well as Secretary of State. "The king asked me who was proposed to be First Lord of the Treasury? I answered that I could not tell, but that it was meant that some one should be in that situation who was on terms of friendship and confidence with both both parties. His Majesty replied it would be very awkward for Mr. Pitt after having been head of that board to descend to an inferior situation at it, and that whoever was First Lord must either be a cypher or Mr. Pitt appear as a *commis*."

On Wednesday, August 22, the Duke of Leeds had an interview with Pitt. Pitt received him very civilly, but did not appear quite at his ease. The Duke told the same story that he had told to the king: "Mr. Pitt listened attentively to all I said, and answered, there had been no thought of any alteration in the Government, that circumstances did not call for it, nor did the people wish it, and that no new arrangement, either by a change or coalition, had ever been in contemplation." On the Duke reminding him of the reported interviews between Lord Loughborough and Lord Dundas, at which Pitt had been present, he said that it was true, but that such meetings had not in view any change of administration. The language both of Pitt and of the king admits of no doubt, and we must conclude that the negotiations for a coalition which have been repeated in all histories of the time have, as far as Pitt is concerned, no basis but the interested imagination and creative memory of Lord Loughborough.

The king remained at Weymouth from the middle of August to the end of September, and during this time home politics were in abeyance, but events were moving rapidly in France. On September 20, the cannonade of Valmy announced, as Goethe said to those who heard it, the birth of a new era; on October 23, a salvo of artillery all along the French frontier announced that the soil of France was free from the enemy. Before the end of September the French armies marched across the frontier. Nice was taken on September 28, Spires on September 30; the attacked became the aggressors, and the French Government imagined a victorious course of mingled conquest and propaganda. These events did not appear to compromise English interests until Dumouriez began to overrun the Netherlands. The battle of Jemappes was fought on November 6, and on November 14 the capture of Brussels laid the whole of Belgium at his feet. These victories encouraged the French to take a higher tone. Chauvelin, who did not like to go to Court for fear he should be badly received, now asked his Government for credentials as Minister of the Republic. He writes to Lebrun on November 3, that the time has come to treat openly with England, and that he wishes for positive instructions.

Lebrun was clear-sighted enough to see the effect which the conquest of Belgium was likely to have in England. He writes to Chauvelin on October 30, "The army of the Republic commanded by Dumouriez is on the point of entering, if it had not already entered, the territory of the Low Countries. It is possible that Dumouriez may conquer them, and in this case it is quite possible that the inhabitants will rise in a general insurrection against the House of Austria. What would England do in this case? Would she feel bound by the convention of November 10, 1790? The Republic solemnly renounces every conquest." The next day, October 30, Lebrun orders Chauvelin to announce distinctly that "the nation will never suffer Belgium to be under foreign influence, and that it will never annex the smallest part to the French Empire." He adds, "now we of course desire for our protection a democratic power on our frontier." On November 6, he shows a still greater desire to know what public opinion in England thinks about the conquest of the Netherlands, and he expresses the same views as before.

On November 10, he writes in a similar strain to Noel. "Our policy is very simple on this point as on all others. We do not wish for conquest; we have no desire to give any nation this or that form of government. The inhabitants of Belgium will choose that which suits them best, we shall not interfere." Interested as the English might be in the fate of Belgium, they were far more interested in that of Holland. Holland was united to us by the closest ties, its friendship was the triumph of our diplomacy, the power of the Stadtholder depended upon our support, to desert it would have been an act of ingratitude as well as of weakness. At Pitt's accession to office in 1783, he found England, after the struggle with America, isolated in Europe. The main jealousy of this country was directed towards France. But France was really weak and anxious to recover something of the maritime power of which England had robbed her. With this object she turned to the strong fleet of Holland; in close alliance with the Dutch she might regain her trade, and even establish a footing in India. The mission of Lord Malmesbury was designed to counteract these plans. Arriving in Holland when the power of the Stadtholder was at its lowest ebb, he reconstructed it, discomfited the Patriot party which was devoted to France, and laid the foundations of the triple alliance between England, Holland and Prussia, which for three years gave the law to Europe. Therefore, although we might overlook the conquest of Belgium, we could not but regard the least attempt upon Holland as a case of war. Yet such was the levity of the French in this serious crisis, that Maret, afterwards Duke of Bassano, who arrived in England about November 8, having just left the victorious Dumouriez, told Chauvelin that Dumouriez had the intention of "throwing a few shells into Maestricht." Chauvelin had sense enough to see that this would make a breach inevitable.

On November 21, Maret, who was on the point of leaving England to return to France by way of Brussels, wrote a letter to Lebrun which exactly explains the situation. He proposes to tell Dumouriez that if he attacks Holland, which he certainly had in contemplation, it will inevitably mean war with England. War is certainly dreaded by the city, even if the Government desire to distract people's attention from home affairs. The *philosopher-general* will not be insensible to these arguments. He will prefer the hope of a general peace to an additional triumph. He then adds with cynical acuteness, "Whether the state of our finances make it impossible for us to go to war, or the fear of letting loose upon society a mob of unoccupied persons by disbanding our armies makes peace impossible, in either case the feeling of England towards us is of the first importance. If we wish for peace, let us make an alliance with England; if we desire war, let us attempt to form a junction which will diminish the number of our enemies and which may embroil England with Spain. Chauvelin, good fellow as he is, is impossible here. Men are prejudiced against him. Send Barthélémi" (the best diplomatist the French possessed, who, in 1790, made the treaties of Bâle with Prussia and Spain) "as ambassador extraordinary, and some one else as subordinate agent. I should be very happy to take this place. Nominate Chauvelin to some first-rate post. Noel could replace Barthélémi in Switzerland." If this advice had been adopted, and, as we shall see, this was very nearly being the case, peace between the two countries would most probably have been preserved.

We now come to the two acts of the French Government which formed the strongest case for grievance on the English side, and which are generally considered as the true causes of war: the decree of November 19, and the opening of the navigation of the Scheldt. Each of these will require attention. The decree of November 19 was passed by the Convention in great haste and under the following circumstances. In the middle of the sitting Rhul rose and stated that the district of Darmstadt, which properly belonged to France by the Treaty of Ryswick, had assumed the national cockade and asked to become French. The Duke of Deux Ponts had marched an army to stop the movement. "The citizens of the Duchy of Limburg, in the district of Darmstadt, ask our protection against the despots; also the club of the Friends of Liberty and Equality established at Mayence have written to ask if you will grant protection to the people of Mayence, or abandon them to the mercy of the despots who threaten them." He concludes thus: "I ask that the nations who wish to fraternise with us shall be protected by the French nation." It will be seen that this proposition goes merely to the extent of defensive measures. It is then moved that Rhul's proposition be referred to the diplomatic committee, which should determine how the French should not only protect but guarantee the liberty of surrounding nations. Legendre supports the proposition. Brissot says that the diplomatic committee is about to speak on the subject on the following Friday (November 19 is Monday). On Rhul urging the cause of the people of Mayence, Brissot asks that the principle of the decree shall be voted immediately. At last Larevellière-Lepeaux, that distinguished member of the Directory, who afterwards complained that it was so hard to found a new religion to take the place of Christianity, and to whom Talleyrand recommended the experiment of being crucified and rising again on the third day, proposed the decree in the following words: "The National Convention declares, in the name of the French nation, that it will give fraternity and assistance to all peoples who shall wish to recover their liberty, and charges the executive power to give the necessary orders to the generals to carry assistance to these peoples, and to defend citizens who have been harassed, or who may be harassed in the cause of liberty." Sergent then proposed that the decree should be translated into all languages and printed. The Convention then proceeded to other business and broke up at five o'clock.

Such is the history of this famous decree. In the French manner of those days a few isolated facts repeated by a member were made the occasion for asserting a number of sweeping generalities, and the terms of the hastily passed decree went even beyond the intention and meaning of those who passed it. Was it worthy of a powerful nation like the English to treat every word of this hasty declaration, "translated into all languages," as if it were the solemn and authoritative voice of a grave and powerful legislature representing an united people?

The opening of the navigation of the Scheldt was much more serious. This is announced to Chauvelin in a letter from Lebrun dated November 27. "The executive council had just freed the navigation of the Scheldt. No injury is done to the rights of the Dutch. Our reasons are that the river takes its rise in France, and that a nation which has obtained its liberty cannot recognise a system of feudalism, and still less submit to it. This need not affect the good harmony which exists between ourselves and England. Engagements which the Belgians entered into before the epoch of their present liberty naturally fall to the ground." He urges Chauvelin to counteract any bad impressions which this may produce, and say that it was done in the interest of the prosperity of Belgium. It was natural that these two measures, following so quickly upon each other, should excite strong feeling in England. The views of the English Government are given in a dispatch addressed to Chauvelin on December 31, signed, indeed, by Grenville, but bearing throughout the stamp of the stern and haughty style of William Pitt. His sentences, when once known, are unmistakable. It states that in the decree of November 19 all England saw the formal declaration of a design to extend universally the new principles of government adopted in France, and to encourage disorder and revolt in all countries, even in those which are neutral. "The application of these principles to the king's dominions has been shown unequivocally by the public reception given by the promoters of sedition in this country, and by the speeches made to them precisely at the time of this decree, and since on several different occasions. England cannot consider such an explanation [as has been given] satisfactory, but she must look upon it as a frank avowal of those dispositions which she sees with so just an uneasiness and jealousy."

With regard to the Scheldt the trumpet-voice of the statesman sounds with no uncertain note. "France can have no right to annul the stipulations relative to the Scheldt, unless she have also the right to set aside equally the other treaties between all the Powers of Europe, and all the other rights of England or her allies. She can even have no pretence to interfere in the question of opening the Scheldt, unless she were the sovereign of the Low Countries, or had the right to dictate laws to all Europe. England never will consent that France shall arrogate the power of annulling at her pleasure, and under the pretence of a pretended natural right of which she makes herself the only judge, the political system of Europe established by solemn treaties and guaranteed by the consent of all the Powers. This Government, adhering to the maxims which it has followed for more than a century, will also never see with indifference that France shall make herself either directly or indirectly the sovereign of the Low Countries, or general arbiter of the rights and liberties of Europe. If France is really desirous of maintaining peace and friendship with England, she must show herself disposed to renounce her views of aggression and aggrandisement, and to confine herself within her own territory, without insulting other Governments, without disturbing their tranquillity, without violating their rights." Chatham could not have spoken more plainly or more worthily. In these sentences is contained the whole opposition of England to the encroachments of the Revolution, to the spoliation of Napoleon.

At the same time it may be argued whether the opening of the Scheldt was a question on which the English were bound to go to war. We appealed on our side to the law of nations, the French on theirs to the law of nature. Both these appeals may be disregarded in the inquiry. Our treaty with Holland of 1788 bound us to guarantee the Dutch possessions from attack or from the threat of attack. But in this instance the Dutch did not protest against the action of the French, nor did they call upon us for our assistance. Therefore it was a matter with which we had no immediate concern. That we should not have considered it as a *casus belli* in the last resort is shown by the fact that negotiations were impending between the Dutch and Dumouriez under the sanction of Lord Auckland at the time when the war eventually broke out. The idea of opening the Scheldt to commerce was not a new one. It had been threatened by Joseph II., and only laid aside upon French persuasion. At this time we had instructed our ambassador at Vienna to inform the Emperor personally that there was no object of his ambition which we should not be ready to further, provided he would break his alliance with France. This had been written by Lord Carmarthen, while Pitt was still Prime Minister. It was scarcely reasonable to regard as an inexpiable insult to England the carrying out by one power of a measure which we had ourselves suggested to another. Other proofs are not wanting that neither the decree of November 19 nor the opening of the Scheldt would have been regarded as sufficient reasons for going to war on the part of England. Chauvelin had a long interview with Grenville on November 29, which left this impression upon his mind. Still more explicit is a letter of Maret, dated December 2, in which he gives account of two interviews, one with William Smith, Pitt's private secretary, and the other with Pitt himself. From the first interview Maret derived the impression that England had negotiated with Spain, that Pitt was extremely reluctant to go to war, and the recognition of the French Republic was not at all unlikely.

The interview with Pitt was more momentous. Pitt began by speaking of his fears about Holland, of his determination to support the allies of England, and to enforce the rigorous execution of the treaties which unite her with other powers. He expressed a sincere desire to avoid a war which would be fatal to the repose and to the prosperity of the two nations and asked if the same desire was shared by the French Government. On Maret giving satisfactory assurances of this, Pitt said, " If the French Government would authorise some one to confer with us, we should be disposed to listen to him, and to treat him with cordiality and confidence." *Maret.* " You speak of a secret agent, there is not such a one here. If there had been one in London, I would rather that he had come here than myself." *Pitt.* " I mean a person with whom we could communicate cordially and frankly, and who would not repel our confidence." Maret said that in that case England would have to recognise the Republic. Pitt replied that that course must be avoided, probably to spare the susceptibilities of the king. " Do not reject this offer, and we will examine everything carefully." Maret said that he would urge Lebrun to send some one. Pitt replied, " Why not yourself ? Write at once to Paris; moments are precious." Maret promised to do so. Pitt spoke again of Holland, and as Maret was going away Pitt called him back and alluded to the question of the Scheldt. Maret avoided discussion on this point, and Pitt mentioned the decree of November 19. Maret gave the same answer that he had given to Smith, namely, that it only applied to powers at war with France; then Pitt cried, " If an interpretation of this kind were possible, the effect would be excellent." Maret assured Pitt that the Government had nothing to do with the decree, that it was the work of a few exalted spirits, made in a burst of enthusiasm, and without discussion. Pitt concluded by urging Maret not to lose a moment in communicating with Lebrun.

This interview shows that on December 1 peace between the two countries was quite possible, that it was ardently desired by Pitt, and that the really burning question was the invasion of Holland, whereas the other two grievances of the Scheldt and of the decree of November 19 might have been satisfactorily arranged. It is tantalizing to reflect how nearly the arrangement which Pitt suggested was taking effect. On December 7 Lebrun determined to move Chauvelin to the Hague, and to authorise Maret to treat secretly with the English Government. He presents his project at the meeting of the executive council, but by some wave of infatuation it is rejected. We may read in the archives of the French Foreign Office the original minute of the Conseil Executif Provisoire, signed by Danton, Barère, and others, which runs in these terms : "The Conseil Executif Provisoire determines that, while making no declaration about Holland, the conference with Pitt may be continued, provided that it is done through Chauvelin, the accredited minister." The French Government probably thought that England could be terrified, that the Opposition were as powerful as they represented themselves to be, and that a revolution in Ireland was imminent—a revolution which Lebrun had certainly been at infinite pain to stir up. Can we wonder that the face of Pitt appeared to Chauvelin to express anxiety, embarrassment, and disquietude. On December 14, Maret saw Pitt again at eight o'clock in the evening. The interview was short. After a few words, Pitt said, "Our conversation must be a private one. I am not authorised to say any more on State affairs.

There exists in the English Record Office proof that the English Government was sincere in desiring the resumption of friendly relations with France, and that in spite of Burke and the *émigrés* they now contemplated sending a Minister to Paris. At the end of the volume of French papers for December, 1792, are the imperfect drafts of two dispatches intended for some one proceeding as envoy to France. It does not appear for whom they were intended, and they have no date.[1] But from internal evidence they may be referred to December, 1792.

On December 15, the day after Pitt's second interview with Maret, the Alien Bill was introduced by Lord Grenville in the House of Lords. The conditions of the Bill were stringent: an account and description of all foreigners arriving in the kingdom was to be taken at the several ports; foreigners were not to bring with them arms or ammunition; they were not to depart from the place in which they first arrived without a passport from the chief magistrate or the justice of the peace specifying the place they are going to; on altering a passport or obtaining it under a false name they were to be banished the realm, and if they returned be transported for life; the Secretary of State might give any suspected aliens in charge to one of his Majesty's messengers, to be by him conducted out of the realm; his Majesty may, by proclamation, order in Council, or sign

[1] M. Lindsay was probably designated for this post.

manual, direct all aliens who arrived since January, 1792, other than merchants and their menial servants, to reside in such districts as he shall think necessary for the public security; they were then only to reside in these places under certain stringent conditions. This measure was strongly resisted in Parliament by Fox and the Opposition, on the ground that the dangers against which it was directed were imaginary, or at least greatly exaggerated. It was supported with vehemence by Burke, who in this debate threw a Brummagem dagger on the floor of the House, saying that we must keep French principles from our minds and French daggers from our hearts.

Events moved hastily towards war. The troubled state of Europe justified calling out the militia. Parliament, which by statute must be summoned shortly after this, met on December 13. On December 15 Noel writes to Lebrun that he has had an affecting interview with William Smith, who is terribly distressed. "It is absolutely impossible for the British Government to bear with Chauvelin, every one says so. Why are you so obstinate? Why plunge two nations into a war?" He writes again on the following day that he has seen Smith again and urges some concessions with regard to the Scheldt. It was afterwards suggested that this question might safely sleep if the executive council did nothing to enforce their decree. The French Government persevered in their system. On January 7 letters of credence were dispatched to Chauvelin and he was ordered to present them. Chauvelin had an interview with Lord Grenville with regard to this on January 13. Both the French and English accounts of this conversation are before us, and they show that Chauvelin was not entirely veracious. His position was indeed a difficult one. The face of Lord Grenville grew dark at the proposal, and he said that he must refer it to his colleagues. Chauvelin began to feel that peace was impossible, and begged for his recall.

On January 20 he received a letter from Lord Grenville, which must have removed any lingering doubt. He had written to ask—first, whether his letters of credence would be received; and, secondly, whether the provisions of the Alien Bill are to apply to him or not; in his present position he cannot possibly be regarded as subject to this law; it would be an insult to his nation. Lord Grenville answers that his letters of credence cannot be received; that as minister from the most Christian king he would have enjoyed all the exemptions which the law grants to public ministers, but that, as a private person, he cannot but return to the general mass of foreigners resident in England.

On January 21 Louis XVI. was executed. It is a mistake to suppose that this event of itself caused the war, although undoubtedly it profoundly affected George III. It was rather used by the Ministry as a popular opportunity for taking a step which had been already decided. The news reached London at five o'clock on January 23. The king and queen, who were going to the theatre, gave up their intention. At the Haymarket it was announced that there would be no performance the next day; upon which the audience shouted, "No farce, no farce!" and rose and went out. On January 24 Chauvelin was peremptorily bidden by an Order in Council to leave the kingdom. He writes, on receiving it, that it will certainly be regarded as a declaration of war, and that it was an unexpected step. This dismissal of Chauvelin cannot be defended. It was a punishment of an insulting nature inflicted on the French nation for having done what the English nation had done a century and a half before—executed their king after trial. To drive an accredited minister from the country as an *ordinary* alien was a blow which no nation could brook, and which the French would certainly not put up with in their present state of feverish excitement. It was, as Chauvelin, said, "*un coup de canon*," equivalent to a declaration of war. It bears rather the trace of the vehemence of Burke and the narrow obstinacy of the king than of the calm self-restraint of the Prime Minister.

If the Government had waited a little longer, this hasty step would have been unnecessary.

On January 22, two days before Lord Grenville's letter, Chauvelin was ordered by his own Government to leave London without delay. Chauvelin met the courier conveying this dispatch at Blackheath. He was to send a note to Lord Grenville, saying that the French are still willing to preserve a good intelligence, and to avoid a rupture. Maret, who was known to be popular with the English Government, was sent as *chargé d'affaires* to pave the way for Dumouriez, who was to come to England after he had visited Holland. The cause of this sudden change must be sought in the internal politics of Paris. The Government was divided between the Girondists and the Jacobins, the first somewhat weakened by their defeat on the king's trial, but still able to hold their own, and anxious for peace with England. The most active of the Girondists was General Dumouriez, who knew that Chauvelin was distasteful to the English Ministry, and he persuaded the executive council to recall him, and to send Maret in his place.

Maret passed Chauvelin on the way from Paris to Calais, close to Montreuil. He and his servants were asleep in their carriages, and they did not notice Chauvelin's liveries, so that it was not until his arrival at Dover on the 29th that he heard of Chauvelin's dismissal. Whatever instructions had been given to him were now useless. He sent a note to Lord Grenville to announce his arrival in England, and waited for new dispatches from Lebrun and for the coming of Dumouriez. It is difficult to say whether peace was still possible. Some statesmen, including Lord Lansdowne, were not without hope of averting war; not so, however, the Prince of Wales. Some one meeting him at supper with the Duchess of York said, "There is a curious report abroad that Marat is come to London. The Frenchman who has arrived is a very different person." Upon which the Prince replied, "We know that well; but if he were God Almighty himself, he comes too late, and perhaps they will ask him to go away. Before three weeks war will be declared. Five of my brothers will fight at sea, I shall leave on March 10 to put myself at the head of the troops on the coast, and 50,000 foreign troops will enter Holland. The time is past; we must make an end of these murderers." At the same time Maret's presence in England caused considerable alarm to the *émigrés*. Maret himself was not without hopes of peace. He said that the sudden dismissal of Chauvelin was regretted by the Ministry as a precipitate act.

In the meantime Chauvelin had arrived at Paris. His report decided the vacillating committee. Dumouriez was ordered to proceed to Antwerp and to invade Holland, and on February 1 war was declared against England and Holland.

We are now in a position to decide the question as to who was most to blame for the rupture. No doubt the English had ample provocation, but it may be questioned whether the English Government maintained to the last that system of dignified abstention and neutrality which they had at first displayed. The death of the king was not so entirely different from the events which had preceded it—the riots of October 5, the acceptance of the new constitution, the storming of the Tuileries on August 10—as to justify action of a new and violent kind. The Ministry exaggerated the importance of French bombast and of English sedition. By allying ourselves with the small but distinguished minority in the French Government we might have restrained their impetuous rivals from provoking two new and dangerous enemies. We ought to have accredited a minister to the French Republic, we ought to have continued diplomatic relations with Chauvelin, we certainly ought not to have ordered him out of the country as a suspected alien. The influence of Burke and the *émigrés* was very powerful, but they warned us against the wrong dangers. We needed protection not against the poison of French Republicanism, but against the rapacity of French armies and of the statesmen who directed them. Could we have remained neutral, France would not have invaded Holland, and the history of Europe might not have been sullied with the crimes of Napoleon. These speculations are of little use; but even to those who believe that what has happened must have happened, it is interesting to trace the momentous effect of small divergencies, and to place our finger on the point at which the scale of fate seemed to tremble as it swerved.

VII.

HUGH ELLIOT AT NAPLES, 1803-1806.[1]

AFTER the rupture of the peace of Amiens war was declared by England against France on 20th May, 1803. The instructions given to Hugh Elliot, the new minister, are dated two days earlier. They point directly to the occupation of the island of Sicily by the English. They state that we do not object to English ships being excluded from Neapolitan ports if French ships are excluded also; but if the King of Naples is forced to admit French ships into his harbours on the mainland, we cannot allow this permission to be extended to the island of Sicily. We shall garrison the forts of Messina, and retain them as long as a French military force shall remain in the kingdom of Naples. Assurances are, however, given that the English will confine themselves exclusively to military occupation, and will not interfere in any way with the civil administration of the country. We shall see in the following essay how this little undertaking was observed.

Mr. Elliot set off from England at two days' notice and embarked on board the *Amphion* (not the

[1] This paper is mainly based on Foreign Office papers preserved in the English Record Office.

Victory, as stated by Lady Minto), to which Nelson had shifted his flag. A disagreeable and stormy passage brought them to Gibraltar on the night of 3rd June. On 11th June, off Cape Zilia, Elliot was transferred to the *Maidstone* frigate, Captain Mowbray, while Nelson sailed to Malta. In preparation for his departure Nelson had given him introductions for the King and Queen of Naples and for Sir John Acton, the prime minister. He landed at Naples on 18th June. On 24th June the new ambassador delivered his credentials in the usual form to the king and queen, the king having returned from Caserta for the purpose. Elliot heard on his landing that General St. Cyr, with an army of 13,000 men, had already taken possession of various ports on the Adriatic; but although it was known that his destination was Taranto, he had not actually crossed the Neapolitan frontier. It was certain that the French would demand the exclusion of English ships from Neapolitan harbours, and although it was judged prudent not to precipitate matters by the occupation of Messina, yet steps were taken in that direction with the cognisance and consent of the Court.[1]

Sir John Acton, the valued and trusted minister of the King of Naples, of whom Elliot gives a most favourable character, was anxious that the ægis of England should be thrown over Naples as well as Sicily. English troops should be disembarked on the mainland, while English frigates patrolled the coast. In any case crews should be ready in the port of Naples to rescue the Royal family from any

[1] Elliot to Hawkesbury, 5th July, 1803.

insult or outrage at the hands of the French.[1] Nelson was not favourable to undertaking too much. He was willing to promise that a ship of war—generally of the line—should always be in the bay of Naples to prevent that "worst of all accidents—the loss of the Royal family." "But it must be remembered," he says, "that although Naples is lost Sicily is secure, whereas if Sicily is lost so is Naples."[2]

The assumed purpose of the French was not to overrun or subdue the whole kingdom of Naples, but merely to occupy the three towns of Pescara, Otranto, and Taranto, which had been in their possession before the treaty of Amiens. By that treaty, they said, the French had been bound to evacuate these towns, and the English on their side to evacuate Malta. The failure of the English to fulfil their conditions had made it allowable for the French to replace their garrisons in the fortresses whence they had been taken. Sir John Acton's letters are expressed in quaint, broken English. He writes to Nelson on 7th July: "Three of these provinces have already received 13,000 men on the abominable and known false pretence. Out of these 4,500 only are French, the rest Cisalpine and Poles. Their behaviour seems rather quiet and careful of paying regards to the Government and people for the moment. The detachment of Otranto shall arrive to that place on July 19, and not before the last days of the month the garrison of Taranto can reach the port." There

---

[1] Acton to Nelson, 20th June, 1803.
[2] Nelson to Acton, 25th June, 1803.

is no immediate danger of an attack upon Sicily, and too great haste in movements might precipitate a catastrophe. "Their Sicilian majesties are of this opinion, and moved by the most fervorous wishes for every preparation to be got ready, but not employed in Sicily till the last moment, on evidence of an attack, as they thing that a time must be given for troops from England or Gibraltar, which succour their Majesties consider as the most necessary and sure mean of preservation of Sicily if Naples is lost!"[1] At this time the mediation of the Russian Government, which was on comparatively friendly terms with Bonaparte, was being used to prevent a French occupation of Naples.[2]

Nelson was keeping a close eye on the French ports, and especially Toulon, to prevent the sailing of any ships. He had only six sail of the line opposed to seven or nine, yet he was able to detach the *Superb* under Captain Keats, "one of the very best officers in his Majesty's navy," to remain a fortnight at Naples, or longer if Elliot particularly wished it.[3] The French had other good reasons for not offending the Court of Naples, because they cherished some hopes of alliance between the two countries. M. Alquier, French minister at Naples, proposed an alliance against the English on the basis of enlarging the territory of Naples at the expense of that of the pope. This proposition was supported by the Marchese di Gallo, but strongly opposed by

[1] Acton to Nelson, 7th June, 1803.
[2] Elliot to Nelson, 7th July, 1803
[3] Nelson to Elliot, 11th July, 1803.

Acton. The king was fortunately firm. He writes to Acton in colloquial Italian: "What glory or honour would there be in joining those who have always done us all the harm in their power to go against the English who have saved us, and with whose help we have recovered our lost kingdom?" The queen appeared to follow in the same direction. In the meantime a resolution was agreed upon between Elliot and Sir John Acton that the Neapolitan garrison in Malta should be sent to the defence of Sicily, that the fortifications of Sicily should be strengthened as much as possible, and that General Oakes should be sent to Messina to give the earliest information of the movement of French troops, in order that English troops might be immediately summoned from Malta.[1] The queen stated frankly to Elliot that she was not English but Neapolitan. She was consistent throughout. She was afraid lest the French should seize Naples and lest the English should seize Sicily. She desired to keep them both for her husband and her son. There was indeed some reason to suspect that the designs of Bonaparte went further afield than the island of Sicily. One of the principle causes of our distrust of the first consul which led to the breach of the peace was the apprehension that he was still bent on the conquest of Egypt. Two French ships coming from Greece had been captured by English men-of-war, one by the *Maidstone* while Elliot was on board, and one by the *Superb*. Intercepted letters revealed that attempts were being made to stir up a revolution in the

[1] Nelson to Sir Alexander Ball, 10th July, 1803.

Morea, and Elliot believed that the eastern ports of Italy might be a more important object to the French than those on the south-west coast.[1]

The plans of Bonaparte soon began to take a new development. In the beginning of August the queen requested Elliot to visit her in her private apartments. She was much agitated and frequently mentioned Napoleon's name in terms of abuse. It soon appeared that the king and queen had both received letters from the first consul in answer to letters which they had addressed to him at the suggestion of Alquier. Bonaparte's letters are well known, being printed in his correspondence. The queen's letter is now, we believe, published for the first time.

General Premier Consul,—C'est comme Épouse, comme tendre Mère de mes enfants, et de mes bien-aimés sujets, que Je vois écris cette lettre. Je compte sur votre grand caractère, que Vous voudrez bien contenter les demandes, que le Roi, mon cher Époux, vous fait.

L'entrée des troupes françoises dans notre Royaume, qui se trouve en paix avec la France, et suit exactement les règles de la plus parfaite Neutralité. Cette entrée Nous ruine et Nous détruit surtout par le poids énorme et inattendu de defraier les troupes. Notre Pays n'a que trop souffert de la Guerre, de l'anarchie, des dépenses trés considerables à la paix, et de plusieurs années de mauvaise recolte, pour être dans l'impossibilité de soutenir ce nouveau poids. Je laisse à part toute discussion de justice et de droit. J'ai trop d'opinion de Votre Esprit, pour n'être pas convaincu, que Vous sentez la force des raisons, que Je pourrois dire. Je parle en Mère

[1] Elliot to Hawkesbury, 26th July, 1803.

de mes Enfants et de mes Peuples. Je vous demande de nous décharger de ce poids des troupes dans un pays neutre et de l'affreuse charge de les entretenir. Je l'espère de Vous General Premier Consul, à qui J'en aurai une vraie Gratitude. Je m'addresse à Vous pour la première fois, avec confiance. Vous soulagerez le Roi mon Époux, et ses sujets d'un fardeau horrible en retirant vos troupes, et Vous pouvez compter entièrement sur le Caractère du Roi mon Époux, qu'il conservera Sa Neutralité stricte et exacte, et Moi et mes Enfants nous aurons une veritable reconnoissance de cette démarche, qui augmentera la haute opinion pour Votre Personne, la considération et l'estime distingués avec lesquels je suis,

G. P. C.,

Etc., etc., etc.,

CHARLOTTE.

These letters had not been shown to General Acton, and there was good reason for it. In the letter to the king Bonaparte urged him to distrust a nation which had always shown so deep a hatred to his house, and which regarded continental powers only as an instrument of hatred against France. To the queen he spoke out more explicitly. He asked how could he have any regard for Naples when it was governed by an English minister, a stranger to the country, whose wealth and affections were concentrated in England. He gives her the sincere advice to remove this minister from her councils. If we dismissed General Acton, the queen argued, who would take his place—Gallo, Castelcicala, or Ruffo? If Acton were to see the letters he would resign. What did Elliot advise? Elliot asked for time for consideration. He learned that General Acton was aware that something strange had happened, and was prepared to give in his resignation.

On 16th August Elliot sent a most astute letter to the queen. He began by insinuating that Bonaparte's letter was inspired by Gallo, who had secret reasons for jealousy against Acton. He therefore advised her to treat it with the contempt which it deserved, but to communicate to Acton its contents. He boldly accepts the statement that Acton is English, and declares that he is all the better for being so. Reviewing the events of the last two months, he urges that the preservation of Naples from French attack has been due to the efforts of Russia and of England. To dismiss Acton would be to throw herself into the arms of France. We must oppose a solid barrier to the torrent which threatened to overwhelm civilized Europe. In obedience to Elliot's advice, Bonaparte's letters were shown to Acton, and the king declared that he would rather abdicate his crown than consent to part with so faithful a servant. Remarking on these events, Elliot astutely says that he is by no means persuaded that Bonaparte thought the dismissal of Acton would be disagreeable to the queen. She had so many new favourites that the absence of an old one might be a relief. While acknowledging the queen's great and pre-eminent endowments, her infinite abilities and activity, and a degree of courage above her sex, with every quality which may enable her to struggle against difficulties, he at the same time acknowledges that in all cases which require discretion, self-command, and prudence she needs to be guided and controlled. Elliot's judgment of her was far more favourable than that of Lord William Bentinck.[1]

The danger of Naples being absorbed by the French was for the present averted. General Acton drew up a careful memorandum for the defence of Sicily, and on 11th November, 1803, Lord Hawkesbury, while assuring Elliot of the full approbation of the English Government, sent him a power to advance to the Neapolitan Government a sum not exceeding £170,000, to enable them to place Sicily in a proper state of defence.[2] Writing on 10th January, 1804, Elliot is able to assure Lord Hawkesbury that the fortress of Messina is furnished with provisions and ammunition for six months; that the guns are mounted and the garrison completed; that everything is prepared for a vigorous defence in case of attack. These arrangements were placed under the supervision of Lieut.-Col. Layard. It happened that the coast of Calabria was in danger of being harassed at this time by Algerine and Tunisian pirates, who took advantage of the European war to infest the Mediterranean. This gave an opportunity of calling out and arming the Calabrian peasantry with the object of preventing or impeding any attempt which the French might make upon Naples. General St. Cyr was at first ordered to resent this measure, but Napoleon, occupied with other designs, adjourned his retaliation for the present.[3]

He was at this moment bending the chief powers

---

[1] Elliot to Hawkesbury, 28th August, 1803.
[2] Hawkesbury to Elliot, 11th November, 1803.
[3] Elliot to Hawkesbury, 5th February, 1804.

of his mind to the invasion of England from
Boulogne. He had induced Spain and Portugal to
co-operate in the English blockade and was forcing
the same policy on Genoa. Elliot believed that he
was also meditating a descent upon the Morea, as the
French bakers in Naples were preparing biscuits for
15,000 men.[1] The letter of Napoleon to General
Brune, ambassador at Constantinople, 14th March,
1804 (*Correspondance*, ix. 290), throws some light
on these projects. The first consul writes that in the
present position of Europe his objective is exclusively
England; that he has at Boulogne transports to carry
100,000 men and 10,000 horses, but that in the future
Brune's mission will acquire a great importance,
whether Napoleon marches on London or whether he
makes peace. Unfortunately the bases of English influence in Naples were not so solid as might be wished.
The queen was surrounded by French *émigrés*, who
traded upon her devotion to the memory of her sister
Marie Antoinette, and whose relations to her were
not always confined within the limits of prudence or
decorum. Strange to say, the French ambassador
was able to work upon the queen through the influence of his countrymen, although his master was at
this very time energetically suppressing their machi-
nations in the neighbourhood of France. One of their
first objects was to upset the influence of General
Acton. The queen became irritated at the resistance
which General Acton showed to her views, and she
seemed inclined to appoint one of her favourites in

[1] Elliot to George Elliot, 8th February, 1804.

his place.[1] Matters reached a crisis at the end of April. A violent altercation took place between General Acton and Alquier, which ended in his ordering Alquier to leave the room. The cause of it appears to have been the demand for the arrest of certain persons whom General Acton was anxious to screen. Acton told his master that he could hold no further communication with Alquier. Alquier threatened to declare war unless Acton left Naples. The queen persuaded her husband to allow General Acton to sail for Sicily, which he did on 24th May, 1804. He still retained the office of prime minister, but the real direction of affairs was in the hands of the French ambassador.[2] The intrigue had evidently been assisted by the Marchese di Gallo, Neapolitan ambassador at Paris, who was known to be completely under the influence of Napoleon.[3] He had written a private letter to the queen that unless Acton was dismissed a declaration of war was certain. When, however, the despatch from Paris arrived, it was found to be of a different tenor. It ordered Alquier not to push any further his personal quarrel with Acton at a time when Napoleon was occupied with objects of much greater importance. When Elliot saw the queen after the receipt of this despatch, she said to him: *Vraiment, M. Elliot, j'en suis au repentir, et nous avons été trompés.*[4]

In an interesting letter dated 15th June, 1804, Elliot

[1] Elliot to Hawkesbury, 5th March, 1804.
[2] Elliot to Hawkesbury, 25th May, 1804.
[3] See *Napoleon Correspondance*, ix. 299.
[4] Elliot to Harrowby, 15th June, 1804.

informs the English Government of the secret reasons which have led the queen to acquiesce in the removal of Acton, and even to desire it. Queen Caroline, although fifty-two years of age, and the mother of seventeen children, had not yet learned to master her passions, and had formed an attachment to a French emigrant officer named M. de St. Clair, a man of no personal or mental accomplishments. Her first object was to banish from Naples every rival with whom St. Clair might previously have intrigued. The other emigrants made use of St. Clair's influence with the queen to obtain distinction or emoluments for themselves. The French ambassador was not ashamed to use the same influence for his own purposes; and all remonstrances on the part of General Acton were useless. Indeed they excited her resentment against her former favourite, a feeling which was fanned by the French party at Naples and at Paris. General Acton, originally invited from the service of Tuscany to reorganize the Neapolitan navy, was able to maintain an equal position between the king and the queen so long as his powers were in full vigour. But at the age of seventy-four, being subject to acute disorders, his temper, his memory and application to business have begun to fail. "He is frequently as petulant and froward in his opposition to the queen as he is easily soothed, deceived, and mastered by her experienced management of every feminine wile and snare." His departure was made easier by the acceptance for himself and his heirs for ever of an income of £6,000 a year secured on a fief in Sicily. At the same time he was the best defence that the English interest can have against the intrigues of Bonaparte, and his loss in this respect was irreparable.

In the absence of General Acton the queen conducted the affairs of government herself "with infinite ability." Elliot saw her every day, and she communicated to him all the dispatches she had received.[1] The English Government expressed their entire approval of Elliot's conduct, and promised a subsidy to the Neapolitan Government of £153,000 a year, to be increased in the event of war.

On 18th May Napoleon changed the consulate into an empire, and in July Alquier presented his credentials as ambassador from the new Government. It was observed that the queen, in her answer to the ambassador's compliments, frequently repeated the expression, "The emperor your master," taunting him with the recollection that he had voted the death of his former sovereign, and had upon all occasions shown himself an ardent republican. The king contented himself with saying, "You will assure the Emperor of the French that my sentiments towards him will never suffer any alteration"—a cleverer remark than might have been expected from him. Indeed the king was brought with the greatest difficulty to consent to receive Alquier at all, wishing to substitute the hereditary prince and to plead illness.[2] Elliot, distracted with the contradictions of the different parties at Naples, determined to ascertain the truth by going to the fountain-head. He

[1] Elliot to Harrowby, 25th June, 1804.
[2] Elliot to Harrowby, 7th August, 1804.

therefore sought an interview with the King himself, although there was no precedent for his ever having treated personally with any minister. The account which Elliot gives of his conversation, if it is to be taken literally, certainly gives a very different idea of King Ferdinand's abilities and power of expression from what is usually supposed to be the case. The king, after declaring his unalterable attachment to the English Government, entered into a most masterly detail of the motives by which his conduct had been guided since the occupation of the Neapolitan territory by the French. He distinguished "with the nicest discrimination" between his feelings as a private man and his duties as a sovereign. Elliot says that he never listened to more "pathetic, affecting eloquence" than when the king told him how often he had been obliged to sacrifice the warmest feelings of his heart to the interests of his people. He had ordered General Acton to leave Naples in order to avoid the disgrace of his leaving at the order of Bonaparte. He then informed Elliot that the Russian Government had determined to recall their ambassador from Paris unless the French troops were withdrawn from Naples. Ferdinand had fully made up his mind to adopt a similar course, and to fortify both Sicily and the mainland, although it would be madness to declare war against the French. He had also directed General Acton to send the *Archimede* and two frigates to Naples in the first week in October, to convey the king to Sicily in case matters between France and Naples should come to an extremity. The king expressed great gratitude for the subsidies received from England, and in conclusion remarked that the queen was the only person who possessed his complete confidence, and that Elliot was to refer to her in all cases that required secrecy and confidence. "Thus, my lord," Elliot concludes, " ended a conference the most remarkable in which I have had a share in the long period of my diplomatic service, and which filled me with surprise and admiration at the king's unexpected display of character and consummate ability.[1]

This is not the place to discuss the complicated diplomatic relations between the Russian and French Governments which took place at this time, nor are materials at present available for the complete understanding of them. It was hoped that Russian persuasion or pressure would be able to preserve the independence of the Neapolitan kingdom. It was therefore with great disappointment that Elliot informed his court on 2nd October, 1804, that on the one hand the Russians had determined not to act without the participation of Austria, and that on the other Napoleon had increased his troops in Italy by eight thousand men intended as an answer to the Russian occupation of Corfu. Napoleon stated at the same time that he intended to keep possession of the ports he had already occupied so long as the Russians continued at Corfu or the English at Malta. A week later we hear of the actual arrival of a portion of these troops. This circumstance led to a most extraordinary step on the part of the Sicilian Government. The queen offered to pay an annual

[1] Elliot to Harrowby, 23rd August, 1804.

tribute to Napoleon on the condition that the French troops should be withdrawn, and that the neutrality of Naples should be secured. The sum proposed was six million francs a year so long as the war should last. Napoleon was at this time occupied with the inspection of the frontiers of the Rhine, and with preparations for his coronation by the pope, so that he did not answer the queen's letter till January, 1805. Before the reply was received the Court of Naples had good reason to regret that the offer was ever made.

Writers on the history of Napoleon have employed themselves sometimes in indiscriminate panegyrics on his career, and sometimes in stooping to collect every calumny with which jealous mediocrity can bespatter the brilliancy of genius. They have taken but little pains to ascertain the secret of Napoleon's plans, and have argued as if that most consummate of rulers were swayed solely by uncontrollable ambition and an irresistible impulse to provoke those whom it was his interest to keep as friends. It will be long before the recesses of his mind are fully fathomed, but there can be little doubt that one of his principal schemes was to form a confederation of the Latin races with France at their head to oppose the solid forces of the northern military powers which threatened to dominate Europe.[1] The neutrality of Naples would have been inconsistent with this scheme, and still more her alliance with England. In a conversation with the Marchese di Gallo at

[1] This view has received unexpected confirmation from the Memoirs of General Marbot.

Paris, Talleyrand laid it down as a determined principle of Bonaparte that he would not suffer either Spain or Portugal or the States of Italy to deviate in any degree from the system of politics adopted by France, which last power, that minister asserted, was to be considered in future as the head of the confederate army of the south of Europe.[1] As the neutrality of Naples was impossible under this view, it is not to be wondered at that the English Government informed Elliot that a peremptory demand for the evacuation of the Neapolitan territories by the French army and the dismissal of the French minister in case of a refusal, would probably be the best way of bringing on the crisis whenever sufficient preparations had been made at home, and there was a sufficient prospect of assistance from abroad.[2] At the same time Elliot was informed of the intention to send five or six thousand English troops to Malta to co-operate with the Russians in defence of Turkey, but especially to defend Sicily if the king should retreat thither.

At seven o'clock in the morning of 12th November, Elliot was summoned to the queen to hear the news that she had just received despatches from Gallo reporting a conversation with Talleyrand. Instructions were to be sent without delay to Alquier to insist upon the Neapolitan Government declaring war against Great Britain. Some British ships had attacked Spanish ships carrying money to Spanish courts. This, Napoleon declared, was contrary to

---

[1] Elliot to Harrowby, 27th October, 1804.
[2] Harrowby to Elliot, 6th November, 1804.

the rights of neutral nations, therefore all neutral nations must resent the insult. There was at this time a considerable trade in salt fish, called *baccaluo*, between Newfoundland and the ports of Italy, and there was some danger lest their ships should be suddenly seized. The king was at Caserta, and nothing decisive could be done till he returned to the capital.[1] In the absence of assistance from Russia and Austria the queen seemed inclined to comply so far as to agree to exclude British ships from Neapolitan harbours. The state of Naples was indeed serious. The French troops in her territory now amounted to 18,000 effective men. The headquarters of the army was little more than a hundred miles distant from the capital, and the troops were so disposed as to be able to concentrate at a day's notice.[2] December 8 witnessed a fresh insult on the part of Alquier. He demanded the dismissal of all the British legation from Naples. This was parallel to the policy pursued by Napoleon towards Wake at Munich, Spencer Smith at Stuttgard, and Rumbold at Hamburg. However, this blustering demand could not be seriously entertained. Great allowances, indeed, ought to be made for the queen at this juncture. The French were only too evidently desirous to occupy Naples. It seemed as if the English might be drawn into permanent occupation of Sicily, making it into another Malta. It is remarkable how firmly the king and queen adhered to the English alliance. Elliot, who was a very acute

[1] Elliot to Harrowby, 13th November, 1804.
[2] Elliot to Harrowby, 7th December, 1804.

observer, makes no such complaints of her tergiversation and want of straightforwardness as we find Lord William Bentinck making at a later period. The course of action which, in resisting the aggression of Napoleon, appeared wise and just to Englishmen did not always wear the same aspect to the statesmen of other countries. This is very evident in the despatches of the Duke of Serra Capriola, Neapolitan ambassador at the court of Petersburg, narrating conversations upon English politics with Prince Garbowicz. Speaking of Mr. Stuart, secretary of Lord Gower's embassy, he says that he is a gentleman of merit, but a firm supporter of the English system of embroiling the continent in a war to make a diversion for itself, but without any views for the benefit of the allied powers, who have sacrificed themselves in the late war and are ready to do the same in the present. He defends the whole of the English system with all its pretensions, to keep Malta whatever it may cost, to consent to no peace without it, to commence hostilities in the kingdom of Naples with the forces already there, little reflecting on the consequences, because, provided that the citadel of Messina is in the hands of the English, whatever complications may happen to the kingdom of Naples will only be a signal for England to turn Sicily to what end it pleases, and as this island is near to Malta, the two possessions will become one dominion." [1] The Russian policy at this time seems to have been to unite with Spain and Naples into a confederacy against Napoleon, the

[1] Serra Capriola to the queen, 7th December, 1804.

counter-stroke to his design of a Latin union. The Russians were anxious to some extent to act with England, but were profoundly impressed with the selfishness of the policy of England, her tendency to aim at private ends, and the chances of her making a separate peace.

At the beginning of January Napoleon's answers to the letters of the king and queen arrived. They are well known, and it is not necessary to describe them in detail. The letter to the king was short and business-like. It attributed the occupation of Italian ports to the treaty of Florence, it announced that the French troops would remain until Corfu was evacuated by the Russians and Malta by the English, and it stated that additional forces would never have been sent unless the Russians had occupied Corfu. It concluded with an exhortation to reject the perfidious advice of England. The letter to the queen was of a very different character. It was long and violent, calculated to leave a sting. "Your Majesty has a mind distinguished amongst women. Can you not then throw off the prejudices of your sex, and can you treat affairs of State as you would affairs of the heart? You have already lost your kingdom once. Twice you have caused a war in which your father's house has narrowly escaped complete ruin. Do you then wish to cause a third? . . . At the first war of which you are the cause, you and your family will cease to reign; your children, wanderers, will beg in the different countries of Europe assistance from their relations. . . . I desire peace with all Europe, with England even, but I fear war with

no one." He then advises her to dismiss the French
émigrés, to recall Serra Capriola from St. Petersburg,
to dismiss Elliot, to give her confidence to Napoleon.
"It is only to a person of a strong and superior mind
that I should take the trouble to write with so much
frankness." The queen in giving these letters to
Elliot shed many bitter tears of grief and indignation at being treated with so much insolence by the
upstart and unfeeling tyrant. The first result of
these letters was to induce the king to call out a
levée en masse of the population if they transgressed
their present limits. The real sentiments of Napoleon
to Queen Caroline may be inferred from a letter of his
to Berthier (19th January, 1805), in which he says:
"Write to General St. Cyr that he is to place no faith
in the protestations of that woman . . . that he is
to insist strongly on General Damas being driven
from Naples, and on Elliot being at least sent to Sicily,
that there is to be a complete disarmament, and that if
he is disobeyed, he is ordered to march on Naples."[1]

At this time news arrived that the French fleet
which Nelson had been watching for so many months
had put to sea from Toulon with a number of troops
on board. Its destination was entirely unknown,
even to the fleet itself. We now learn from Napoleon's
correspondence that it was a part of a combined
attack, in conjunction with the rest of the French
fleet from Brest and the Spanish fleet from Ferrol,
on the East Indies and the coast of Ireland.[2] Nelson

[1] *Correspondance*, xi. 119.
[2] We find that Gallo had a suspicion of the attack on
Ireland. Elliot to Harrowby, 9th February, 1805.

believed that it was directed against the Morea or perhaps Egypt, and therefore continued to search for it in a wrong direction. A storm dispersed the Toulon fleet, and it was obliged to return to harbour. Nelson says of this: "These gentlemen are not accustomed to a Gulf of Lyons gale; we have buffetted them for one-and-twenty months and not carried away a spar." Napoleon writes in something of the same strain: *Quelques mâts de hune cassés, quelques désordres dans une tempête, qui accompagnent une escadre sortant, sont, pour un homme d'un peu de caractère, des événements d'une nature fort ordinaire. Deux jours de beau temps eussent consolé l'escadre et mis tout au beau. . . . Mais le grand mal de notre marine est que les hommes qui la commandent sont neufs dans toutes les chances du commandement.*[1]

The effect of Napoleon's orders to St. Cyr quoted above is seen in a letter from Elliot to Lord Mulgrave, 16th February, 1805:—

This morning I received a letter from the queen, written in the greatest agitation, on the account of the arrival of one of General St. Cyr's aides-de-camp from the French army in Puglia, asking for a categorical answer in three days' time to the four following demands.

1st. That the population of the province should be disarmed.

2ndly. That the Neapolitan army should not be allowed to recruit.

3rdly. That General Damas should be sent into exile.

4thly. That the British minister, Mr. Elliot, should be obliged to quit Naples.

These demands are accompanied by the menace on the

[1] Napoleon to Lauriston, *Correspondance*, xi. 136.

part of General St. Cyr of commencing hostilities if they are not complied with.

Her Sicilian Majesty has since sent the Chevalier Mendici to confer with me upon these violent propositions and upon the nature of the answer to be sent to General St. Cyr with which Prince Parolo will be dispatched this evening to Puglia.

It happened that Count Kaunitz was then at Naples travelling with his wife. He offered his mediation with the French, the result of which was that the demand for Elliot's removal was withdrawn, but that Damas was forced to send in his resignation. He left Naples for Sicily on 8th March, still nominally retaining his post of inspector-general of the Neapolitan army.

On 5th March, 1805, Lord Mulgrave wrote to Mr. Elliot that a number of troops would immediately be despatched to Malta, by which at least five thousand men would become disposable for the occupation and defence of Sicily, either in the event of the King of Naples again returning to that island, or for the preservation of it by a British force from any attempt which the French general might make to possess himself of it. Lieut.-Colonel G. Smith was sent to Naples to confer with Elliot as to the best means of effecting the object they had in view.[1] Sir James Craig was placed at the head of the expeditionary force. His instructions state that the protection of Sicily is the first object which he is to have in view. This is to be done either with or without the request of the King of Naples. The second contingency is to be

[1] Mulgrave to Elliot, 20th March, 1805.

considered to arise (1) if British ships are excluded from Neapolitan harbours; (2) if any attempt on Sicily is made by the French; (3) if there is reason to suppose that any such attempt is likely to be made. In these cases it is to be clearly understood and made known that the island is only held by the English for the King of Naples, and on his behalf. Lord Nelson is to co-operate with Sir J. Craig in every respect. Further and most secret orders inform Sir J. Craig that his troops may also be employed either for the defence of Naples if that is attacked before Sicily, or in co-operation with the Russian and Austrian armies in northern and southern Italy if the French should withdraw from Naples. The despatch is dated 29th March, 1805. Colonel Smith arrived at Naples and was cordially received by the two sovereigns. On his departure from Palermo the king gave him a letter of introduction to General Acton.

The assumption by Napoleon of the title of King of Italy dates from 18th March, 1805. He set out to be crowned at Milan at the end of the month, and entered Milan on 8th May. It was natural that these events should have a serious effect on the impressionable nature of the queen. In a moment of impulse she ordered the immediate departure of Prince Sherbatoff from Naples because he had formerly killed the Chevalier de Saxe in a duel, thus risking a serious breach with one of the few powers who were friendly to her. Elliot had some difficulty in explaining the matter at St. Petersburg.[1] Immediately after this

[1] Elliot to Leverson Gower, 14th May, 1805.

the British man-of-war, *Excellent*, having left the
Bay of Naples, she imagined that it was done to give
the Russian men-of-war then in the harbour the opportunity of seizing the Neapolitan ship *Archimede* as
a reprisal. In consequence the *Archimede* was kept
under arms all night expecting an attack. This
paroxysm of suspicion was either preparatory to or
part of a serious illness, during which the queen was
delirious.[1] On 26th May Napoleon crowned himself
King of Italy in the church of St. Ambrose at Milan.

Prince Cardito was sent to attend the coronation, but
he had orders not to acknowledge the title of the King
of Italy except in concert with the Court of Vienna.
Napoleon's wrath knew no bounds. He denounced
Queen Caroline as a new Athalia, and said that he
would not leave her enough Italian soil even for a
grave. Talleyrand declared to Gallo that if he did
not receive new instructions by 16th June at Bologna,
war would be declared.[2] General St. Cyr was sent
off hastily from Milan to his Neapolitan command.
Elliot asked General Lascy, the commandant of the
Russian forces, if he would assist Naples in case of
an attack by France, and whether he would advise
the recognition of the King of Italy or not. Lascy
recommended compliance, but Elliot believed that
this would only result in a very short respite.
Eventually Gallo received orders to present himself
at Bologna and to do what was required of him.
Napoleon's language was just as violent as before.
It seemed likely that, having failed in his attempt to

[1] Elliot to Mulgrave, 28th May, 1805.
[2] Elliot to Mulgrave, 11th June, 1805.

get rid of Elliot, he would now insist on the removal of the queen.[1] Alquier returned from Milan on 5th June. On the following day he sought an audience with the queen, in which he overwhelmed her with every insult and intimidation. He repeated in all their naked crudity the expressions which Napoleon had used towards her, which had been softened in the despatches of Gallo. She fell into violent hysterics and was confined by illness at Caserta for ten days. On 16th July the queen repeated the substance of this interview to Elliot. Napoleon had threatened that he would march on Naples, depose the Royal family, and proclaim the hereditary prince. Napoleon refused to allow Circello to become foreign minister—unless, indeed, this was an invention of the queen's, who did not desire to see him appointed. To add to these troubles, a terrible earthquake took place a few minutes after ten on 26th July, which destroyed a large number of buildings, and about four thousand people.

The pressure of circumstances drove the Neapolitan Court into tortuous courses. On September 10, 1805, a secret convention was signed with Tatishcheff, by which Naples joined the coalition between Russia and England, and placed its forces under the command of General Lascy. Pains were taken that Alquier might not even suspect such a step. On the other hand, on September 21, Gallo in Paris agreed to sign a convention with Talleyrand by which, on a promise of neutrality, the French troops should be withdrawn from Neapolitan territory. At the last

[1] Elliot to Mulgrave, 2nd July, 1805.

moment two conditions were added : one a refusal to recognise the English occupation of Malta, and the other the complete banishment of General Acton. Gallo could not sign the convention with these conditions without the especial command of his sovereign. He therefore wrote to Naples strongly urging the queen's consent. Napoleon's object was to obtain the assistance of St. Cyr's army in the war against Austria. Couriers with despatches from Talleyrand and from Gallo reached Naples on the morning of October 4. A delay of only forty-eight hours was allowed, which would expire at midday on October 7. The deliberations of the council were prolonged far into the night. At last the king agreed to ratify the convention—"complying with the request of the highwayman who holds a pistol to your head," as the queen wrote to her daughter the empress.[1] Three days later a Russian ship entered the harbour with instructions for Tatishcheff to do everything in his power to prevent an agreement between France and Naples. All that now was possible was for the king to declare that the convention with France had been extorted from him by force and had no validity. Napoleon on his side was delighted at the convention. Writing from Haag, near Wels, on November 2, 1805, he orders Talleyrand to print the treaty in the *Moniteur*, preceded by a short article to show that the emperor had thus given a new proof of his moderation, considering that the conquest of Naples would put obstacles in the way of a general peace.

[1] Helfert, p. 186.

Sir James Craig reached Malta with six thousand English troops about the middle of July, and immediately notified his arrival to Elliot. A good deal of discussion took place as to the best means of employing these troops in the service of the allies. Elliot writes to Craig on August 4, 1805, that General Lascy is a thoroughly honest and upright man, a brave soldier, and an experienced officer, but his health is completely broken. He has not the faculty of expressing himself fluently or with precision in any language with which Elliot is acquainted, but his ideas are certainly clearer than his words, and there is no reason to apprehend from him any species of trick or underhand dealing. He is an Irishman by birth, and an Englishman in his heart. He is every day expecting to hear that his reinforcements have arrived at Corfu, and that Russians and Austrians are preparing to act together in the north of Italy. It is Lascy's opinion that the British troops should act as an independent body in conjunction with the peasantry of the Calabrias, while the Russians attack the main body of the French. The Neapolitan troops who are not fit for the field should remain in the garrisons. Sir James Craig should send an accomplished English officer to co-operate with Lascy. If there is no one else available, Colonel George Smith would perform the duties very well. The first notice of the secret treaty with Russia is given by Elliot on August 26, when he informs Lord Mulgrave that the king has secretly appointed the Prince de Luzzi and the Marquis di Circello to negotiate a treaty with M. Tatishcheff. A previous

despatch, in which the purpose of the treaty had
been mentioned, is not forthcoming. The full powers
are written in the king's own hand and sealed with
his private seal, in order to conceal knowledge of
the transaction from the public; but Elliot is much
afraid lest the secret should ooze out from the
foreign favourites of the queen. On September 12
Elliot is able to announce that the secret convention
had been signed the day before. The Russians had
been anxious that Elliot should take part in the
convention, but he thought it better not to do so
without direct orders from his Government. He
preferred to let the Russian minister take the lead
in order that his country might be more deeply committed to the protection of Naples without having
it in her power to reproach England for drawing
Naples into the war. Elliot therefore avoided even
seeing the convention before it was signed. Two
other reasons were that a participation in the treaty
would have implied a large augmentation of pecuniary assistance, and that he did not altogether
approve of the plan of the convention, which was to
put Naples actively forward in the conduct of the
war. The British Government will have to decide
whether they intend to favour the neutrality of the
Two Sicilies as they have hitherto done, or to grant
him such supplies as may enable him to take the
field with efficiency.[1] Unfortunately we possess no
account from Elliot of the negotiations which preceded the signing of the convention of neutrality
with the French. The ciphers he possessed were

[1] Elliot to Mulgrave, September 12, 1805.

so old that he was afraid to entrust any important secret of state to them. The fact of the treaty having been signed is only mentioned in a letter of October 14, but the step had Elliot's full approval. He informs his Government that it will not prove injurious to the interests of Great Britain nor to those of its allies.

On the very day that the ratifications of the convention were exchanged, General Lascy left Naples on board the *Krepka* for the Ionian Islands. The expedition sailed from Corfu on October 22 : thirty-eight transports sent by England to embark the Russians, six ships of the line, and nine frigates, two regiments of grenadiers, two of fusiliers, and two of chasseurs, 3,000 Albanians, two battalions of artillery, and thirty-six field-pieces; all under the command of General Anrep. On October 31 they reached the harbour of Syracuse, where they were to meet the English.[1] All circumstances for their joint co-operation had been duly weighed and were finally settled.[2] The English forces, 6,000 strong, sailed from Malta on November 6, and, delayed by contrary winds, did not effect their junction with the Russians till November 7. The French army had entirely evacuated Neapolitan territory when Lascy returned to Naples accompanied by Sir James Craig and General Stuart. The allied fleets eventually appeared in the bay of Naples on November 20, having been long detained by strong northerly winds. The Russian forces consisted of

[1] Helfert, p. 189.
[2] Elliot to Mulgrave, November 14, 1805.

13,000 men, the British of 8,000. Six thousand Neapolitans were marched into the Abruzzi. A reinforcement of several Russian battalions of infantry and some cavalry was daily expected to arrive from the Black Sea, and would probably disembark in La Puglia. A new levy of 30,000 Neapolitans was ordered to strengthen the army.

Unfortunately these measures were too late. On October 20 had taken place the disastrous capitulation of General Mack at Ulm. On October 30 the Archduke Charles was entirely defeated by Massena in the battle of Caldiero; on November 8 he was retreating between the Piave and the Tagliamento; on November 20, the very day of the disembarkation of the allied troops, the French general Serres took possession of Venice. On December 2 was fought the decisive battle of Austerlitz, which led to the peace of Presburg. Elliot, writing to Lord Mulgrave on December 10, in ignorance of the last of the events, speaks as follows:—

From the above statement your Lordship will be pleased to observe that the forces already assembled, or likely soon to be brought together in the south of Italy, by the allies, would have been sufficient, not only to have afforded security to both the Sicilies, by effectually covering this kingdom, but might also have contributed to have a most essential diversion in favour of the Archduke Charles, in the north of Italy. The misfortunes, or misconduct, of the Austrian generals have, however, in their fatal consequences surpassed all calculation, for, in the interval that elapsed from the time of embarkation of the troops at Corfu and at Malta to their arrival here, the formidable force of the Austrian monarchy appears to be dissolved, I am tempted to say, in the words of Shakespeare, It has vanished "like the baseless fabric of a vision."

Vienna, the Tyrol, and the Venetian States, are in the hands of the enemy, while the Archduke Charles, with the only remaining army, that we know of, belonging to the House of Austria, is supposed to be retiring to Hungary, leaving the whole peninsula of Italy open to the inroads of any degree of force it may suit the convenience of Bonaparte to assemble for the purpose of completing the conquest of Italy.

At the date of my writing this letter, no accounts of an authentic nature, have as yet reached this capital, of the actual march of any considerable body of French forces from north towards the south of Italy.

A formal intimation has indeed been given at Rome to the papal Government of the expected arrival of Eugene Beauharnois at Bologna, to take the command of 30,000 men in the ecclesiastical States; but I do not apprehend that a serious attack will be made upon this country, by a force which I conceive as being not adequate for the purpose of ensuring its conquest. Should the Austrians be forced to sign a separate peace, or should, from other circumstances, Massena have it in his power to detach a considerable part of his army towards the south of Italy, it will in that case be indeed doubtful whether resistance ought to be attempted in this kingdom, or whether it will not be more prudent to confine the efforts of the allies to the defence of the Calabrias and of Sicily.

The news of the Anglo-Russian expedition reached Paris on the very day of Austerlitz. Gallo did not know what to say in defence of his conduct. His mistress had given him the vague direction " to act according to the dictates of prudence." Vengeance was not long delayed. Napoleon wrote to Talleyrand on December 14: *Une fois tranquille sur la Prusse, il n'est plus question de Naples; je ne veux point que l'empereur s'en mêle, et je veux enfin châtier cette coquine.*[1] Again, on December 23 he writes: *Je vous recommande expressément de ne point parler de Naples. Les outrages de cette misérable reine redoublent à tous les courriers. Vous savez comment je me suis conduit avec elle, et je serais bien lâche si je pardonnois des excès aussi infâmes envers mon peuple. Il faut qu'elle ait cessé de regner. Que j'en n'entende donc point parler absolument. Quoi qu'il arrive, mon ordre est précis, n'en parlez pas.*[2] Finally, in the *Bulletin de la Grande Armée*, dated Schönbrunn, December 26, 1805, we find it announced that General St. Cyr is marching at full speed on Naples to punish the treason of the queen and to drive from the throne the criminal woman who has so shamelessly violated everything which is sacred amongst men. When intercession was made on her behalf to the emperor, he replied that if the nation had to support a thirty years' war so monstrous a perfidy could not go unpunished. "The Queen of Naples has ceased to reign: this last crime has filled her destiny to the full; let her go to London to increase the number of intriguers and to form a committee of sympathetic wits with Wake, Spencer Smith, Taylor, and Wickham. She may summon to her councils also, if she thinks right, Baron Armfield, Messieurs de Fersen and d'Entraigues, and the Monk Morus."[3] A pro-

[1] *Correspondance*, xi. 478.   [2] *Ib.* 497.
[3] *Ib.*, 503.

clamation to the same effect was published in the *Moniteur* on February 1, 1806.

There is little more to relate in this painful history. On January 6 an *aide-de-camp* of the Emperor Alexander brought orders to Naples for the Russian troops to retire immediately to Corfu. On January 8 Cardinal Ruffo was sent by the queen with the most humiliating offers of submission to Cardinal Fesch and Alquier at Rome. She was ready to exclude the English from her harbours, to give up all her ships of war, to allow French troops to occupy all her fortresses, to abdicate the crown, and commit the government to the crown prince. The only answer that she could anticipate was that they had no power to treat. The English troops set sail on January 20, and the Russians on January 23. Before their departure they broke down the bridges and ferries over the Garigliano, and killed the horses which had cost the Neapolitan Government so dear. In the meantime the Royal family were making preparations for their departure. Napoleon made no answer to the queen's letter; he forbade Cardinal Ruffo to come to Paris. His wish was to drive the king away and to bring the crown prince prisoner to Paris. He urged his brother Joseph, who had been nominated his viceroy, to conquer Sicily with all speed. It might easily be done in this moment of confusion with 15,000 men. Eventually at 2 a.m. on January 24 the king embarked with a small suite on board the *Archimede*, and sailed for Sicily, leaving the crown prince as regent. The French army, 40,000 strong, crossed the Garigliano on February 8.

Three days later, at four o'clock in the afternoon, the queen, accompanied by her three daughters, Christina, Amélie, and Isabella, went on board the *Archimede*. At the same moment her two sons, Francis and Leopold, embarked on the *Minerva* for the gulf of Policastro. The little squadron lingered long in sight, and the queen could not persuade herself to leave the beloved scenes which she was never to see again, until the capital had been occupied by the French, and her personal safety was in danger. Mr. Elliot accompanied her to Palermo.

VIII.
HUGH ELLIOT IN BERLIN.

THIS episode from the earlier life of Hugh Elliot is interesting in itself, and throws light upon his character.

No diplomatic story is better known than that of Hugh Elliot stealing the despatches of Arthur Lee at Berlin. The most graphic account is to be found in Carlyle's "Frederick," vol. vi., page 557. He describes how the American war is raging and blundering along. The devoted colonists have their Franklins, Lees, busy in European courts. "Help us in our noble struggle, ye European courts; now is your chance on tyrannous England." He says that the British Cabinet had got it into their sagacious heads that the bad neighbour at Berlin was in effect the arch-enemy, and probably the mainspring of the whole matter, and that it would be in the highest degree interesting to see clearly what Lee and he had on hand. Order is therefore given to Elliot, "Do it at any price;" and finally, as mere price will not answer, do it by any method—steal Lee's despatch box for us. Carlyle says further that Elliot had no appetite for the job, but that orders were peremptory. "Lee is a rebel, *quasi* outlaw, and you must." Elliot thereupon hired or made his servant hire the chief housebreaker or pickpocket in the city. He is told that Lee lodges in such and such an hostelry; bring us his red box for thirty hours; it shall be well worth your while. "And in brief space the red box arrives. A score or two of ready writers are ready for it, who copy all day and all night, till they have enough, which done, the Lee red box is left on the stairs of the Lee tavern. The box locked again and complete, only the Friedrich-Lee secrets completely pumped out of it." Carlyle goes on to tell us that this "astonishing mass of papers" is still extant in England, in the Eden House archives. That he has seen the outside of them, but not the inside, but that he is able to say from other sources, which are open to all the world, that the discovery had no value, but that the only question mooted between Lee and Frederick was the conclusion of a treaty of commerce. He says, further, that this surprising bit of burglary was done on Wednesday, June 25, 1777, and that the box, with the essence pumped out, was restored the following night.

This account is as inaccurate in every particular as Carlyle's historical statements very often are. The British Cabinet did not consider Frederick as their arch-enemy, nor were they more afraid of him than of the Courts of France and Spain. There was no order given to Elliot to steal the despatches, but only a general warning that Lee and Sayre were in Berlin, and that they must be carefully watched. Elliot contrived the whole job himself. No professional housebreaker was employed. When the despatch

box arrived, it was received not by a score or two
of ready writers, but by four Englishmen of good
family. They copied not all day and all night for
thirty hours, but for about six hours. The despatch
box was not left on the stairs of the hotel, but given to
the landlady by Elliot himself. There is no astonishing mass of papers, but nineteen documents, the titles
of which, with most of the documents themselves, are
at present at King's College, Cambridge. Finally, the
robbery took place, not on Wednesday, June 25, but
on Thursday, June 26, 1777, and so far from the documents being of no importance, they were admitted
to be of the highest importance by Lee himself.

A different account of the matter is given by Lady
Minto, in her life of Hugh Elliot. Her story is that
a German servant of the ambassador, having heard
him say at his dinner table that he would gladly give
a sum of money to any one who would bring him the
papers of the American envoys, waited for no further
authority, but, in the most imprudent and reckless
manner, broke into the apartments occupied by the
Americans in their hotel, entered the room by the
window, forced open a bureau, and carried off the
papers it contained. When the theft became known
Mr. Elliot declared that he considered himself solely
responsible for what had occurred. One of his servants had been led to commit the act by Mr. Elliot's
own imprudence. No time had been lost in restoring
the papers to their rightful owners.

A third account is given in Bancroft's "History of
the United States," vol. vi. page 123. He says that
Elliot, then British minister in Berlin, at a cost of

one thousand guineas, hired a burglar to steal the papers of Arthur Lee, but, on his complaint to the police, sent them back and spirited the thief out of the kingdom. The rash envoy attempted to throw on the officiousness of a servant the blame of having stolen the American papers, which he himself received and read. Another account is to be found in a work of Friedrich Kapp, called "Friedrich der Grosse und die Vereinigten Staaten von Amerika." He tells us that Arthur Lee was at dinner in the Hotel Corsika, Brüder-Strasse No. 2, when the English ambassador, by means of a servant, opened his door with a false key, broke open the desk which was in the room, and stole a portfolio. Lee got up from table sooner than usual, and met Elliot on the stairs on the way to his chamber. Elliot, he remarks, was a very unskilful thief; that when he heard that Lee had hastened with a complaint to the police, he became very much frightened, and instead of securing his prey and studying it carefully, he got rid of it and sent back the papers to Lee's door in less than half an hour. Frederick the Great himself gives an account of the transaction which is as far from the truth as those which we have already quoted. Writing to his brother, Prince Henri, on June 29, 1777, he says: "The English ambassador, in the absence of the American agent Lee, went to his hotel and stole his portfolio, but he became frightened, and instead of opening it threw it on the steps of the house. All Berlin speaks of the occurrence. If one were to act with strictness, I should have to forbid this man the Court because he has committed a public robbery, but in order to make no noise I suppress the matter." At the same time he writes privately on July 1 to his ambassador in London, Count Maltzan, "Oh, this worthy scholar of Bute, this incomparable man : your goddam Elliot. In truth Englishmen ought to blush for shame that they sent such ambassadors to a foreign court." All these accounts are very far from the truth. The papers disclosing the true story were discovered by me in the autumn of 1887, and with their assistance I will now proceed to give a narrative of what really happened.

Arthur Lee was a native of Virginia, and was born on December 20, 1740. He was educated at Eton College, and was afterwards sent to Edinburgh to prepare for the medical profession. Having taken his degree as doctor, he travelled in Holland and Germany, and then returned to his native country, where he began to practise, but afterwards determined to devote himself to the study of the law, and in 1766 went over to London and became a student in the Temple. He continued to hold correspondence with his brother and several other persons in America on the political state of things in England and on the affairs of the colonies. In the spring of 1775 he was appointed agent in London for the colony of Massachusetts in succession to Benjamin Franklin, and, in December of the same year, the committee of secret correspondence in America requested him to act as their agent in London, and to send them any information which he might think important. When the young Republic was attempting to obtain assistance from European powers, they sent commissioners to the Court of France, and Jefferson declining the appointment, Arthur Lee was put in his place; this was on October 22, 1776. Lee went to Paris, where he met the other commissioners, Franklin and Deane. In the spring of 1777 he went to Spain to obtain assistance from the Spanish Government for the United States, and in this object he was partially successful. Shortly after returning to Paris he set out for Berlin, where he arrived on June 4. He travelled by the circuitous route of Munich and Vienna, driving, we are told, in an English post-chaise painted deep green, with the letters " A. L." in a cypher. His companion was to have been Carmichael, but Sayre, an alderman of London, devoted to the American cause, was substituted at the last moment. Lee and Sayre lodged, as we have before said, at the Hotel Corsika, in the Brüder-Strasse, a small street near the king's palace, in which the principal hotels of that time were situated. In 1777 there were no hotels in the Unter den Linden.

Hugh Elliot, at this time a young man of twenty-five, had been sent as minister to Berlin, where he arrived on April 1, just two months before the American envoys. His instructions, dated March 3, are in the Record Office, but do not differ from the ordinary run of such documents. The Earl of Suffolk was then Secretary of State who had charge of the Foreign Department. On May 9, 1777, he wrote to Elliot in the following terms :—

Messrs. Carmichael and Lee, two of the rebel agents, are said to have quitted Paris in order to attempt some negotiation at the court where you reside. These two persons are not on good terms with each other; the first of them has the best abilities, and is most in the confidence of his principals, Messrs. Dean and Franklyn. The other, however, is more immediately in the commission of the rebel Congress, and was lately employed in their service at Madrid, but was not suffered by the Spanish ministers to open his business. I am not yet informed of their views at Berlin, but should conjecture that they had general instructions to hold out false ideas of the progress of their rebellion towards independence and of the commercial advantages in their power to grant, with a view to obtain in return money and experienced officers. You will, of course, give every proper attention to their conduct, and to the impression which it may make.

On May 30, he writes again :—

I now find that Mr. Sayre (and not Mr. Carmichael, as was at first proposed) accompanies Mr. Arthur Lee to Berlin. His Majesty's ambassador at Paris has already communicated to you the supposed object of the rebel agents in this mission, and I have only to add with regard to Mr. Sayre, that he is a man of desperate fortune, but with the disposition rather than the talents to be mischievous. His personal vanity is at the same time so great, that he talks of going forward to Petersburg, in order to try the effect of his address and figure at that court.

It will be seen that in these letters there is no indication that Lord Suffolk ordered Elliot to take the strong measures which he eventually adopted.

On June 6, two days after Lee's arrival, Elliot writes from Berlin in the following terms :—

Two persons alighted at an inn the day before yesterday, who call themselves Americans. One of them is Lee, mentioned in your lordship's letter No. 1; the other is Sayre, the banker, who travels under the name of Stephens. They are said to have come from Vienna by way of Prague and Dresden, and give out that they are to stay here about a fortnight. Their servant, who arrived in town some time before them, went immediately to the Marquis de Pons, the French minister, to whom he gave letters. Lee himself carried a letter to M. de Schulemburg, by whom he was received, although that minister in the evening turned the conversation towards the report prevailing of the arrival of American agents, that he might have an opportunity of assuring me he was perfectly unacquainted with the truth of it. Mr. Zegelin, formerly minister of the court at Constantinople, who possesses a great share in the king's confidence, and in consequence of being employed in his most secret transactions always resides at Potzdam, came to Berlin unexpectedly the day before Lee, and is now lodged at the same inn and upon the same floor. It will be exceedingly difficult if not impossible to discover negotiations carried on through so private a channel. The appearance of emissaries from the rebel Congress is the general topic of conversation, but as any knowledge of their character is totally disclaimed by the Ministry, from whom I continue to receive every mark of attention, I have no other line to take than that of watching their motions in private with all possible diligence.

On June 10, he gives this further information :—

I am not yet able to give your lordship any authentic account of the particular object which the American agents have in view at this court. It is probable nothing will transpire till the King of Prussia is returned from

Pomerania. I am well assured that Lee has brought a letter from the rebel Congress, but it is not supposed that any answer will be given to it. He has had some conferences with M. de Schulemburg, but though received politely he is said to have met with little encouragement, and had no hopes given him that his proposal would be accepted by his Prussian Majesty. Sayre and he talk of going to Potzdam about the time of the king's return, which is fixed for Saturday next. In the meantime they employ themselves in making inquiries of the different manufacturers at Berlin concerning the prices of cloth and linen; and I make no doubt if they pay ready money but they will be supplied with what quantities they please.

And on June 19 he writes as follows:—

M. Hertzberg told me yesterday at dinner, loud enough to be overheard by the French minister, that no permission had been sent to Embden to receive American privateers, etc. Mr. Sayre continues at Berlin, and often sends letters to M. de Schulemburg's department and receives answers from it. He has also written two lately to the King of Prussia, but I cannot give your lordship any information of their contents.

In the meantime Lord Suffolk had written the following instruction from London, dated June 20:—

I have secret and certain information that Mr. Arthur Lee's journey to Berlin was the result of a correspondence which had been carried on some time between the other rebel agents at Paris and Baron de Schulemburg, who you know possesses very good abilities, and is supposed to be much in his Prussian Majesty's confidence. The object of that correspondence on the part of the rebels was to obtain some public countenance of their cause at the court of Berlin, with a view to make it the pretext for a similar avowal at other courts. His Prussian Majesty however would not give any sanction to an indecency so derogatory to the sovereign character in general; and though the proposal of the rebel emissaries to make some agreement respecting tobacco (which had been thrown out as the lure on their part) was not rejected, they were informed that any person sent by them to treat thereon at Berlin must be content to remain incognito.

The robbery of the papers took place on Thursday, June 26, and of the details of this transaction there are no particulars whatever in the papers which are preserved in the Record Office. From the state of the binding it can easily be seen that the volume which ought to contain the documents has been tampered with, but a happy accident has enabled me to discover the very papers which by some unknown means were removed from their proper depository.

On June 28, 1777, Hugh Elliot writes the following letter in cypher to the Earl of Suffolk :—

(Most Secret.)

My Lord,—I have only time to inform your Lordship that I have taken copies of several papers belonging to Lee which contain some important information respecting the connections of France and Spain with the rebels. I am sorry to add, that by any accident I may be subjected to considerable trouble from the consequences, and perhaps lose my situation. I will write in full upon this subject, either by the next post or by a courier. In the meantime I presume to observe that the most confined

secrecy on this subject is material. I have the honour to be, with the greatest truth and respect, my Lord,
Your Lordship's
Most obedient, humble servant,
H. ELLIOT.
Right Honourable Earl of Suffolk.

The robbery had taken place three days before. Mr. Liston, who in early days had been Elliot's tutor, was at this time attached to the embassy at Berlin. Elliot sends him to London with the papers he has copied, ordering him to give a verbal account of the means by which they were obtained. By great good fortune I discovered, in a country house occupied by a descendant of Hugh Elliot's, the narrative which was taken down from Liston's lips for the information of the king and ministers, and which has hitherto eluded the curiosity of historians. It runs as follows:—

Mr. Elliot having, by the activity and address of a German domestic, gained the servant at the inn where the rebel agents lodged, and having heard that Lee had long entered in a journal at night the transactions of every day, determined if possible to possess himself of that journal. He was informed that Lee kept it in a portefeuille which was sometimes locked and sometimes not, but that the door to the chamber was always locked when Lee was about. His next step was to get false keys made both to the door and to the bureau. Hearing now that both Lee and Sayre were going to M. de Launay in the country, where they generally stayed till eleven at night, he sent the German servant to bring off the papers, but strangers were just arrived and the man could not get in at the door. He therefore entered the room at the window of the first floor, opened the bureau with his key, found the portefeuille with the key in it, and brought it away out of the window without being seen, except by one of the people who were gained. This was about four o'clock, and Mr. Elliot was at dinner with Sir Trevor Corry, Mr. Bernier, Mr. Liston, and Mr. Harvey, member for Essex. They were all enjoined the most sacred secrecy, and set to copying instantly: and Mr. Elliot went about to pay visits and show himself, which he did till eight in the evening, when he called at the inn on the pretence of visiting Lord Russborough, son of Lord Milltown. He found Lee and Sayre that moment arrived, and with Lord Russborough, and knowing the papers not to be yet replaced, had nothing left for it but to join them and to endeavour to amuse them with conversation, which he did for near two hours (without any introduction or acknowledgment of each other's names, but merely as men happening to meet who spoke the same language). About ten o'clock Lee got up and said he must go to write. Soon afterwards Mr. Elliot heard a violent clamour in the house of "a robbery, the loss of papers, etc." He now drove home, and finding the most material papers copied, resolved to send back the whole parcel immediately. They were accordingly delivered (by Mr. Elliot himself, disguised) late that night to the mistress of the house, who was in the plot, and said they were brought by a porter, who left them and ran off. The instructions from the Congress were accidentally left behind, and were sent afterwards, from which circumstance it was supposed that this was the only paper that had been read.

Lee now made his complaint to the Governor of Berlin, and to the lieutenant of the police. The waiter of the inn and Lee's servants were seized and examined. They confessed that a servant of the English minister had tampered with them, but to no purpose; this was reported to the king, and Mr. Elliot learnt that M. de Hertzberg was to desire him to give up his servant to be examined. This, however, he had guarded against by directing the man to fly out of the country, and he is now with Mr. Matthias at Hamburg. He then went himself to MM. de Schulemburg, Finckenstein, and Hertzberg, and attributed the whole to the indiscreet zeal of the fugitive servant.

Copies of nearly all the documents carried by Liston are now accessible, but, what is more important, I am able to give the list of the whole.

1. Letter from Schulemburg to Franklin and Deane at Paris. Dated Berlin, March 15, 1777.
2. The Answer. Dated Paris, April 19, 1777.
3. Letter from A. Lee to Count Schulemburg. Dated Paris, May 8, 1777.
4. Note to Count Schulemburg from A. Lee. Dated Berlin, June 5, 1777.
5. Letter to Count Schulemburg from A. Lee. Dated Berlin, June 8, 1777.
6. The Answer. Dated Berlin, June 9, 1777.
7. A. Lee's Reply. Dated Berlin, June 10, 1777.
8. A. Lee's Answer to a Letter of Count Schulemburg's of June 18. Dated Berlin, June 20, 1777.
9. A. Lee's Memorial to his Prussian Majesty.
10. A. Lee aux Ministres du Congrès.
11. Letter from A. Lee to the Right Hon. the Secret Committee of Congress. Dated Paris, April 13, 1777.
12. A. Lee's Letter to Señor Don Diego Gardoqui, Madrid. Dated Paris, ——.
13. A. Lee's Letter to Señor Don Diego Gardoqui, Madrid. Dated Paris, May 13, 1777.
14. A. Lee's Letter to Señor Don Diego Gardoqui.

15. Postscript from Mr. Grand to Arthur Lee at Strasburg. Dated Paris, May 16, 1777.
16. A. Lee to M. de Grimaldi, at Rome. Dated Berlin, June 21, 1777.
17. A. Lee to Dr. Franklin. Dated Vienna, May 28, 1777.
18. The Instructions of the Congress to their Commissioners.
19. Mr. Arthur Lee's Journal of all that passed among the Commissioners with the French Ministers, the Congress, Holland, from December 16, 1777.

Three other despatches were also conveyed by Liston, which once existed in the Foreign Office archives, but which, as I have said above, exist there no longer.

(Most Secret.) Berlin: July, 1777.

My Lord,—I am happy to inform your Lordship that the inconveniences I apprehended when I wrote last from my having possession of Mr. Lee's papers are not like to take place. Mr. Liston will set out immediately to carry copies of them to England, and will give any further accounts that may be wished of the transaction. I hope the interesting nature of the information acquired will excuse the irregularity of the mode adopted. As Mr. Liston takes purposely a roundabout road, he may probably arrive some days later than this letter. I have the honour to be, with the utmost truth and respect, my Lord,

Your Lordship's most obedient humble servant,

H. ELLIOT.

Berlin: July 2, 1777.

My Lord,—I have the honour of inclosing several papers of importance I have obtained copies of at con-

siderable risk and some expense. Mr. Liston, the bearer of this letter, will give your Lordship an account of all the particulars relating to them. I have the honour to be, with the greatest truth and respect, my Lord,
Your Lordship's most obedient humble servant,
H. ELLIOT.

(Most Secret.) Berlin: July 2, 1777.

My Lord,—As Mr. Liston will have the honour to deliver this letter, I shall not enter into any minute detail of the transaction mentioned in my two last. He can give every information your Lordship may require with respect to the manner of acquiring the papers. I shall only mention the conduct I have held since.

Such strong suspicions had fallen upon a servant of mine who was actually employed in bringing them to me, that I thought it my duty to take a step I had previously resolved upon in case a discovery was likely to be made. I waited upon the minister, and declared that what had happened had been occasioned by my imprudence in having shown too great inquisitiveness concerning Mr. Lee and Mr. Sayre; that a person employed to give an account of their motions had from over-officiousness committed this unwarrantable action; that though the papers had been sent back as soon as I knew what had been done, yet I felt myself so much to blame that I could not help begging leave to represent to his Prussian Majesty, either in person or through the minister, that my court had no knowledge of this affair, that I alone was in fault, and that if his Prussian Majesty chose, I was ready to ask my recall, and to submit to any decision he might think proper to give.

The day after, I received for answer that the king could not help looking upon what had been done as *fort vif, fort précipité*, that as I had declared my court was totally ignorant of this affair, *il ne la réleveroit pas*, but advised me to take care that nothing of this kind should happen for the future.

If I might be allowed to express to your Lordship what appears to me becoming of his Majesty's dignity upon this occasion, I should not hesitate to beg that I might be ordered to tell either the King of Prussia himself or his minister, that although the King of England is sensible of the indulgence shown me by his Prussian Majesty, yet he disapproves of my conduct in this business, and his Majesty offers to nominate another in my place if I have made myself disagreeable to his Prussian Majesty. Whether this will be accepted or not I cannot determine with certainty, though I am rather inclined to think it will not. I make no apology to your Lordship for having risked everything when I thought his Majesty's interest so essentially concerned. I knew that by the sacrifice of an individual every public inconvenience could be prevented; and as I have not scrupled to make that sacrifice when called upon, I flatter myself I have not forfeited your Lordship's protection or my sovereign's approbation.

Mr. Liston will inform your Lordship, that matters were so arranged as to make it appear that I had not had time to peruse the papers, and will explain in full every circumstance of this affair.

I am much obliged to Sir Trevor Corry, Mr. Bernier, and Mr. Liston for their assistance in copying the papers. The expense incurred by gaining some, silencing others, and different articles, amounts to five hundred pounds.

I have the honour to be, with the utmost truth and respect, my Lord,

Your Lordship's most devoted humble servant,

H. ELLIOT.

Carlyle has told us that Elliot was induced to undertake this work by Lord Suffolk against his will.

There lies before me the original letter of Lord Suffolk's upon the subject, which tells an entirely different story. The part which concerns Elliot runs thus :—

Charleton : July 14, 1777.

I have ruminated much on Elliot's adventure, and think it won't end as quietly as he imagines. His secret is in too many hands. I applaud his zeal, but I don't mightily affect a dasher; and though I wish to encourage the former, I by no means wish to encourage the latter. All steps whatever relative to this strange business must wait my return.

When Lord Suffolk returned from the country, the matter was without doubt fully discussed between the king and his ministers, and the result was the following despatch from Lord Suffolk to Elliot, which is still in its place in the Record Office, and which is eminently fitted to be published in a blue book.

St. James's : August 1, 1777.

Sir,—Mr. Liston arrived from Berlin on the 11th past, the morning of my departure into the country; but the despatches which you had transmitted by him were immediately laid before the king, and I have now received his Majesty's sentiments on their contents. It gives me real concern when I find it my duty to convey any intimation of his Majesty's dissatisfaction with the conduct of a minister whose zeal in the public service is as little doubted as his ability, and who, by an excess of the former quality, has been induced to swerve from that discreet regard to his own situation and the dignified principles of his Court, which ought in every moment and on every occasion to regulate both his actions and his language. You will easily conceive that I allude to the expression which you confess yourself to have hazarded at your table, " that you would gladly give a considerable sum of money to anybody who would bring you the papers of the rebel agents." An expression which, however it might arise in the warmth of conversation, and might be in itself without further meaning, was highly improper to be used by the representative of a Court which has disdained and will ever disdain to tread the crooked paths of duplicity and treachery. The very wish that suggested the language, so improper in itself, would have been peculiarly improper at a Court which was acting on the occasion with the utmost frankness and friendship to his Majesty and his kingdoms, and with a due attention to its own dignity and the royal character in general. It is, however, but justice to you to admit that you are not liable to this part of the charge after having explained that you spoke in reference only to Mr. Arthur Lee's journal of his proceedings, *before* he went to the court of Berlin.

I insist so long on the expression above mentioned from an equitable anxiety to construe and consider that expression unconnected with the violent act which it occasioned ; for that act certainly carries a very different aspect when supposed to originate in your servant's mind from the accidental overhearing of your table conversation, to what it would have done if it had appeared to be a settled plan to obtain the portefeuille, begun by your suggestion and conducted by your contrivances. As, however, in the course of accidental events, there was but too much reason to put the latter interpretation on what passed, the part you took, of stating your own story, fully and frankly, to the Prussian ministers, was certainly the wisest that your peculiar circumstances would admit. And the reparation which you offered by your proposal to solicit your own recall in case your part in the transaction should have made any unfavourable impression on his Prussian

Majesty's mind, was no more than our Royal Master would have been disposed to grant. But the generous answer which was returned to you on the part of his Prussian Majesty prevents this unpleasant consideration; and the caution, to discourage for the future such vivacity in your own language, and so criminal an avidity in the conduct of your dependents, with which the answer was accompanied, comes with so good a grace, that it must, I am sure, be constantly remembered by you. It remains only for you to take some natural occasion of mentioning to the Prussian ministers the sentiments of your Court on this business, as I have already done to Count Maltzan. Upon the whole, I may now very sincerely congratulate you on the fortunate conclusion of these embarrassments, every culpable part of which his Majesty will fully forgive, in consideration of the zeal which occasioned them.

I am, etc.,
Suffolk.

This very nearly completes the story, but it is satisfactory to learn that Elliot was not only forgiven by the king but received an extra £500 as payment for what he had done. Mr. Harris, afterwards Lord Malmesbury, a near relative of Elliot's, was on his way to St. Petersburg in the first week in October. He carried with him the following letter for Elliot :—

St. James's : October 7, 1777.

Sir,—In addition to what I have already written to you with regard to the late transaction respecting the papers of the rebel agents, I use this conveyance to inform you (in further proof that the exceptionable circumstances in that business are entirely overlooked in consideration of the loyal zeal which occasioned them), that the king has been graciously pleased to take notice of the great expenses in which you involved yourself, and has directed the amount to be made good to you. I have accordingly received his Majesty's gracious commands to pay one thousand pounds to your agent, and I sincerely congratulate you on this close of our correspondence upon an enterprise which, as it could not be conducted without your making improper confidences, could never have been justified [but] by the completest success.

It is scarcely necessary to make any remarks upon this story, of which we now know the whole truth. If the Americans had been recognised belligerents, and Lee and Sayre their accredited agents, it would have been probably within the rules of international law to treat them as Elliot treated them, although the neutral Court might have resented the action of the ambassador in any way that it pleased. It must, however, be remembered that the Americans were at this time not belligerents but rebels, and that Lee and Sayre were in the position of Irish Home Rule leaders at the present day, seeking for the active co-operation, if not the armed interference, of a foreign but friendly power against their own country. At the same time actions like these are to be judged not by definite rules but by the impression they make on the moral sense of mankind. If it be the first rule of an ambassador's conduct that he should on no account exhibit an excessive zeal, Elliot may be judged to have transgressed this precept. He was, however, quite a young man, and his later history shows him to have been, if one of the most erratic, at the same time one of the most brilliant and successful of English diplomatists.

When the foregoing facts were laid before the Royal Historical Society, Mr. C. A. Fyffe made the following remarks on them, which are of great value.

All had had their admiration for Dick Turpin and Jack Sheppard, and it would be a shock to some to find that their glories must be shared with an English ambassador. He saw no use in calling things by their wrong names. Elliot chose to act as a thief; and the revered George III., with that arch-Pecksniff the Earl of Suffolk, gave him £1,000 for doing so.

The reference to the rights of belligerents seemed to him quite erroneous. When France and Germany were at war in 1870, the French and German ambassadors in London had no more right by international or any other law to steal papers from one another's houses than they had to blow one another's brains out. Then to take the case of rebels. Suppose that in 1861 the Confederate Agents, Messrs. Mason and Slidell, instead of being captured by Commodore Wilkes on board the "Trent," had prosperously reached the Langham Hotel; that while they were there the United States minister had bribed the waiters and chambermaids, made false keys, and stolen their papers; and finally that he had been caught, sneaking back in disguise with the despatch-box. Should we ever have heard enough of Yankee blackguardism and the baseness of republics? Should we ever have been sufficiently thankful for our own highmindedness? The world would have reeked of it to this day.

He agreed to this, that, low as Elliot's conduct was, Lord Suffolk's hypocrisy was even more disgusting. "A Court which has ever disdained and will ever disdain to tread the crooked paths of duplicity and treachery!" Talleyrand was never more shamelessly cynical. The real excuse, such as it is, must be sought in the fact that all the Courts of that time were about equally unscrupulous in their methods. Any scoundrelism was thought fair (he used this word for want of a better) in diplomacy; and though Frederick called Elliot a "goddam Englishman," and possibly resented his housebreaking in his own capital, he would not in his heart think the worse of Elliot for it,—on the contrary, he probably thought him a sharp fellow. Frederick himself, Joseph of Austria, and Catherine of Russia, habitually employed people to steal despatches and rob mail-carts. There are plenty of allusions to this even in those State papers of the time which have been published. Though Joseph or Catherine robbed from one another on occasion, they actually had an understanding that papers stolen from third parties, if they could not be deciphered by the comparatively dull people at St. Petersburg, should be sent to the more practised hands at Vienna, and an interpretation be there made for the common benefit. References to this will be found in Vivenot's "Confidential Letters of Thugut," the Austrian minister; and he suspected that, if only for lying's sake, Thugut sometimes gave the Russian Court odd interpretations of the papers they had sent to him to decipher—if indeed the Russians did not manufacture bogus papers in order to mislead *him*.

Are thievery and tricks like Elliot's now practised by the British Government? He believed not. Pitt did a great deal to check this, and to make such words as "honour," "good faith," which had been mere ridiculous sounds to Suffolk and George III., realities in the action of the English Government. In the long struggle with France, when every base means was employed by successive revolutionary Governments, Pitt saw how important it was that there should be one European Power which, in its methods, should hold fast, not only in profession, but in deed, to fair and honourable dealing. Judging from things in the English records of that time, he believed that Pitt would summarily and for ever have dismissed any English ambassador who should have stolen like Elliot. Pitt was beset by people, refugees and others, who were ready to carry out any enterprise against the French Republican Government, and afterwards against Bonaparte. As the murder of the French envoys in 1799 at Rastadt shows, robbery of papers easily passed into assassination; and events like this probably strengthened Pitt's natural hatred for the dishonourable ways which diplomacy had hitherto sanctioned. Under enormous difficulties, from 1793 to 1815, the British Government, though often violent and high-handed, refrained from the meaner tricks of political business. He was speaking of its foreign policy, not of Ireland. Of course attempts were made to bribe the enemy's generals. This is a recognised part of the operations of war. In the invasion of France in 1814 a sum of £100,000 was offered, though in vain, to the commander of Strasburg. The only interest attaching to the matter is that the Englishman concerned in it was that model of respectability, the late Lord Aberdeen, whose despatches are the authority for the statement.

IX.

QUEEN CAROLINE OF NAPLES,
1811–1814.

SOME time ago the editor of the *Historical Review* placed in my hands about thirty letters addressed by Queen Caroline of Naples, wife of Ferdinand IV., to Mr. Robert Fagan, who was consul-general in Sicily at the beginning of the century.[1] The letters range in date over about a year, from March, 1812, to April, 1813. Most of them are in Italian, a few only in French. They are full of denunciation of the queen's wrongs and of abuse of Lord William Bentinck. There is one letter of his Lordship's in which he vies with the queen in strong expressions. Lord William writes from Palermo, September 26 [1812], to Mr. Fagan: "I have read your note just now informing me of the queen having sent to you to say that the hereditary prince was declared to be so ill as to be unable to hold for the

---

[1] These letters to his grandfather were kindly placed at my disposal by Mr. Louis Fagan, of the Print Room, British Museum, who adds that Robert Fagan was born at Cork, and died in Rome August 16, 1816. Besides his other occupations, he was distinguished as an amateur artist, and in 1812 exhibited in the Royal Academy the portrait of Lord Amherst's children.—EDITOR, "HISTORICAL REVIEW."

future the reins of government. This must be one of her lies, of which she deals out a great abundance. I think it will be better to put an end to the negotiations which she takes either for the want of decision or of instruction, and therefore if she sends for you again I beg you will not go to her." Although it was obvious from the correspondence that the relations between Lord William and the queen were of anything but an amicable character, it did not appear easy to determine who was in the right. Lord William has always had the reputation of a just and upright man and a good officer. Queen Caroline receives a good character from the hands of her German biographer Helfert. I felt that it would not be fair to write upon a subject with one-sided evidence in my hands. I therefore made a careful study of the correspondence relating to Sicily in the Public Record Office from February, 1811, to June, 1813. Even then it was not easy to come to a decision. Those who were best acquainted with both sides of the case seem to have condemned the queen. At the same time great allowance must be made for an impulsive, passionate nature coming into violent conflict with a cold and obstinate Englishman. In this dilemma I determined to lay the facts before my readers, and allow them to judge for themselves. It will probably be found that the inevitable force of circumstances is more to be blamed than either the lady or her adversary.

Naples did not become involved in the troubles which followed the French Revolution until nearly ten years after its outbreak. In 1798 the king of the Two Sicilies joined the coalition against France. The Neapolitan army marched into the Roman territory under the command of the king. No time was lost by France in avenging the insult. The army retreated, the old king returned to Naples in the clothes of a lord-in-waiting, a terrible insurrection broke out in the capital, and the Royal family took refuge, December 21, 1798, in the *Vanguard*, Nelson's flagship, which three days later sailed for Palermo. The lazzaroni did their best to resist the French, they broke open the prisons and let out the convicts, but could not stand against regular troops, and on January 23 Championnet was after a severe struggle master of the city. The Parthenopean republic was established by the French, and Ferdinand IV. did not return to his country till after the signing of the peace of Amiens in 1802. He was brought back with great rejoicings by British ships and under British protection. Queen Caroline, who had left Palermo two years before for Schönbrunn, hastened to join him. The first results of the breach of the peace of Amiens have been narrated in a previous essay.

It would have been difficult for the most keen-sighted statesman to foretell on which side victory would incline. The whole strength of England, Russia, and Austria was ranged against Napoleon. Prussia was only waiting for the first gleam of victory to join the coalition. How could France, scarcely recovered from serious defeats, stand against such combined efforts? All these plans were disconcerted by the marvellous rapidity and good fortune of the

French emperor. On November 5 the last French troops crossed the frontier of Naples on their way to the north, but a fortnight before the whole army of Mack had capitulated at Ulm; on November 20 the combined English and Russian fleets sailed into the Bay of Naples, and Alquier demanded his passports. Twelve days later the battle of Austerlitz was fought, and on December 29, the day after the signing of the peace of Pressburg, Napoleon issued a proclamation to his army that the dynasty of Naples had ceased to reign. The allies on whom the queen had relied began to desert her; the English troops sailed to Sicily, the Russians to Corfu. On February 8 the French army again crossed the Garigliano, and four days later Ferdinand and Caroline set sail for Sicily. Joseph Bonaparte was made king of Naples, to be succeeded two years later by Murat. From this time the situation is a very complicated one. Joseph and Murat are both convinced that Naples is a valueless and incomplete possession without the addition of Sicily. The Neapolitan sovereigns in Sicily are supported by English arms. Sicily was regarded by the English partly as a third station in the Mediterranean besides Gibraltar and Malta, and partly as a point of departure for harassing the French in Sicily. Ferdinand, or rather Caroline by whom he was urged, disliked the French and English equally. She was German by birth and Italian by education. Her great desire was to have her own way, and be restored to the position, which she had held for so many years, of queen of the Two Sicilies. She was willing to be friendly with either party who would secure that end; she was the enemy of whichever party was for the moment the most likely to deprive her of her crown and of her remaining possessions. Joseph and Murat were open enemies, but the English might at any moment put an end to the sovereignty which they had already reduced to a shadow, and annex Sicily as they had annexed Malta. Nor was it certain that Sicily might not at some time or other be surrendered by the English as the price of peace. Such an arrangement had been discussed between Lord Yarmouth and Talleyrand in 1806, and the negotiations had only been put an end to by the death of Fox. The connection with England was indeed a material advantage to the Sicilian Court. By the treaty of commerce signed between England and Naples in 1808, we had undertaken the defence of Messina and Augusta, which required a garrison of at least a thousand strong; we also covenanted to pay the Court a yearly subsidy of £300,000, to date from September, 1805, the date of the landing of the Anglo-Russian forces in Naples, and eighteen months later this sum was raised to £400,000. Notwithstanding this liberality the queen's demands for pecuniary aid were persistent and importunate.

The peace of Vienna, which followed the battle of Wagram in 1809, affected the relations of the Sicilian Royal family to Napoleon. The reconciliation between France and Austria was confirmed by the marriage of Napoleon with Marie Louise, whose mother was Maria Theresa, the daughter of Ferdinand. Thus the great emperor became the grandson of Queen Caroline. Although Murat, king of Naples, had married another Caroline, the sister of Napoleon, who combined the beauty of the family with the talent of her brother, relations were not always very smooth between his great protector and himself. His haughty spirit led him to aim at a more independent kingship, and the favour of Napoleon might at any time be changed into wrath and revenge. It was natural that Queen Caroline should not neglect the opportunity which her connection with the French imperial Court offered of regaining her coveted palaces. Lord Amherst, writing to Lord Wellesley on February 8, 1811, says that he has further information of an arrangement between Naples and Austria, by which Naples is to be restored to Ferdinand IV., and that a prince of the house of Austria is to be placed on the throne of Sicily. "This project is to be put into execution by means of German troops, to whom it is imagined that the Sicilians would oppose less hostility than to an army consisting of French and Neapolitans." The inhabitants of Sicily are to be deprived of arms; the *levée en masse* of the population, which had been so potent an instrument against the French, is to be discouraged. The queen is constantly corresponding with Vienna in cipher, notwithstanding her solemn promise, after the marriage of Marie Louise, that she would break off all connection with the Court of her birth—the pledge given in March, 1810, both by the king and queen, of unshaken loyalty to the alliance with Great Britain. He adds: "If your Lordship asks me how I can reconcile these assurances with the engagements now supposed to be entered into with our enemies, I answer that I believe jealousy of the designs of Great Britain predominates in the queen's mind over the hatred she may entertain for Bonaparte; and with respect to his Sicilian Majesty—never doubting for a moment the loyalty and fidelity of his principles, I think deception may be practised towards him, and that a plot may be carried on in which he is no partaker."

Just at this time another matter caused additional strain to the relations between the English and Sicilian Governments. Sicily had for a considerable time possessed a parliament of estates of the medieval and feudal type. It consisted of three arms or branches, the barons, the clergy, and the tenants of the crown. Among the last were the most important towns under the presidency of the prætor of Palermo. The parliament met every four years, and in later times consisted of 62 prelates, 124 barons, and 46 deputies from the crown lands. The Prince of Butera, as holding eighteen fiefs, had command of as many votes. The different branches of the assembly met and voted separately. During the vacation of parliament a committee of three from each arm watched over the expenditure of the taxes and the execution of the laws.[1] The time had come when a new parliament was to be summoned. It was opened by the crown prince in the grand hall of the Royal palace at Palermo on January 25, 1810. A yearly subsidy of 250,000 ounces had been voted in 1802 and 1806. The parliament was now ordered

[1] Rotteck and Welcker, ix. 63. Helfert, p. 429.

to increase this to 300,000 ounces, and to give besides a donation to the queen and one to the crown prince on the birth of his infant daughter. After three weeks, the parliament had only voted a little more than half the sum asked for; on June 13 the king declared his intention of summoning a new parliament, which was to correct abuses and equalize taxation. The king promised on his side to employ in future none but Sicilian ministers. This promise, however, was not fulfilled. Mendici, the minister of finance, was removed, but the Marchese Donato Tommasi, a Neapolitan, was appointed in his place. When the new parliament came together, it was found to be less willing to vote money than its predecessor, and it proposed a reform in taxation, which was accepted by the king. The needs of the Court continued to be as pressing as ever. The English subsidy was granted for certain well-defined purposes, and, as we shall presently see, was suspended on the ground that its application had been improperly altered. On February 4, 1811, Tommasi took strong measures for bringing money into the Royal coffers. An edict was issued which imposed a tax of one per cent. on all money payments of every description whatsoever. Further, a proposal was made to sell by lottery a large amount of property belonging to religious orders. 15,000 tickets were to be issued at ten ounces each, which would bring in a sum equal to £112,500.[1] The edict imposing the tax was entirely unconstitutional. Only four cases existed in which the authority of parliament could

[1] Amherst to Wellesley, March 26, 1811.

be dispensed with in raising supplies—an enemy in the country, an insurrection, the captivity of the king, and the marriage of his daughters. No such exercise of arbitrary authority had been known since the war of the Austrian succession. The measure was a great hindrance to commerce, and specially injurious to the numerous English firms settled in the island. Immediately on the appearance of the edict, forty out of the fifty-seven barons of which the military arm was then composed, with Prince Belmonte at their head, drew up a protest against it. They commanded amongst them 160 votes out of the 275 which were assigned to their order. The population found means to evade the edict. Business arrangements, which before depended on law, were now left to rest on the good faith of the contracting parties. The protest of the barons was presented to the king, but the tax continued to be levied. The lottery project failed; only a small number of the tickets were taken up.

If we are to believe our agents, the eyes of the Sicilians were turned with hope to the English Government. Lord Amherst had been recalled, and Lord William Bentinck, who was to take his place as civil and military governor of the island, was looked for with impatience, as pursuing a more energetic exercise of English authority.

Lord William Bentinck's arrival (says Mr. Douglas, writing on June 22, 1811) is expected with a degree of *anxiety* which nobody can conceive but those who are on the spot. The Sicilians look up with eager and *gasping hope* that he may be bearer of instructions to adopt a lofty and decisive tone which may compel the Court to the adoption of a milder system of government. I can assure you most positively that the majority of the Sicilians will be satisfied with nothing less than *the British flag flying all over Sicily*. It is impossible that things can go on as they are at present. Last year when I made the tour of the island I found the universal cry to be, " *If the English will not take Sicily, the French must.*"

These expressions of opinion, whether true or false, were not calculated to influence the queen favourably towards the English, and she had been the more alarmed by a discussion which took place in parliament upon the Sicilian subsidy on May 1. In the meantime she determined upon a bold stroke. On July 19 a Royal decree directed the arrest of five of the principal barons who had signed the protest, Princes Belmonte, Villarmosa, Villafranca, Petrulla, and Aci.[1] They were carried off by a Sicilian corvette under the guns of Admiral Boyle's flagship to be confined in various Italian islands. Three days after this event Bentinck reached Palermo.

Lord William Charles Cavendish Bentinck, second son of the third Duke of Portland, was born September 14, 1774. He served in the Scots Greys under the Duke of York in Flanders, was attached to the army of Suvoroff in Italy, was from 1804 to 1807 governor of Madras, and commanded an English brigade at the battle of Corunna. He had therefore enjoyed ample experience both of civil and military commands. He was a just and upright man. His chief defect was that he was too much

[1] Douglas to Wellesley, June 24, 1811.

of an Englishman, and was apt to consider narrow English remedies as a panacea for all political diseases whenever they might arise. He had received very ample instructions both open and secret. He was to be at once ambassador and commander-in-chief, to exercise all the functions which had been separately performed by Lord Amherst and Sir James Stuart. His first attention was to be directed to the subsidy. That was to be devoted to the payment of the Sicilian army and navy in due proportions, and an account of expenditure was to be rendered to the English Government every three months. There is a grave suspicion that these conditions had not been complied with; if Bentinck finds them justified, he is to threaten the suspension of payment. The due application of the subsidy for the defence of the island is regarded as the keystone of the alliance. At the same time other important matters will claim Bentinck's attention. The discontent of the Sicilian nation, arising from the exclusion of Sicilians from the government and the employment of Neapolitans, from the neglect of the advice of parliament and the imposition of arbitrary taxes, is of serious moment to English interests. The feudal rights of the nobility and the privileges of corporations are serious hindrances to the development of the country. The irritation caused by these evils is so great that there is danger of a revolution; the queen is jealous of English influence, and is afraid that she and her husband may at any time be sacrificed to France. Bentinck was to remove if possible the causes of this jealousy. He was to give a solemn pledge that so long as Ferdinand was faithful to England, the English Government would under all circumstances maintain his right both to Sicily and Naples, and at any rate secure him in the possession of Sicily. But the Court must be willing to listen to English advice. England does not wish to interfere in the internal government of Sicily, except where abuses jeopardise the defence against the common enemy and the security of the English alliance. It is absolutely necessary that Sicilians should be admitted to the ministry, and that the orders of parliament should be attended to. If the neglect of these measures should lead to a revolution, English arms could not be used to put it down. On the other hand, if the king will listen to English warnings, the British forces will be employed in the protection of his person and Government, in maintaining his just and legitimate authority in Sicily, as well as in the defence of the island against the enemy.

Bentinck had a weary task before him. He was to give advice which might be good and was certain to be unpalatable. He was to offer it with discretion and temper. It was only too probable that the discretion and temper would be such as instigated the severity of John Knox towards Mary Stuart. On this first occasion Bentinck only stayed a month in Sicily. He did his best to induce the king and queen to revoke the obnoxious edict, to recall the exiled barons, to allow Palermo to be garrisoned by British troops, and, it is said,[1] to send a Sicilian contingent

[1] Helfert, p. 436.

of 120,000 men to strengthen the British army in Spain. His advances were met with an absolute refusal. On August 27 Lord William, having given a brilliant ball on the previous evening, embarked on board the *Cephalus* and sailed with great haste to London. The queen was in a deep state of dejection. She wrote on August 30 to the emperor at Vienna: "I am almost forgotten by my enemies, but pressed down and trodden under foot, robbed and almost dethroned by those who call themselves our friends and allies, for whom we have sacrificed so much. Will your Majesty grant me a refuge in one of your cities, Brünn, Graz, or Salzburg, to finish my unhappy life there?"[1] Shortly after this she had a dangerous attack of illness. On September 16 she took an emetic against the advice of her physicians, and, experiencing no relief, she drank twenty-four glasses of water. Soon after this at two o'clock in the afternoon, whilst she was conversing with the Marchese Tommasi, she fell down senseless. She was with difficulty carried by five persons to a sofa. After some time she came to herself and sent for her confessor and her children. She took an affectionate leave of them. To her eldest son she recommended her dearly beloved youngest son Leopold and the *émigrés* who had accompanied her from Naples. She bade Leopold, then twenty-one years old, to behave well. To her favourite daughter, the Duchess of Genevois, she said, "Mimi, you have always been very good to me"; and to Marie Amélie, duchess of Orleans,

[1] Helfert, p. 439.

afterwards queen of the French, "I thank you also, my dear Emily; live happily." "Pray for me, my children," she concluded; "I stand in great need of your prayers." At ten o'clock she had another attack, and the last sacraments were administered to her. Soon after this she asked to be bled in the foot, which had relieved her in a similar illness at Leghorn. Next day she was much better, and in a day or two was out of danger. We shall see, however, that this illness was only the beginning of the end.

At the beginning of November, 1811, it was known in Palermo that Lady William Bentinck, who had remained behind in that city, was expecting her husband to arrive about the 20th of that month. He did not actually reach Sicily till December 7. He came with very precise and not very agreeable instructions. He had informed his Government that Sicily was by no means in a satisfactory state of defence, that the military force raised by the English subsidy was, in the event of an invasion, more likely to be a hindrance than a help, while the discontent of the population against the Government prevented efficient co-operation against an enemy. Acting on this advice, Lord Wellesley determined that the subsidy should be suspended from October 1 until Bentinck should think it advisable to resume it. The exiled barons were to be recalled, and persons opposed to the English to be removed from the Ministry. His instructions further reminded him that there was grave suspicion, but no absolute proof, that the queen had conducted a treasonable correspondence with the

French. He was to watch carefully for evidences of guilt, but was to understand that the English troops were in no case to be used to silence the Court of Palermo. If all advice failed, they were to be transferred to some spot where they could be of greater use. The placing of the whole disposal of the subsidy in Bentinck's hands gave him immense authority.

Bentinck was also ordered to superintend a plan for wresting Italy from the French, which has been little noticed by English historians. Archduke Francis of Este (afterwards duke of Modena, now a young man of two-and-thirty) had formed the design of collecting an army in Sardinia for the invasion of Italy. The English Government instructed Bentinck to render what assistance he could to the enterprise. On his former journey to Palermo he had stopped at Cagliari to gain what information he could about the archduke's armament. He reported favourably of him, said that besides the loss of his dominions he had a special grievance against Napoleon for having deprived him of his betrothed bride, Marie Louise. His plan was to collect an army of Austrians and Italians who were disgusted with Napoleon's Government. He looked especially to the Dalmatians, whose country had recently been annexed by France, to form the nucleus of the conspiracy. With an army of this kind he would rouse a national insurrection in Italy against the French such as they were already contending with in Spain. The first idea had been to make the Ionian Islands and the Island of Lissa on the coast of Dalmatia the principal rallying point of the archduke's armament, but subsequently the Island of Sardinia was preferred. Bentinck was entrusted with £100,000 to spend on the enterprise, and £50,000 for the defence of Sardinia. He was authorised to promise the archduke £5,000 a year if he should engage in actual warfare in Italy. Bentinck was to decide upon all measures which it might be desirable to take. At the same time the people of Italy must not be excited to any exertion which they may not think necessary for their own safety and interests. The principal reliance of Italy must rest upon the unanimity, courage, and perseverance of her own people in applying the resources of their country against the common enemy with the necessary precautions of prudence. The season and mode of resistance must be chosen by them on the spot. It would be wrong to afford any assistance to a partial attack or premature project which should neither unite the energy and zeal of the great body of the people, nor be founded on a due sense of the difficulties and dangers of such an enterprise.[1]

Bentinck's first step on his arrival was to inform the Marquis Circello, the prime minister, that the subsidy had been suspended. Two days later he was presented to the king and queen. Knowing that the queen was really the mainspring of the Government, he was anxious for a conversation with her as soon as possible, and this was arranged for December 13. Bentinck, on being introduced, said that he wished to see her Majesty as soon as possible on his arrival, as she had been the last person he had taken

[1] Lord Wellesley to Lord W. Bentinck, October, 1811.

leave of. The Prince Regent of England was actuated solely by friendship and regard, and never had any other object in view than the honour and independence of the King of Sicily. Here the queen stopped him, and asked him if he were an honest man and could make such a remark. For six years it had been the settled wish of the English to take the country. Fox *le spirituel* had said so, Moore *le Jacobin enragé* did not deny it, Drummond *qui parlait comme un fou*, Stuart, and Bentinck himself were all working to the same end. She had always said so to her ministers, who first thought her mad, but now admitted that she was right. How had the English behaved with regard to Spain? Prince Leopold had been invited by the Spanish ministry, and they refused to let him go. Sir John Stuart had remained at Ischia inactive with 23,000 men, when there were only 3,000 French in Naples. On Bentinck urging the employment of Sicilians, she said that the king ought to be allowed to choose his own servants. The council consisted of Butera, Cassaro, and Parisi, who were Sicilians, Circello, *qui est une bête*, Medici, who was an able man, and Artali, minister of war. "As for him," she said, "he is a fool whom you may boil, cook, and roast if you please." It would be impossible to compose the council of Sicilians, from the difficulty of finding persons who could read and write. Cassaro was an honest man, and, she added ironically, "a great genius. He has a sublime idea of geography; he would think it quite natural if you told him that the English squadron had just anchored in the Port of Vienna." She would be very glad to see Prince Belmonte in the ministry, because he would immediately turn against the English. In the very room in which they were now standing he had cautioned her against the English, who wished to reduce the sovereign to the condition of a nabob. It was quite impossible either that Bentinck could command the army or that the barons should be recalled. She had never corresponded with Napoleon nor with his granddaughter; Napoleon was a *coquin*. She would leave the country, not to beg her bread in England or Italy, but to go to Germany, and hoped that a frigate would not be refused her to take her to Durazzo or Constantinople. The king might do as he pleased; perhaps he would abdicate in favour of his son. The conversation lasted two hours. It left the impression on Bentinck that, with exceeding good abilities, she probably never had any common sense, and that her mind, enfeebled by age (she was now fifty-nine years of age), by vast quantities of opium and the operation of violent passions, had reached a state little short of actual insanity.[1] Two days before this interview the queen had sent for Fagan, the British consul-general, with whom she had quarrelled, and whom she had not seen for a year.

There is no doubt that Bentinck and the English Government believed firmly that the queen had carried on treasonable correspondence with the enemy, with Murat certainly, if not with Napoleon. It is difficult from the materials at hand to get a clear idea of when this was, but there seems to be evidence that during the year 1811 tolerably frequent com-

[1] Bentinck to Wellesley, December 26, 1811.

munications were kept up between Palermo and Naples. A small felucca mounting one or two guns would sail from Naples to Palmerola, the westernmost of the Ponza group; thence it would proceed nearly due south to Ustica, a small isolated island lying due north of Palermo about five hours' sail. The emissary would remain ten or twelve days at Palermo, and have frequent interviews with the queen three hours after sunset. The emissary would return by the same route. Prince Ascoli was in the secret, and one Castroni conducted the correspondence. The letters were sealed by a lyre with the inscription *Nous sommes d'accord*. It appeared that Napoleon had promised the queen compensation for herself, and a niece of his own for Prince Leopold if she would co-operate in driving the English out of Sicily. Murat was to march his troops down to Reggio, while the Sicilian troops attacked the English and favoured the landing of the French at Messina. The fleet had been corrupted, and two battalions devoted to the queen had been formed under the supervision of the police. There is so much converging evidence for a design of this kind that the charge is probably not without foundation. It is corroborated by the remarkable conversation between General Donkin and General Goldemar which will be found at length at the end of this essay.

Another charge was of a totally different character. A certain Baron Jacobi, a German diplomatist, was overheard at Messina giving utterance to designs for turning the English out of Sicily. It was said that in pursuance of a secret article of the treaty of

Vienna, Naples and Calabria were to be restored to King Ferdinand, while Sicily was given to one of the emperor's brothers. The arrangement was sanctioned by the Court of St. Petersburg, and Baron Jacobi was sent to Palermo as the envoy of Austria.[1] Whatever might have been the result of either of these plans, they were frustrated by the arrival of Lord William Bentinck. After listening to all the evidence Bentinck informed his Government that it was his decided opinion that a treacherous correspondence had been carried on with the enemy. He felt that energetic measures were necessary for the security of the island, and deprecated the limitations of his instructions. He ordered up a regiment from Malta to Messina, and collected transports at Milazzo and Palermo. He considered that in " listening to the call of the whole country " the British Government was fulfilling the duties of a good and great nation.[2] Admiral Fremantle was also in favour of energetic measures. He felt sure that there had been treachery on the part of the Sicilian Government, but up to the present he had not discovered any document which would criminate any part of the Royal family.

Bentinck had a second interview with the queen on January 2, 1812. She expressed great anxiety for an accommodation; she had always been English by sentiment, and " now," she said with a smile, " I must be English by necessity." She would not oppose force. She had persuaded the king not to abdicate, but to return to Palermo for his birthday.

[1] Violland's declaration, Sicily, vol. 78.
[2] Bentinck to Wellesley, January 1, 1812.

He was now, she said, at the Ficuzza, a shooting-box in the mountains about six miles from Palermo. She had never corresponded with France, and in future no vessel should go to Naples without a passport from the English admiral, and no letter without being shown to Bentinck. She hoped that Bentinck would come to her at all hours without notice and speak without restraint. Bentinck took care not to irritate her, and the interview passed off quietly. From the palace he went to Circello, who announced to him the king's design to appoint him captain-general under certain restrictions, and showed him a plan for a new administration. This was to add four new members to the council, but not to change any of the ministers except the minister of war. Bentinck said that the arrangement was entirely unsatisfactory. He declined to give his objections or to propose names, but said that Prince Cassaro should be consulted. The next day Circello showed Bentinck a list of names which Prince Cassaro had suggested for the Ministry. Bentinck, however, had previously seen Prince Cassaro, and had heard from him that he had neither been consulted nor had approved of the names. Bentinck, feeling that whilst the barons remained in exile Prince Cassaro was the only person who could be trusted to oppose the queen's measures, urged him to take the three departments of finance, war, and the interior, leaving the Foreign Office to Circello. After some hesitation he accepted.

On January 5 Bentinck accepted an invitation from the king to visit him at the Ficuzza, where he stayed a night. The king did not talk on politics;

this was left to the Duke of Ascoli. The duke abused the queen roundly; he said that she was surrounded by a crowd of villains and the dregs of Naples, whom he was ashamed to see in her antechamber. She was a woman with whom nothing could be carried on, whose intentions varied every five minutes, who speaks " to you, to me, to the porter, the priests, with a crowd of rogues and villains, believes what each one says and changes with each of their opinions." He said that the king would never consent to Prince Cassaro holding these offices, as both the king and the queen disliked him exceedingly. The only hope lay in the queen's death, which might not be far distant. On returning to Palermo Bentinck informed Circello that if Prince Cassaro were not appointed to a principal place in the Government he would leave Palermo for Messina that day week. On January 9 the Court gave way. Bentinck's arrangement was carried out except that Gargoles, " a spy and a creature of the queen's," was made minister of war.[1] Notwithstanding this submission Bentinck gave orders for the garrison of Milazzo to sail to Palermo, Milazzo being reinforced from Messina.

On January 16 by a Royal decree the hereditary prince was appointed vicar-general and *alter ego* of the king with full powers. This was attributed to the king's state of health, but Bentinck in a despatch of January 17 gives a graphic account of the means by which it was brought about. On the 10th he paid the prince a visit by invitation, and had a very long

[1] Bentinck to Wellesley, January 11, 1812.

conversation with him. The prince repudiated the suggestion that his mother had corresponded with the French, while Bentinck disclaimed any desire to acquire the island on the part of the English. Bentinck urged that the king should abdicate, and that the barons should be recalled. The prince was afraid of the revolutionary character of the barons, and did not believe in the existence of popular discontents. Bentinck said that the only way to drive the French from Italy was to hold out liberty and a constitution to the nation. Bentinck left the prince with the impression that he had never spoken with a person more dispassionate, honest, and apparently well-meaning. After this conversation the prince went to his mother, fell down on his knees and urged her to retire from public affairs; he would now accept the transfer of the Royal authority, which the king had already offered him three times. The queen was very angry, and reproached her son in the bitterest terms. However, next day Circello came to Bentinck to say that the queen was going to the Ficuzza to persuade the king to transfer everything to the prince, and that he hoped that he would countermand the troops, which was done accordingly. Fortunately they had not sailed from Milazzo.

Two days later Bentinck saw both the prince and the queen. The prince had by no means got over his treatment by the queen, although he said that she was the kindest of mothers. The queen asked Bentinck what was to be done. He advised abdication, which the queen would not hear of. She was deeply moved, and said that the English wished to dethrone the king and his family. She abused Napoleon, and said that if she had ever thought of selling Sicily it would have been to the English. At last she became very wild. She said that there was only one way to save the king's honour, that he should place himself at the head of his army to reconquer Naples, and if necessary die like Tippoo Sahib in the breach. Bentinck said that the king could do as he pleased with his own troops. She asked Bentinck to write it down, and forced a pen into his hand, but when he refused she wrote herself, "Lord Bentinck declares that he does not object to the expedition to Naples." "This," she said, "will leave you in complete possession of Sicily, which you will not dislike." The king came to Palermo on the 14th, when Bentinck says that the queen made a last attempt to persuade him not to surrender his authority. This, however, is very doubtful. On the 16th, as we have said above, the prince was appointed *alter ego*. The king retired to the Ficuzza and the queen to Santa Croce. The first acts of the prince were to appoint Bentinck captain-general under the orders of the king, to recall the barons, and to repeal the obnoxious one per cent. tax. Bentinck was offered a seat upon the council, which he declined. In consequence of these measures the subsidy was ordered to be paid in full as before. Nevertheless Bentinck still continued to suspect the queen. The prince defended her, saying that injustice was done her, that she did not interfere with him, and that it was hard that she should not be left in quiet in her retirement.

At Messina, whither he had gone upon business,

Bentinck heard detailed accounts of the queen's correspondence with the enemy. She had written to Murat, to Napoleon, to Marie Louise, to offer to give up the island to the French if some compensation could be found for her husband and herself. The kingdom of Holland had been suggested. The correspondence was carried on with melodramatic secrecy. Letters were written in lemon juice or pricked in from holes which could only be seen when held to the light. Muffled messengers met the queen in the suburbs of Palermo. Seals were broken in half to be used as tokens. It is difficult to say how much of this was true. Without doubt the queen would have been happy to exchange the position of a prisoner for one of independence. It was one thing to scheme these plots, another to carry them out. Bentinck, however, could make no allowances. Castlereagh, the new foreign minister, was a harder man than Wellesley. On March 16 Bentinck wrote to the queen that he had evidence of a direct correspondence with the French, which, however, he could not divulge, and that she must retire from the neighbourhood of Palermo to a more distant part of the island. The prince wrote warmly in his mother's defence; he demanded proof of treasonable correspondence, and warned Bentinck against the falsehoods of infamous persons. The queen was quite ready to quit the island when the season permitted, and when she had ascertained whither to go. "My lord," he concludes, "if we wish to produce real good and quickly, which I do not doubt, let us unite, let us proceed, and spare me the pain which steps of this nature cause me. Let my parents be respected and you will find me entirely yours." Bentinck now insisted on the Ministry being changed. Belmonte took the place of Circello, Villanuova of Tommasi, Aci became minister of war instead of Castellentini, Cassaro was made minister of justice. He also continued to insist upon the queen's retirement from Palermo. On April 17 he wrote to Padre Cacamo, the king's confessor, to request him to persuade his Majesty to remove the queen from the island. Cacamo answered that he could not interfere in a matter which was alien to his character and his conscience. A week later Bentinck wrote to the king himself, urging that a parliament was about to meet, and that it could not deliberate in security unless the queen were absent. A copy of this was sent to the queen, who replied with great dignity and force. She says that the difficulties of the situation do not arise from her, but from the nature of things, that his charges against her are the invention of her personal enemies, that public opinion is really with her. "Let Lord Bentinck be at last convinced," she concludes, "that the daughter of Maria Theresa may be oppressed and calumniated, but never dishonoured." It is to this period that the first letter of the queen to Fagan belongs. She pours out her heart to him in confidence, and bewails her unhappy fate. She is ready to die like her unhappy sister Marie Antoinette, but she will do her duty till the grave. She declares that she has never swerved in her attachment to the English alliance, that she has been always loyal and true. It is gratifying to find that Fagan's

services in this respect were not unappreciated by
Bentinck, who writes on May 7 to request that his
salary may be raised on the ground that he has been
employed in the most confidential communications
with the queen, has gained in a great degree her
Majesty's goodwill, and in the delicate and embar-
rassing business with which he has been entrusted
has acquitted himself to Bentinck's satisfaction.
Sicily could hardly be said to flourish under British
government; the loaf got smaller and dearer every
day. Sicilian troops were transported under General
Maitland to Spain, where they were shut up in the
walls of Alicante by the French. The queen's letters
to Fagan of this period are full of warm-hearted
affection for him and his family. She complains
bitterly of her ill-health, of her fever and want of
sleep, which she ascribes to her troubles. Bentinck
soon obtained what he desired. The queen joined
the king at Ficuzza, and when he went to Solunto
for the tunny-fishing she repaired to the villa of La
Bagaria, which is only at a little distance. About
this time she received a long-expected letter from
the Emperor of Austria offering her a home in Germany if she wished for it.

Castlereagh, who had become foreign minister in
January, 1812, was more likely to urge Bentinck to
strong measures than his predecessor Wellesley.
The "Hints on the Improvement of Sicily," which
are printed among his papers, viii. 224-232, although
their author is unknown, were certainly read and
studied by him. Their general drift is that we
should anglicise Sicily as much as possible, if we do

not actually annex it. The chief instrument of amelioration was to be the introduction of a constitution on the English pattern, which was regarded at that time as a panacea for all political ills. Bentinck's new instructions of May 9 order him to make the army a thoroughly national force, to introduce a regular system of paying, clothing, and arming the troops, to make such reforms of the Sicilian constitution as may insure the affection of the people, and make the Neapolitans anxious to receive equal advantages together with the return of their lawful sovereigns. Bentinck says (June 30) that he was at first opposed to the idea of an English constitution on the ground of the people not being fit for it, but as he always says that the queen was in favour of it whereas her protests against it were continuous, much weight cannot be attached to that assertion.

The Sicilian Parliament met on June 18, and the groundwork of the constitution had been in discussion for some weeks before. The principal authors were Princes Belmonte and Villa Hermosa. The strong wish of the hereditary prince to attempt the reconquest of Naples at a time when Murat was absent on the expedition to Russia was made a lever for pressing the acceptance of reforms. The French government in Naples, however unpopular in some respects, had certainly ameliorated the general condition of the people, and if the Bourbons wished to return it could only be with a constitution. Sixteen resolutions were drawn up to be submitted to the parliament as a basis for the new constitution. 1. It is to embrace the English constitution "from the first line to the last," with such modifications as the parliament may consider necessary. 2. All feudal rights and distinctions are to be abolished, and the whole population of Sicily declared equal before the law. 3. The nation, being free to elect its prince, elects, subject to the observance of the present constitution, Francesco Borbone, all other claims to the throne being declared void. 4. That public lands henceforth belong to the nation, but are assigned to the decent support of the Royal family. 5. Forest laws are abolished. 6. Only Sicilian subjects can have any public employment. 7. The chamber of ecclesiastics is abolished and incorporated with the chamber of peers. 8. The legislative power rests with the nation meeting in parliament with the consent of the king. 9. Parliament is to determine the number of the army. 10. The king may not leave the kingdom without the consent of the parliament, and if the throne become vacant the nation may elect a new king. 11. The nation is to pay dowries for the king's daughters, but they are not to be married without the consent of the nation. 14. Parliament is to meet every year. If the king does not summon it, the chancellor is to do so. 15. The person of the sovereign is sacred, but the ministers may be impeached. 16. The minister of marine shall always be chosen from the Commons, and the ministers of grace and justice from the Lords. These bases were afterwards modified, and eventually the constitution was passed in fourteen articles.

The preamble states that the constitution of England is to be the basis of the Sicilian constitution, except as regards religion, which is to be Roman Catholic as heretofore. 1. The legislative authority belongs exclusively to parliament, but the sovereign has a veto. 2. The executive authority is vested in the person of the king. 3. The judicial authority is distinct from and independent of the executive and legislative authority. Judges and magistrates may be removed by the House of Peers on the accusation of the House of Commons. 4. The person of the king is sacred and inviolable. 5. Ministers and public functionaries may be impeached by the parliament. 6. Parliament is to consist of two houses, peers and commons. Ecclesiastics are to sit with the peers. 7. The barons are to have only one vote apiece. 8. Parliament is prorogued by the king, but must be convoked every year. 9. The crown lands and other national resources are to be administered by the nation, who shall also determine the amount of the civil list. 10. No Sicilian shall be punished except by law. Peers are to be judged by peers. 11. The feudal system is to be entirely abolished. 12. Certain ancient rights on land are to be abolished with compensation. 13. Money bills must originate in the Commons, and must be approved or vetoed by the Lords without amendment. 14. The parliament shall have the right of adding to or amending the constitution. Of these articles, all but three received the Royal assent. No. 10 was vetoed, and 9 and 13 were deferred for future consideration.

It is not difficult to imagine the feelings of the queen during this time. On June 16 she writes to Fagan : " The day after to-morrow the extraordinary parliament is to open which is to bring about the happiness of Sicily. Such are the repeated assurances of Lord Bentinck, who has, indeed, forced and brought about the holding of this parliament. I repeat what I have so often said, and what I deeply feel, it will never bring about the happiness of the people, but act as the cause of many evils." She was, however, little able to give effect to her opinions, being at this time terribly in debt. She turned to Fagan as to a confidant whom she could trust, and by his advice wrote him a letter to be shown to Lord Bentinck. Her public letters are always in French and are signed Charlotte, which was not one of her names, whereas her private letters are in Italian and are signed Caroline.[1] Her letter of June 21 asks for an advance of £100,000, to be repaid by deducting £50,000 from the subsidy for twenty months. She says what civil things she can to the English, and goes so far as to hope that the new constitution may be on the English model. In her private Italian letter she tells Fagan how much it has cost her to write this, but beggars must not be choosers. She also hints that the collections of Capodimonte transferred to Sicily in 1798 are worth a million sterling, and might, if deposited in a London bank or sold, secure her an income of £50,000 a year. There is a list of her debts in the Record Office which amounts to 154,000 ounces.[2] Bentinck requested Fagan on July 9 to tell the queen that he could not pay so large

[1] She was christened Maria Karoline Johanna Josephe Antonia.

[2] The Neapolitan ounce at this time was worth about 13s. 4d.

a sum of money without the authority of the English
Government, that he had given her advice which she
would not take, and that, although he should be glad
to extricate her, he did not see how it was to be
done. The queen replies on July 14 that she has no
objection to an application being made to the English
Government, who are, indeed, the cause of her misfortunes; and she encloses the list of her debts as
given above. On July 30 she writes a private letter
to Fagan, of which, however, there is an English
translation in the Record Office, that she has persuaded the king to seek an interview with Bentinck,
which she trusts will improve the relations between
them. An account of what passed is given in a letter
from the queen to Fagan of August 4.

I beg you, without fail, to return me either the whole
letter, or at all events as soon as possible the annexed
paper. We live in doubtful times when no one should be
trusted, and I wish this confidential paper to be returned.
I return you many thanks for your letter of August 3, and
I am much obliged to you for the interest which you
evince for me on every occasion. I saw Lord William
Bentinck on the 1st of this month; I had great difficulty
in persuading the king to the interview, which I had
conceived would be useful. The conversation between
the king, Lord William, and Mr. Lamb lasted three complete hours, during which I was in the greatest agony,
knowing well that everything depended upon the result
of it; from its length I was induced to flatter myself that
the conference would be amicable, but it had scarcely
finished when the king removed these hopes. I confess
I was annoyed at finding myself at dinner in company
with those who had effected our destruction and dis-

honour, and as I am of a candid and sincere disposition, I dare say that my looks betrayed my feelings; during dinner, however, reflection soothed them, and when it was over, I begged Lord William and Mr. Lamb to walk into my room, where he sat down without uttering a word; a repulsive silence. I begged him to speak to me, and for the honour of Great Britain to consider what might be beneficial to her ancient ally; he continued mute as a stone, and at last I said to him that I had a right to expect that he would converse with me on friendly terms; he then loosed his tongue, and in the most bitter manner, with a sarcastic smile, he assured me that he never expected and certainly never wished either to see me or to speak with me, and this he urged with a tone and manner which was not customary, even among equals, before the general revolution of Europe. We passed then to the subject of the parliament, and he constantly repeated, without entering into any detail, *il faut sanctionner*. I took the trouble, by an exercise of patience which shortens one's life, to explain to him that he did not defend the rights of the king, his ally, at whose Court he was accredited, to which he answered " that he had used every means in his power to defend the nation." I said that only a few factious individuals were defended by his Lordship's measures; that the nation, the provinces, the second order, and the people, all cried out against this aristocracy; he replied " that the whole were happy and content, and that only a few alterations were required to introduce the English constitution." I said that I did not know what his Court would say, finding that, instead of rendering Sicily happy, he had established a destructive aristocracy, which had disgusted and perhaps revolutionised, the provinces, and facilitated the introduction of the French. He asked me, in a tone of irony and reproof, what I should say if the parliament had unanimously asked for the English constitution: I with perfect composure answered that I should say, I consider it a meanness in a nation already having a constitution to seek for another, but that I should prefer the English constitution to those fifteen articles, a shapeless machine, which had deprived the king of all that belongs to him, of his authority, his revenue, honour, and his pre-eminence, restoring and confirming at the same time the oppressive baronial rights. He continued to say it was the best, and I, not being able to concur with him, said that I was resolved to depart from this island, but in one of our own frigates, which was competent to my honour. In short, Lord William was stern toward me, manifesting ill-will and spite, and I see that for me all is useless; I am miserably rewarded for enthusiastic Anglomania. These are facts. Reflection upon what would be said in England, when it becomes known that she is the protector of aristocracy, induced him to send to tell the vicar that if he would accept the English constitution entire, he would in that case sustain the veto against the other demands of the parliament. With this assurance the prince came on August 2, and laying a paper before the king, he, constrained by necessity and by the urgent circumstances of the case, subscribed it. I send it you in the greatest confidence. I have told you only facts, and I abstain from mentioning my reflections, which are very painful, and the truth of which time will prove. My health, respecting which you show so much anxiety, suffers much; sleep has forsaken me, and the air disagrees with me, but I have not time to think of those things; my mind is tortured to see our ancient allies behaving towards us in a manner which our enemies, the French, never even contemplated, during the two long periods that they sojourned in the provinces of Puglia.

I now propose to give information of all that is passing to England, and to our other allies, and to request an asylum in my country, where I may end my unhappy life in peace, at a distance from the infamous cabals and intrigues of this place. Were it not for the absolute impossibity of maintaining myself, I would not accept of a penny from the nation who have behaved so ill to us; but I am a mother, I have children, and cannot cut short my days; I must therefore wait for the pension which our rebellious subjects shall assign to us. All these are melancholy reflections. I cannot, in honesty, withdraw myself from unhappy Sicily, without discharging my debts; I conceive myself honourable, and I wish to conclude my unhappy career as such.

I am near my unfortunate and honoured husband, a king of fifty-four years' standing, a true lover of the happiness of his subjects, perfectly just, a true and sincere friend and ally, and after all treated as he has been by his subjects and allies! But he possesses a strong sense of religion, which affords him consolation. I cannot deny that I feel this treatment very sensibly, nor do I think we are yet at the end of our miseries, they have gone too far to stop. We have lost Sicily, and every reasonable hope of recovering Naples. All is lost to us. This is a melancholy but just picture of our situation; I trace it for a friend, whom I have known to be honest, loyal, and sincere, which I shall ever remember with gratitude. A thousand compliments to your wife and your daughter, and believe me with esteem your grateful friend, CAROLINA.

The criticisms of the queen upon the new constitution were not too severe. The sudden abolition of feudal and other customary rights of property caused great discontent amongst the persons affected by it. A large bottle full of gunpowder and pieces of iron was thrown on the night of August 12 into the House of Parliament. By an accident it failed to explode. It was attributed to the Duke of Crano, who afterwards confessed the crime; but it was an expression of the general discontent. Many of those best able to judge thought that the idea of forcing a constitution similar to that of England on a foreign people was absurd, that many parts of it were not suitable to the continent. An Englishman, writing from Palermo on August 26, 1812, says: "To copy a law verbatim and to apply it to a people in totally different circumstances is to counteract and spoil the very effect we intended. . . . In one moment is overturned the whole fabric of an ancient government which has existed nearly ten centuries, without opening one of its records nor examining the foundations on which it rested, and with the same precipitation it is voted that the British constitution is to be adopted. . . . Lord William Bentinck in allowing such resolutions to be formed has proved himself extremely unacquainted with two material points—the Sicilian Government which he has overturned with a view of reforming, and the British constitution which he thinks he has been establishing." Blaquière tells us, writing in the middle of July, that he had received a number of letters from Sicily which all concurred in representing the state of the island, if possible, more deplorable than ever, and that every one from the monarch to the peasant was opposed to the new arrangements.

On August 19 the queen writes to Fagan as follows:—

I have received your consoling and honest letter, and I am infinitely obliged to you for it, but the day of August

19 has extinguished in me every hope of relief, and has overwhelmed me with the deepest despair. For two days the vicar has been writing the most violent letters, saying that he wishes to act as he pleases, or that he will throw up the charge, and leave the king to contend for himself; moreover, he gives a most frightful description of the great violence of Bentinck, and says that if the king returns to authority he will be constrained to act in the same way, adding a long detail of the most unpleasant subjects in order to dissuade him from returning to the Government. Cacamo and Cassaro have come here this morning: the latter has represented in such a dreadful light the contest which is inevitable with Bentinck, and the necessity of conceding everything immediately, that the king, losing himself through consternation, has confirmed and even exceeded the powers which he gave to the vicar on January 16; he has conceded to Bentinck seven thousand men, to be paid from our subsidy, and has given him full power over the Royal household; in short, the king has not entirely abdicated, he has done the same thing, and we may say, *consummatum est*. For my part I feel their malice towards us more than ever; every sacred duty of probity should induce Bentinck to arrange the payment of my debts at the expense of England, in which case he will obtain my departure from Sicily, but I will not go while I have a grain of debt, wishing to conclude honestly, having lived so. It appears to me that they have already done us mischief enough in thus perfidiously depriving us of a kingdom, and in using every sort of infamous intrigue to annihilate us entirely. We are ruined and undone, at the mercy of fifty revolutionary regicides, who will make us grieve while they are protected by the minister of Great Britain, our ally, who supports the regicides, and who has destroyed the principles of a son who has hitherto been obedient and dutiful, but now a traitor and a revolutionary! In short,

he has rendered me truly miserable, and I see no hope except in my immediate departure from Sicily, otherwise they will commit the most barbarous outrage against my innocent person. I confess to you that my mind is agonised. I foresaw every misfortune, I perceive that the parliament is literally attacking the sovereign authority. I cannot express my affliction and despair, which I am assured proceed from the minister of our faithful ally. Adieu.

Believe me your good mistress,
CAROLINA.

On September 13 Bentinck sent a letter to the king at the Ficuzza saying that he had positive orders from his Government that the queen was to take no part in public affairs. The queen interpreted it to mean that she must leave Sicily, and that night she had a fit of apoplexy. Bentinck remarks upon it: "It has recurred within two days of the time when she suffered a similar attack last year. Upon this occasion the fit has been much less severe. She was yesterday [September 14] very much recovered." He says also that her abstinence from public affairs can only be accomplished by her leaving Sicily. Such is the unanimous opinion of the public as well as of all the ministers as well as of the prince himself. "But desirable as this event would be, I do feel very great reluctance to enforce it at the queen's time of life; in the state of her health, and at this advanced season, such an act might appear cruel. But I mean to require that her Majesty shall fix her residence at a greater distance from Palermo, where, as the king will not accompany her, her influence will no longer be exercised in that quarter where it has been always so pernicious."

In the middle of September the prince was attacked by a serious illness. The account which Bentinck gives in a letter to Castlereagh of October 9 is so characteristic that it is worth while to print it in full.

Palermo, October 4, 1812.

My Lord,—I have to acquaint your Lordship that the hereditary prince has been attacked by a severe illness, which for some time threatened the most serious consequences; it began by spasms in the stomach, which it was apprehended from their commencement might be dangerous. On September 22 the queen came to the palace, and the day after the violence of the attacks was so much increased that the greatest apprehensions were entertained as to the result. This state continued with little intermission during the four following days. The symptoms were of a nature so like poison that it was generally believed arsenic had been administered; and such is the opinion entertained of her Majesty's character, that the general suspicion was fixed upon the queen. During the agonies of the prince, she sat by his bedside without either speaking or moving a feature. When the physicians declared his life to be in danger, the prince wept, and her Majesty shed tears, requesting those present would observe how much she was affected. On the physicians pronouncing their opinion that the prince had taken poison, she turned to him and said, "Have I ever been deficient in affection to you?" to which he answered, "No, madam." The result of the illness has destroyed every suspicion of it having been caused by poison, but it is certain that the impression was very strong upon the mind of the prince himself. In a conversation with the

Prince Belmonte during his illness he did not disguise the suspicion, and in speaking of the Prince Belmonte, who has lately suffered much from ill-health, he said, "*Pauvre Belmonte, nous sommes attaqués par la même maladie.*" The queen herself imprudently contributed to give currency to this report, with the view of throwing the odium upon the exiled barons, whom she accused of wishing by this means to obtain the regency for the Duke of Orleans. Her Majesty did not scruple to tell the hereditary prince that he was reported to have been poisoned by the Duke of Orleans, and said to the Duchess of Orleans that it was supposed to have been done either by herself or by the duke. On the evening of the 26th the prince's danger was so imminent that the king was sent for from the Ficuzza, and arrived the next morning; in the interview with the prince he testified the greatest interest and affection for him; they mutually shed tears, and it was not till the morning of the 28th, when his Royal Highness was considered out of danger, that his Majesty left Palermo, and was followed by the queen the day after. The hereditary prince has since retired to a country house near Palermo, and his health has considerably improved. This removes the apprehensions which were excited by his illness at a time when the residence of her Majesty about the person of the king had so strengthened her dominion over his mind, that the loss of the prince might have been expected to be the signal for the adoption of new measures the most inimical to our interests and policy. But I regret to say that the prince's close attention to the details of business, which his habits of suspicion prevent him from entrusting to his ministers, added to the anxiety he has experienced from the opposition of his parents, and the painful struggles which her Majesty has lost no opportunity of exciting between his filial piety and the duties of his situation, have so far impaired a constitution not naturally strong, that he is by no means to be considered as a good life, and the recurrence of the same attack, which there is much reason to apprehend, may suddenly plunge us into difficulties and embarrassments from which we have so narrowly escaped.

I have the honour to be, my Lord, your Lordship's most obedient humble servant, W. C. BENTINCK.

Surely a statesman with such deep-seated prejudices against the queen was entirely unfit for the delicate situation in which he was placed.[1] A letter of the queen to Fagan of September 28 expresses great distress at the calumnies of which she had been the object, and unbounded confidence in Fagan's friendship and affection.

A letter of Bentinck's to Castlereagh of October 24 gives a very naïve and full account of his efforts to get the queen away from Palermo. On September 13 he wrote to the king on the subject, but received no answer. Then came the illness of the prince. The arrival of the queen at Palermo to see her son stimulated Lord William to new efforts. He sent for the Marquis de St. Clair, a friend of the Royal family, and told him his difficulty. On the 24th Prince Cassaro brought him a message from the king, saying that he had heard Bentinck was going to write to him again, and that he did not wish to receive any more impertinent letters from him, but desired to see the proofs he had against the queen, whom he wished he would leave quiet. After some conversation, Bentinck insisted not only that the queen should go away,

[1] The hereditary prince died November 8, 1830, at the age of fifty-three, the father of seven sons and seven daughters.

but that the date of her departure should be fixed. Cassaro saw the queen, who replied that she would stay with the king till the spring, when they would both leave the island. This was at the very time when the prince was in the greatest danger. On October 9 Bentinck wrote a letter to the king; three days afterwards it was returned by the hereditary prince unopened. In the letter which enclosed it the prince declared that the queen had never interfered with him. Bentinck then went to Circello, the ex-minister, who refused to interfere. On October 15 Bentinck, undaunted by these rebuffs, rode down to the Ficuzza, twenty-three miles distant, taking with him a letter for the king. He had not been ten minutes in the antechamber when he saw the queen going into the king's room. Father Cacamo, the king's confessor, then appeared and said that the king could not receive Bentinck unless he promised not to enter upon business. At the same time the king sent a dignified message:—

The orders of your Court direct you to require the queen's absence from Palermo, her removal from the seat of government, her non-interference with affairs of State. His Majesty has secured these points, has resigned the reins of government to the vicar-general, and considering himself as a private individual has retired from business, taking under especial guidance and protection her Majesty his wife. Being under his protection, he is responsible for her actions. His separation from her Majesty cannot be admitted, but in order to remove all doubt of her interference in State affairs it is intended to transfer her abode to Santa Margherita the first day in November, there to remain until after the shooting season, and in the spring of the year her Majesty proposes retiring to the continent.

Bentinck then sent Cacamo to ask whether he was to understand that the king would not admit him to his presence. The king returned answer that he was still king, and that it did not suit his convenience to receive Bentinck. He would let him know his intentions through Prince Cassaro, but that he would never be separated from the queen. Bentinck then said that if he did not receive an answer in two days he should have to adopt other measures. The confessor, alarmed at his violence, went again to the king, and after a considerable delay returned with the reply that his Majesty would receive no peremptory terms, and that he would never be separated from the queen. The confessor offered an interview with the queen, but that he declined, "as it would be painful to both parties, and would not be attended with any advantage." After Bentinck's departure the king sent for Princes Cassaro and Circello, and they brought back word that the queen was going to Santa Margherita, about forty miles from Palermo, and intended going to Vienna in the spring. Bentinck exacted an assurance in writing that the queen would remain at Santa Margherita and not return to Ficuzza. The king afterwards disclaimed the authority of the two noblemen to give any such assurance. A letter of Queen Caroline's to Fagan of October 9 declares that she will never desert her husband, but will do her duty as wife, mother, and honest woman, and that in the fulfilment of what she thought right she was ready to suffer *anything*. Another letter of October 31 is very touching. She is full of gratitude to Fagan. If Bentinck had only had more knowledge of mankind, and had acted towards the king with uprightness and cordiality, things would have gone differently. She expresses a great respect for Lady William Bentinck, and will not invite her into the savage desert of Ficuzza; but as the queen is going for ten days to Palermo, before her departure for her new exile, she hopes to have a visit from her. She is indignant at the letter which Bentinck has written to the prince. "I am sorry for his Lordship, who, being deceived with respect to me, persecutes me in a manner so indecent and so prejudicial to the dignity of the British nation and its good faith towards a faithful ally."

After paying a last visit to Palermo the queen retired with her husband to Santa Margherita, a lonely country house in the neighbourhood of Girgenti. All provisions had to be brought on the backs of mules. The queen herself was borne thither in a litter, and soon after her arrival was dangerously ill. Husband and wife were sorely pinched for means. In December they removed to Castelvetrano in the south of the island, about eighty miles from Palermo. The removal of the queen did not expedite the working of the constitution. On December 7 Bentinck complains to Prince Belmonte that the acts passed in the last session of parliament had not yet received the sanction of the vicar-general. About the same time he suggested to the English

Government that they should facilitate the queen's departure from the island by granting her an allowance on that condition. He cynically adds: "The state of her Majesty's health is such that she would in all probability receive the allowance in question for a very few years."[1] The home Government, who were in constant communication with Prince Castelcicala, the Sicilian minister in London, were anxious on the one hand to escape the odium of coercing the queen, and on the other to maintain the full authority of Bentinck. Then Castlereagh, writing on December 5, admits that he has told Castelcicala that the Government do not insist on the queen leaving the island provided she keeps aloof from public affairs. However, on February 9, 1813, he writes to Bentinck, that in consequence of the new representations he has received from him he has informed Castelcicala that the queen must leave the island, and that he proposes she should go to Vienna rather than to Sardinia. At the same time he warns Bentinck that all expression of using force must be avoided, and that no restraint must be placed on the return of the queen. On January 4 the queen came to the Ficuzza, which Bentinck immediately complained of as a breach of agreement. He called on Princes Cassaro and Circello to enforce their written undertaking, but it will be remembered that the king had repudiated their promise as soon as he heard of its being given. The Duke of Orleans (afterwards Louis-Philippe) took the opportunity of giving the hereditary princes some good advice. The best plan was to

[1] Bentinck to Castlereagh, December 10, 1812.

submit to Bentinck; the English Government would have their way, and would make Sicily subordinate to their political views. If they had intended to take the island, they would have done so long ago. The Royal family were entirely dependent on the English Government. How could it be otherwise when they received a large English subsidy, and were protected by a large English force? "Make yourself," said the duke, "*l'homme des Anglais*: if you oppose them, you can do them no harm, you will only irritate and annoy them, and you may lose your crown, whereas an opposite course will secure you peace, happiness, and prosperity." The position of the prince was a very uncomfortable one. He was anxious for more power or for none at all. Let the king either abdicate or resume the vicariat; the present state of affairs was unendurable.

It was soon to be put an end to. On March 9 the king appeared suddenly at the palace in Palermo, announced that his health was recovered, and that he assumed the reins of government. He sent for the ministers and told them that he only intended to sanction such parts of the constitution as were analogous to that of England. Princes Belmonte and Cassaro said that the hereditary prince had taken great pains to ascertain the analogy and to adhere to it strictly. The king said he was sure that it was otherwise. On the same day the queen left the Ficuzza for Castelvetrano. On Prince Belmonte remonstrating, the king said that Bentinck might do what he pleased. Europe would judge between them. He was determined not to give way. In the evening the king went in state to the cathedral, where a *Te Deum* was performed for the recovery of his health and his resumption of the government. Masses of people were assembled. The king was received with acclamations even in the church. Two days later there was a stormy interview between Bentinck and the king. The minister said that the English Government would never permit the constitution to be destroyed. The word "permit" made the king very angry. "I am a simple man," said Bentinck. "I am more simple than you," broke in the king, "I am more honest than you." Bentinck bowed, and the king corrected himself. "I am honest, you may be also." Bentinck referred to the old story of correspondence with the enemy. "Neither I nor my Government," said the king, "have ever been faithless to the alliance. I cannot listen to such language; write what you have to say," and hastily left the room. There was great agitation in the streets. Cries of "*Viva il re!*" were mixed with shouts of "*Fuori gli Inglesi!*" On March 13 Bentinck sent a letter to Prince Belmonte to say that unless a guarantee were given that the new constitution would be observed he should consider the alliance at an end. The letter was presented to the king on the 14th, and he prepared an answer on the day following. Belmonte declined to present, and with Ruggiero Settimo resigned his office. Bentinck then stated that another day's delay would be fatal. The Duke of Orleans held long conversations with his father-in-law. On the 16th Bentinck sent his ultimatum to the king by Mr.

Lamb, insisting on the establishment of the vicariat, with a promise from the king not to resume the government without the consent of England, and an undertaking that the queen should leave the island. The first point was conceded readily enough, but there were difficulties about the second. After considerable pressure the king said that he would next morning send positive orders to the queen to go immediately to Cagliari, but that if she refused he could not compel her. A promise was then extorted from him that if Bentinck used force to carry out the king's orders the king would not oppose it. Next day the king retired to his country house at Colli.

It is difficult to criticise these transactions. There is no proof whatever that the king intended to destroy the constitution; indeed, his professions were of an entirely opposite character. Even if the queen had advised him to resume the government whilst she remained at Castelvetrano she could have little influence over its deliberations. It is difficult to resist the conclusion that Bentinck acted both with passion and prejudice; indeed, his feeling towards the queen amounted to a monomania. On March 23 the country was without a Government, the king was in the country, the prince had no power assigned to him, and the ministers had resigned their offices. "I have determined," writes Bentinck on that date with something of vindictiveness, "to require the queen's immediate departure from the island; she is the sole cause of all the delay, difficulty, and embarrassment that have so extraordinarily impeded the establishment of the new constitution. Her Majesty will go to Cagliari." Yet in the very next sentence he complains that the acts of the last parliament which terminated five months ago have not yet been sanctioned, which could only be the fault of the hereditary prince and not of the queen.

On the very date of this despatch Bentinck sent Lieutenant-General Macfarlane to the queen to tell her that she must leave the island as soon as possible. At the same time he marched three battalions of English troops, with cavalry and artillery, to Corleone, in the centre of the island, about forty miles distant from Palermo. Macfarlane's instructions were to listen to no excuses, to insist upon her going to Cagliari, and to secure her departure in a week or ten days at the farthest, as soon as the ships have arrived. He is to avoid force if possible, but "if unfortunately her Majesty will not consent to your proposal, you will act promptly and decidedly with the troops at your disposal." On March 25, the morning after his arrival, Macfarlane saw the queen. She at first received his message with composure and indifference, she disputed Bentinck's authority, and said that she would leave Sicily at her own time, in a Sicilian ship, with officers of her own nomination. Macfarlane then hinted at the employment of force, and mentioned the march of the troops. She became deeply affected, said that she was in the worst state of health, and could not move without danger to her life, that she had lately been seized with a spitting of blood, and that it would be adding cruelty to insult to use force against her at such a moment.

On the following day she was extremely affected, but composed and softened. She conjured Macfarlane not to bring the troops into Castelvetrano. The general pressed her to fix a day for her departure. After great pressure she said, "I give my honour that I shall be ready to depart by the middle of April, but I hope I shall have the whole of that month, because I shall then have better weather, but I must go to Trieste and not to Cagliari." Macfarlane repeated that he had no authority to prevent the troops from coming to Castelvetrano, and he left the queen " excessively agitated and in a flood of tears." Macfarlane begs Bentinck to change the place of her destination from Cagliari to Trieste or Fiume; she will then go much more quietly. At the same time he orders the troops to advance to Santa Margherita, but he fears that too much pressure may bring about a "return of the *convulsions* to which her Majesty is subject, which may retard our proceedings." On the day of this interview the queen drew up a dignified paper saying that after mature reflection she had determined to retreat to the only country suitable to her, being compelled by the minister of his ally, the King of Great Britain, to leave her family, her husband, and her dominions, but she must be treated with the respect due to her rank. She demands as conditions: (1) a frigate commanded by officers of her choice and the convoy of a ship-of-war; (2) a promise to take her to the nearest port from which she could reach Vienna; (3) a satisfactory arrangement for paying her allowance; (4) the payment of her debts by the Sicilian Government; (5) the payment of the wages of those who accompany her; (6) the sending of Prince Moliterno to Vienna to prepare for her arrival. She promises if these conditions are fulfilled to embark in the month of April, she does not mind from which port.

By March 29 Bentinck had received Castlereagh's despatch preferring that the queen should go to Vienna, but for some reason he continued to insist that she should first go to Cagliari or Malta. This formed the subject of a conversation between Macfarlane and the queen on the evening of March 31. "Why," she said, "should Lord Bentinck wish me to go to Cagliari, when Lord Castlereagh has decided that I should go to Vienna?" "The queen now asked me whether a letter from herself to Lady William Bentinck would have any effect in obtaining a change of sentiment in your Lordship. I answered that I had every reason to think that you were fixed in your determination." On April 4 the queen learnt that Bentinck conceded this point. She was ready to go by Lissa or Constantinople, but she could not start till the 25th (the Sunday after Easter), when her Easter devotions would be completed.

On April 8 General Macfarlane arrived at Palermo, bringing a letter addressed to Bentinck by the queen. It was couched in the same dignified tone as others which we have quoted, and asserted her willingness to leave Sicily if a proper allowance were made and proper arrangements provided for her journey. The crown prince, to whom the letter was shown, wrote :—

My feelings of filial affection, attachment, and of gratitude to a tender mother, induce me to request that you will use every possible means to mitigate the pain of this separation from her family which your Government requires, considering it necessary to the common interests. You should consider, my Lord, that a queen at her advanced age cannot undertake so long and so difficult a journey without certain comforts and conveniences which, even upon the most economical scale, require an expense proportionate to the length of the journey.

He goes on to express a hope that this may be provided by the generosity of the English Government. Bentinck eventually determines to allow her 1,000 ounces a month, £8,000 a year, paying the first year in advance, the continuance of the pension to be conditional on her good behaviour.

On April 16 the queen wrote a farewell letter of twenty pages to Mr. Fagan. It was written in French and signed Charlotte, and so was evidently intended to be shown to Bentinck. There is, indeed, a complete copy of it in the Foreign Office. In it she complains of the cruel conduct of her allies the English, and of the baseless calumnies of which she has been the victim. She relates the whole story of her political life; how her influence with the king, which is now thrown in her teeth, was employed to prevent him from acceding to the *pacte de famille* which cost her the favour of her father-in-law Charles III., and of Louis XV. and Louis XVI. In the war of the revolution Naples had supported the cause of the allies with a large fleet and army. She had received the English fleet on its way to Egypt, and had undergone great sufferings in 1798 for her attachment to the English and Russians. In 1804 Naples suffered from the breach of the peace of Amiens, but the queen had been faithful, as long as she was able to remain so, to the cause of the allies. She had received them on November 19, 1805, yet when they departed in January, 1806, they caused every kind of damage. In Sicily the strong places were occupied by the English troops. The queen, although seeking to be a good ally to the English, did not wish Sicily to become an English province. For seven years she had suffered nothing but calumny and persecution. The rest of the letter is occupied with the details of the journey, and with a request that something will be done for the Neapolitan pensioners who are dependent upon her. The letter is reasonable and dignified, but is open to the charge that its principal object was to extort money from the English Government. Indeed, she asks for the loan of a million sterling, to be repaid by instalments in eight or ten years. We know already the sum which Bentinck was ready to accord.

The absolute necessity of finding funds for the queen's journey and the incidence of some military operations against the Italian islands appear to have caused a certain amount of delay, which was further extended by the queen's illness. On Monday, May 15, she wrote to Fagan that she is in bed with a very severe attack of fever, and that the next day she will summon the English and Palermitan doctors to show that she is not shamming. On the 18th Dr. Calvert, the physician to the forces, visited the queen in conjunction with Dr. Greco, her private physician, and certified that she was ill of an intermittent fever, which had continued five days and which prevented her from embarking. He trusted that she might recover in a few days. Bentinck was not at all disposed to receive this opinion without question. He wrote to Macfarlane that the queen would certainly not leave Sicily if she could help it; that her body and mind were so deranged by the use of opium that a stranger might be mistaken as to the state of her health, and that this is the reason for her calling in Dr. Calvert. Bentinck is so certain of this that the general is "positively directed to require her Majesty's embarkation whenever Dr. Calvert shall state that it can be effected without danger to her Majesty's life. Public considerations imperiously demand that feelings of mere personal convenience should not be listened to." If the queen is too ill to go to Constantinople, she can sail to Cagliari or Zante. If the queen is quite unable to travel, Castelvetrano must be occupied by British troops, all the "bad subjects" by which she is at present surrounded must be forced to leave the island, and the queen's communications, "personal as well as written," must be vigilantly watched, and must, if necessary, be placed under military control. This unfeeling letter is written on May 24, just after Bentinck had heard that the queen, although following Dr. Calvert's treatment exactly, was mending very slowly, and that a squadron of Algerine men-of-war was cruising off Girgenti.

At the beginning of June, Bentinck left Sicily for

the island of Ponza, where he was to meet an emissary from Murat, who was at that time contemplating defection from Napoleon. Bentinck appears to have regarded with favour the surrender of Naples to Murat, but refused to give up Sicily. At the same time Napoleon ordered Murat to have 20,000 men in readiness for the invasion of Sicily in conjunction with the Toulon fleet.[1] Bentinck was of opinion that half that number could conquer the island, and Sir Edward Pellew declared that he could not prevent the Toulon fleet from evading him, although he might be able to overtake it in Naples harbour before Murat's troops could embark. Thus at the very time of his leaving the island the queen was between the double danger of the French and the English. Peace and war were equally fatal to her dynasty; the only question seemed to be whether she would lose one of her crowns or both. Lord Wellington's reply to Bentinck is characteristic: "In answer to your Lordship's despatch, I have to observe that I conceive the island of Sicily is at present in no danger whatever." The account of the queen's final departure is contained in a despatch from Lord Montgomerie to Lord Castlereagh, June 19, 1813. Helfert[2] states that she paid a last visit to Palermo, which appears to be contradicted by Montgomerie's evidence. The English vessels had to go round to Mazzara on account of the Algerine squadron mentioned above. The queen stayed at Mazzara from June 5 to June 14 "engaged in religious devotions," Whitsunday falling that year

[1] Napier's *Peninsular War*, v. 434.
[2] Helfert, p. 534.

on June 6 and Trinity Sunday on June 13. On Monday, the 14th, at eleven o'clock, after having heard mass and received the benediction in the cathedral, she walked down to the beach accompanied by all the Chapter in their full robes and carrying lighted torches. She entered the boat of the English man-of-war *Unité*, Captain Chamberlayne steering. In her suite were her son Prince Leopold, the Prince of Hesse Philippsthal, the Countess San Marco, and the Marquis St. Clair. At four o'clock the vessels set sail, and, the wind being favourable, they were soon out of sight.

We must follow the actors in this history a little farther. The absence of the queen made matters no better, but, if possible, worse than before. Four days after her departure from Mazzara there was a popular rising in Palermo, and the Belmonte Ministry was overthrown, to be replaced by men more devoted to the crown prince. Bentinck returned from Spain on October 4 and attended a council on the 9th. The parliament was to meet next day, but Bentinck insisted on proroguing it until he had time to confer with the majority of the Commons. This step was hardly in accordance with the traditions of the British constitution. When parliament met, the ministers, being found in a minority, were dismissed by Bentinck's advice, and a few days afterwards the parliament was dissolved. Bentinck then issued a proclamation that "until the glorious work of the constitution so happily begun in the parliament of 1812 shall have been regularly completed," he shall govern the kingdom by martial law. He had now found out what he might have discovered earlier, that Sicily was not fit for self-government in the English sense, and that the difficulties of carrying it out were not caused by the queen, but by the inherent weakness of those entrusted with power. On his return from Spain he sees " a degree of alienation towards us on the part of the people. Experience has shown the weakness and incapacity of the country. Among the higher orders there is no courage, no steadiness, very little instruction, and no knowledge of public business. Among the lower there exist a general distrust and hatred of the higher ranks, no good faith and no public spirit." " The prince himself is the weakest of his subjects." The late ministers, " the best men in the country, have altogether failed ; their failure arose from their own personal weakness." The people are " clamorous for all the advantages of freedom, but nobody will submit to the sacrifice, nobody will pay or serve ; this is, shortly, the state of the country."

The daughter of Maria Theresa would have read these sentiments with full approval, but would have wished that wisdom had come a little earlier for her own sake. She reached Zante on her journey of exile on June 19, and left on August 3. A fortnight later her frigate anchored in the roadstead of Tenedos. Here she was delayed nearly a month by the objections made to her frigate sailing up the Dardanelles, and she did not arrive at Constantinople till September 13. After many changes of plan, and much interruption from bad weather, she reached Odessa in a small sailing boat on November 3 and underwent forty days' quarantine. During this delay she heard the welcome news of the battle of Leipzig. She left Odessa on December 18 and travelled by Nicolaieff and the Ukraine to Podolia, where she was entertained at Christmas by Count Potocki and his charming wife. On January 7, 1814, she touched the soil of her own country, and reached Vienna on February 2. The first week of her sojourn must have been cheered by the news of the victory of the allies in France, of the abdication of Napoleon, and of the peace of Paris. Her return to Sicily and Naples now seemed secured. When all danger from the side of Napoleon was past, the English had no more interest in Naples. On July 6 Ferdinand IV. again took to himself the reins of power, to the delight of the populace, and with the full approval of Bentinck. Bentinck's successor A'Court complained that not a day passed without a flagrant violation of the constitution; but Castlereagh had the good sense to reply to him, that the English could not think of supporting the constitution by force of arms. "We must let the king now administer his own Government, and our minister, I conceive, must try to withdraw himself from the character he has lately filled of being head of a party." On August 19 the Sicilian frigate *Minerva* accompanied by a British man-of-war sailed from Palermo for Trieste, to bring back Queen Caroline and her son Leopold to their own country. But fate had ordained otherwise. On the morning of September 8 the queen was found senseless on the floor of her bed-chamber, her hand stretched out to pull the bell, and her lips opened to utter that cry for help which no one was to hear.

The following conversation took place between General Donkin and the French General Goldemar, February 25, 1812. Donkin had been charged with establishing an exchange of prisoners and had come over to Messina to ratify it.

G. Ma foi, il faut avouer, Général, que vous avez bien mené, et fait bien éclater l'affaire de ces Messieurs que vous avez dans la Citadelle. Dites-moi un peu, quand est-ce que l'on décidera de leur sort ?

D. Vraiment, M. le Général, je n'en sais rien. Nous attendons incessamment les ordres de Lord William Bentinck là-dessus, et nous sommes également prêts à les fusiller ou à les pendre, comme Son Excellence ordonnera.

G. Bah ! vous ne ferez ni l'un ni l'autre. Sitôt que j'ai vu que ces maladroits n'étoient pas pendus tout de suite, j'ai dit à Manhès : " Je te dis bien, mon ami, que Lord Bentinck ne punira pas de mort ces gens-là. C'est un fier calculateur que ce diable de Bentinck, et il a quelque objet en vue avec la Cour ; il pardonnera à ces gens pour obtenir quelque chose de plus de la Cour." Mais dites-moi, Général, ce coquin de Giuffré (here on pronouncing his name he burst out into a long string of oaths and execrations against our faithful Giuffré, stamping, and a good deal agitated) oh ! ce villain-là—malpeste ! s'il fût venu seulement une fois de plus chez nous, il auroit été fusillé. Depuis plusieurs jours je le soupçonnois, et j'ai fait voir à Manhès que ce B— là nous jouait ; ah le sac. . . . (more oaths and execrations) ; mais, Général, comment est-ce que vous ne payez pas cet homme-là après le bon service qu'il vous a rendu ? Il se plaint à tout le monde de vous, comme il faisoit de Manhès, qu'il n'étoit pas assez payé. Il ne faut pas imaginer cependant que ce coquin vous soit absolument fidèle ; il vous a trompé en certaines choses—et vraiment trompé, je vous l'assure, foi de militaire—il vous a trompé—il ne vous a pas tout dit et à présent il se récrie contre vous et dit que vous le payez fort mal.

D. Quant à cela, Général, il a bien raison de dire qu'il n'est pas payé *par nous*, mais sûrement il ne se *plaint* point de cela. Nous ne lui avons jamais donné un sou—non, pas un sou—depuis neuf mois qu'il nous sert fidèlement, et pour deux raisons—

1° Parce que nous le faisions payer passablement bien par *vous autres* pour les contes bleus que je vous envoyais de tems en tems par ses mains—par exemple—pour la nouvelle que je vous envoyais de l'embarquement du 62me à Milazzo 3 jours *après son départ*, et quand j'étois bien sûr que le coup seroit frappé sur vos côtes—vous avez payé à notre Giuffré pour ce joli morceau quatre-vingts onnces—et le lendemain vous entendez que notre débarquement avoit eu lieu, et que nous avions fait le diable parmi vos barques et bâtiments à Palinuro.

La 2me raison que nous avions pour ne pas payer Giuffré étoit que ce brave jeune homme s'obstinoit toujours à refuser l'argent. Dix fois je lui ai offert 200, 300, 400 piastres, mais il refusoit toujours, disant : " Je sers ma patrie et les Anglois : quand j'aurai bien fini cette besogne, alors, donnez-moi, s'il vous plaît, un petit emploi et je serai content."—Voilà, Général, pourquoi nous ne l'avons pas payé.

G. (During this Goldemar was very impatient, but at last said) " Général, il faut avouer que nous avons été joliment joués (a long oath), mais joliment—il est inutile de vous le cacher—et je vous dirai franchement que ce fut un coup de foudre pour nous que cette arrestation—pour moi, j'en ai été *vraiment malade* pendant quinze jours ; j'avois la fièvre—et pour 24 heures, ni Manhès, ni moi, osions nous parler, l'un l'autre—ah ! ! ! F— (a long oath). (At these *Nuts* I could not help allowing rather a strong expression of gratification to escape me, but ended by saying) :—

D. Pardonnez-moi, mon Général, je regrette beaucoup d'avoir contribué à votre maladie—mais vous auriez fait autant pour moi; à présent vous n'avez qu'à établir une autre et plus sûre correspondance.

G. Ne craignez pas—allez! ne craignez pas—elle est déjà bien établie, et en très-bon train—nous sommes supérieurement servis; je vous assure —et par un moyen que vous ne connoîtrez pas si tôt. (After this he made a transition to Palermo—and after expressing himself in terms of the highest admiration of Lord W. Bentinck having accomplished what he had without bloodshed, he added): "Diable, j'ai toujours craint l'arrivée de votre Lord Bentinck. Dans son absence il y avoit vraiment de beaux moments—mais, de très-beaux moments. Si nous eussions pu décider cette villaine Cour à éclater; mais cette B——sse la Reine avec son machiavélisme a manœuvré, et manœuvré tant, que voilà ce diable de Bentinck que revient, et alors je dis à Manhès que l'affaire étoit finie : je me rappelle bien de ce Bentinck dans l'Italie—et à Vienne—Sacrebleu! comme il a mené son monde dans ce tems-là! il a fait des choses dans ce tems qui lui ont fait autant d'honneur comme négociateur qu'elles nous ont fait du tort—mais—dans son absence—nous aurions dû faire beaucoup si cette femme se fût décidée seulement : votre armée étoit perdue et la Sicile à nous!

D. Ah, mon Général, pas si vite—une armée de vingt mille hommes ne se perd pas si facilement.

G. Vingt mille hommes? bah! mais vous avez très peu de Cavallerie—bien peu. . . .

D. Je ne dis pas cela; mais soit—regardez nos montagnes : à quoi serviroit une Cavallerie nombreuse ici dans un tel pays? vous êtes trop bon militaire, et avez trop fait la guerre des montagnes, pour croire que nous manquons de Cavallerie pour le service que nous aurons à faire quand vous viendrez — mais — dites-moi — la Reine — ne savez-vous pas?—Oui, sans doute vous saurez pourquoi elle n'a pas voulu se décider—c'est-à-dire à entrer en correspondance avec vous : elle est Autrichienne, trop altière. Elle a trop de la fierté de sa famille pour vouloir entrer en correspondance avec un Roi vassal et subalterne tel que Murat : si elle daignoit entrer en correspondance de tout avec quelqu'une des couronnes de nouvelle date, ce seroit avec Buonaparte *lui-même*, et non pas avec un de ses Lieutenants—(I said this to pique him, and make him come out with something. It had the effect.)

G. (After swelling and blowing out his cheeks): Ah ! la vilaine menteuse—Ah ! la fière putain—*Elle dit cela* : elle ment ! F——, elle ment. Si elle dit qu'elle n'a pas voulu entrer en correspondance avec mon souverain ! (There the murder came out ; this really is pretty convincing.) Non, non—c'étoit son—machiavélisme qui a différé le coup jusqu'à l'arrivée de votre Bentinck—et alors il était trop tard : l'affaire est finie ; mais une chose je vous dirai : vous croyez avoir affermi votre pouvoir en Sicile, n'en croyez rien : tant que restera cette femme, vous ne serez jamais tranquilles—vous êtes trop loyaux— vous êtes trop faciles à croire. Je vous le répète, tant que restera en Sicile cette femme-là, elle vous tourmentera ; c'est un feu sous la cendre. Si vous voulez être tranquilles, chassez-la—envoyez-la à Vienne. (After this the conversation took a miscellaneous turn during which Goldemar spoke a great deal of Buonaparte, and mentioned some instances of his tyranny and injustice to *his army* which are truly astonishing. This gave me an opportunity of sounding him about Murat's feelings to Bonaparte.) He said :

G. Quant à l'Empereur, il n'est pas possible de lui être personnellement attaché—il est le plus grand égoïste qui existât jamais : cet homme ne pense, n'agit, ne vit que pour lui seul.

D. Je suis bien aise, Général, que sur le continent vous commencez à connoître son caractère ; il y a bien longtems que vous êtes les victimes de son ambition, qui n'a d'autre objet que son propre agrandissement. Je suis seulement étonné que ceux qu'il a décorés du titre de *Roi* ne désirent point l'être en *effet*—par exemple, Murat—comment diable peut-il se contenter comme il est—maître titulaire d'un beau pays, Rome sous sa main, et Eugène Beauharnois prêt à lui donner la main ? Je parle d'Eugène B—— parce qu'il n'est pas possible que ce jeune homme ne soit, à cœur, l'ennemi implacable de Buonaparte : un fils ne peut jamais pardonner l'insulte qu'a soufferte sa mère.

G. Oh!—mon Général (soupirant), que voulez-vous—il y a des obstacles—des liens—des rapports entre l'Empereur et mon maître !

D. Des liens ! des rapports ! vous vous moquez de moi, M. Goldemar—vous ne voulez pas très sûrement me prêcher la morale, et me parler de *liens*, de reconnoissance, de l'honneur—et tout cela, si nécessaire, en vérité entre nous autres en vie privée : vous ne voulez pas me parler de cela entre deux souverains, quand il s'agit de *l'indépendance* d'un d'eux ? Si vous raisonnez de cette manière, vous avez très peu observé tout ce qui s'est passé sur le continent depuis vingt ans.

G. Mais il faut avoir des *forces* pour une telle entreprise.

D. Ah ! pour cela, je ne m'en mêle pas. Ceux qui préfèrent l'indépendance à l'esclavage doivent penser aux moyens pour élever leurs peuples, et se fortifier contre leur dominateur; pour moi, je vous avouerai franchement, mais comprenez bien, je ne parle ni le langage de mon Gouvernement, ni de ma nation peut-être généralement, mais je parle de moi-même—mon propre sentiment est que j'aimerois mille fois mieux de voir Murat indépendant que vassal : s'il étoit indépendant, il deviendroit, malgré tous les préjugés, l'allié *naturel* de l'Angleterre. N'importe, soit-il Murat, soit-il un Bourbon—le *souverain* de Naples *indépendant*, ou se débattant pour son indépendance, devient, *de facto*, l'allié des Anglois : c'est contre la domination universelle de Buonaparte que nous nous battons —et tout homme qui a le courage de s'élever contre ce colosse a droit, non seulement à notre admiration, mais aussi à notre secours : comprenez bien, je parle théoriquement. Quant à mon Gouvernement, ou les Anglois en général, je ne sais pas s'ils seroient de mon opinion ; mais vous, Général — vous, dites-moi franchement, non pas comme François ou général napolitain, qu'est-ce que vous pensez de moi, politique ?

G. Oh! ma foi (after considerable luctation), il y a beaucoup de raison en ce que vous dites ; mais il y a des rapports—des difficultés. (He here fell into a silence of a quarter of an hour, the longest interval of *lingual* repose he enjoyed while here, and the conversation took another turn. He execrated war and, like every other French general I ever met with, prayed for peace that he might go and live quietly. I forgot to mention that in speaking of Murat's situation I observed to him that he could not be ignorant of Bonaparte's intention to transport him to Poland ; that Bonaparte was afraid of Murat's growing popularity at Naples, and that before long he would have his order to march.)

G. Pour cela, Général, ce changement n'aura très sûrement pas lieu : mon—le Roi ne souffrira pas cela, il a un caractère très ferme, et il y a un *point* au-delà duquel un homme ne veut que l'on le pousse. L'Empereur, nous le savons bien, a *envie de transplanter Murat*, et le projet a déjà été entamé ; mais il ne poussera pas l'affaire au bout : il sait de quoi le Roi est capable, et ne le poussera pas aux abois. (*Here* there is a thing to be seen ; a project of B's determined on, and which the victim is resolved to resist.) He mentioned the address with which Bonaparte had *again* put off war with Russia, and alluded to this as a thing *we must* be acquainted with. He did not speak of it as *news*, but as a thing we no doubt were well aware of.

The foregoing will give an idea of the *feeling* in Naples about that country, Bonaparte, and Sicily. All his conversation was in the same strain, more or less. He certainly spoke with very great freedom against Bonaparte, and entered so fully into the satire of some of the *Ambigus* he found in his bedroom in my house, that he sat up reading them, he told me, till two in the morning, and I gave him every number I had—about fifteen.

N.B.—The above, as is evident, is written at a gallop, without pains or correction. I hope it is legible. Goldemar has just left me, and this is the moment to fix his conversation: by to-morrow one-half would have evaporated. (Signed) R. DONKIN.

REPUBLICAN GOVERNMENT.

THERE is probably no question which deserves the attention of politicians at the present time so much as that of republican government. We are often told that England is practically a republic, that the monarchy is an antiquated institution which some day or other must disappear. If we are not already republicans, we regard a republic as an eventual necessity. Its realization is only a question of time. Some of us would wish to hasten that period; some of us to retard it; but we all regard it as our fate. We live in a democratic age, and the republic is the government best suited to a democracy. We accept the idea of it either with hope or with apprehension as best suits our temperament or our principles. If this idea of things is in any way true, it surely behoves us to consider what we mean by a republic, and by what practical means a republic can be introduced, or the government of one carried on. My object now is not to argue either for or against a republic; I shall discuss as little as possible whether England would be better governed under a republic or not. I only wish to suggest certain considerations with regard to republican government which must be taken into account before we seriously think of establishing one anywhere. I confine myself in the main to determining what is meant by a republican government, and what are, as far as history and experience teach us, the only possible forms under which a republic can exist.

I suppose that we mean by a republic a form of constitution in which the government is exercised by the voice of all for the benefit of all, in which all men are equal before the law, in which birth confers no privilege, and in which every one has a chance of rising to any position, even the highest. Such a government is inconsistent with the existence either of an hereditary monarch or an hereditary aristocracy. Such governments have always excited enthusiasm, and it is not easy at first sight to see where this enthusiasm has come from. It has been largely connected with the glamour which attaches to the histories of Greece and Rome. Greece is certainly for us the mother of literature and art; the Greeks were the first people who discussed political questions in a scientific manner. Aristotle was the first political philosopher worthy of the name. Marathon and Plato are watchwords of liberty; the world is even now better for the stand which a small handful of free Greeks made against the servile bands of barbarians hurled against them by a despot. Many of the Greek city States were republic, and we imagine that it is to this circumstance that the glory of the Hellenic world is due. But we must remember that Sparta was certainly not a republic, but a dual monarchy in form, and a close aristocracy in fact, and that Leonidas, who held the pass of Thermopylae with his three hundred, was a king. Aristotle also was the tutor of Alexander the Great; and the King of Macedonia, although much abused by Demosthenes, was largely instrumental in spreading Hellenic culture and civilization throughout the ancient world. Further, it may be considered doubtful how far even cities like Athens were republic in our modern sense. In the first place, they were cities, and cities of a limited size. Aristotle tells us that no city should be so large that the whole number of inhabitants cannot be addressed at the same time by a single man. They were also slave States, in which the slaves largely outnumbered the free population. Further, the idea of representation was unknown; none took part in the government except those who could be actually present in the assembly. Nor is it certain whether the best authorities in Greece would have agreed that a republic should be democratic, or that it was desirable to have a democracy at all. Aristotle classifies governments as the rule of the one, the few, and the many; but he says that each of these three forms may be either good or bad. Democracy he classes as a bad form along with oligarchy and tyranny; the good form of government by the many he calls *politeia*, a word which is translated into Latin by respublica, but is not represented by our word republic. The best translation of it is polity or government, that is, the well-ordered rule and the due subordination of interest on a popular basis in a city State. Therefore the republics of Greece, however much they may contribute to our just enthusiasm for freedom in general, do not help us much in deciding that a republic is the best form of government which mankind are capable of adopting. Nor is the example of Rome much more to the point. The Roman republic has indeed left a glorious name in history. It conquered the ancient world. It laid the foundation of the best system of jurisprudence which mankind has ever seen. It inaugurated a fabric of administration which has been a model to all those communities who have been destined by nature or by providence to establish an empire over subject peoples. In the darkest days of despotism patriots have always turned to the bright examples of Roman history, to heroes many of them legendary, who regarded life as a cheap ransom for freedom. But here large deductions must be made. It may be doubtful whether Rome was ever a democratic republic. Slaves, which were seventy-five per cent. of the population, were always excluded from power; so were women. The history of Rome is occupied by struggles between the two orders of patricians and plebeians, the one trying to retain power, the other to secure it, and these struggles were not over when the republic was merged into the empire. The democracy of Rome did not conquer the provinces nor did it maintain them when conquered. The exigences of foreign warfare obliged the Romans to break through their most valued safeguards against the over-weening power of individuals. It is the great merit of Julius Cæsar to have seen that the empire gained by a republic could only be maintained by an emperor; and to have conceived the lines on which alone imperial government could be founded. The magnificent organization of the Roman world, one of the greatest civilizing agencies which mankind has ever witnessed, was the work of the emperors. Rome therefore, like Athens, although it has much to teach us of the evils of despotism and of the benefits of liberty, can afford us little if any knowledge as to the desirability or the method of establishing a democratic republic. We are apt to be misled by a confusion of ideas. The greatness of Athens and Rome was founded in both instances upon the expulsion of kings. The name of king was hateful to both peoples. In Rome it was never resumed even when the monarchy was restored. But the kings, when they were expelled, were despots, armed with spiritual as well as temporal power, who respected neither the liberties nor the lives or property of their subjects. The Romans had no conception of a constitutional monarchy; when it was their interest to have established one, they blundered again into despotism.

After Greece and Rome we come to the Italian republics of the Middle Ages. There were city States without slaves, and there is a remarkable similarity between them and the city republics of ancient Greece. Indeed the only adequate illustrations of Aristotle's political theories in modern history are to be found in these republics; but they can hardly be taken as democratic republics. Some of them were never democratic at all, but were always under the influence of a dominant family and took the side of the emperor against the pope. Even Florence was democratic only for a very short space; its government, at first confined to a few privileged families, was gradually extended till it reached the hands of the mass of the people; but almost at this very moment it came within the grasp of the Medici, who eventually moulded it into something which was indistinguishable from a monarchy.

Besides the political fallacies which I have endeavoured to expose there are others which concern the literary and artistic development of republics. It is often asserted that the highest culture of literature and art goes hand in hand with popular freedom, if not with the fervour, of religious belief. Whether this was the case in Athens or not, I am unable to state. My own view of the age of Pericles differs from that usually held. I think that in Athens the sudden ripening of the highest art was due to an individual rather than to a popular movement. But in Italy it can be said with certainty that the only connection between the expansion of art and the expansion of freedom was in that one had a bad influence over the other; one grew as the other declined. Raphael, Michael Angelo, and Leonardo served selfish tyrants and worldly popes. In fact, men will always do that which they find to be most interesting or most amusing. If politics are interesting, the best minds will take to them; if business, as in America, is more exciting than politics, it will attract the services of the best minds. When, under a bad form of government, participation in politics is impossible, and business does not exist, the noblest minds will devote themselves to literature and art, unless indeed the form of government is so bad that literature and art cannot breathe under it. When the national consciousness becomes thoroughly corrupted by the loss of habitual power and self-respect, the most active minds of the nation will either leave it or wallow in self-indulgence and extravagance, in gambling and in lust. I have I hope now shown that although much of our enthusiasm for republican government is derived from the memories of Athens, Rome and Florence, yet few practical arguments can be drawn from the history of these States which would lead us to prefer a democratic republic to a constitutional monarchy.

Passing to more modern times, we have before us the great example of the Dutch republic of the United Provinces. It is respectable in its origin and glorious in its history. Founded upon the ardent love of religious freedom, it attained a position in Europe to which neither its size nor its population entitled it. It is difficult for us nowadays to realize that Holland was ever a first-class power. During the seventeenth century it was the refuge of all who were persecuted for their religious or political opinions, monarchs as well as philosophers. It gave William III. to England, and it may well have inspired republican statesmen with the conviction that their utopias were not impossible. Yet there are several reasons why the example of Holland is not of any special service to the democratic republican of to-day. In the first place, it was a federation, and a federation of the loosest kind. America and Switzerland are both federations. There are many reasons why it is easier for federations to be organized as republics than as monarchies, and the success of the new republic in Brazil may possibly depend upon whether it is or is not organized as a federation. In the next place, Holland was never a democracy without passing into a monarchy. Its history is very curious and instructive. Comparatively weak in itself, it was forced to depend largely on its two more powerful neighbours, England and France. France desiring that it should be as weak as possible, encouraged jealousies between the provinces and undermined the authority of the stadtholder, who held something of a regal position. England desiring that Holland should be strong, encouraged the power of the stadtholder and succeeded sometimes in giving the republic almost the form of a monarchy. The separate provinces were governed by a jealous oligarchy of merchants, who regarded the common people with a hatred which was fully reciprocated. The stadtholder depended on the democracy. In a time of peace the oligarchy raised its head and the stadtholder was depressed; in times when war threatened the voice of self-preservation demanded a stronger government, the democracy triumphed over the abused oligarchy, but in its triumph went far to create a monarchy. The government of Holland thus far may be said to have oscillated between a Whig oligarchy and a Tory democracy, neither of these forms approaching our ideal of a democratic republic.

We next pass to America—to a republic created by the thinkers who learnt philosophy in Holland and experience in England. From the rebellion of 1776 arose the American constitution based upon the fundamental principle that all men are equal. Here we have for the first time in history a genuine democratic republic, with neither an oligarchy nor a stadtholder; undoubtedly a most important epoch in the history of the world and one likely to produce far-reaching results. What then has the democratic republic of 1776 to teach us at the present day? Nothing; and for two reasons : it was federal and it was a failure. The federal tie between the thirteen provinces was permissive and not compulsory; taxes were not paid, contingents were not provided, laws were not enforced, parliaments were not attended. After ten years' trial the failure became so glaring that a revision of the constitution became absolutely necessary. A president had to be elected, who was invested for a limited period with more than the power of an English sovereign. Alexander Hamilton, the most vigorous critic of the old constitution, desired to establish something even more closely resembling a monarchy. This second constitution has now lasted for just a hundred years, and has contributed to the marvellous prosperity of the great continent of the West in a way in which no other form of government could have contributed. Undoubtedly republicans look mainly to it when they advocate that form of constitution. We shall presently inquire in detail what are the lessons which we are able to derive from it.

The revolution in France was the natural consequence of the revolution in America; but the French Revolution did not at first lead to the establishment of a democratic republic. The National Assembly formed out of the States-General soon transformed itself into a constituent assembly for the purpose of drawing up a new constitution. During this period the Royal power still remained unimpaired in theory and only slightly weakened in practice. The result of its labours was the creation of a constitutional monarchy which was ineffective from its birth and which never came into active operation. The Royal authority, a mere shadow after the flight to Varennes, was formally abolished after the tenth of August. A period of anarchy succeeded. The Directory, which was in some sense a democratic republic, besides being occupied entirely with military triumphs and defeats, was avowedly only a transition to a more permanent state of things, while the consular government of Siéyès, intended by its author to be a democratic republic of the most elaborate and efficient kind, was turned by the astuteness of Napoleon into something scarcely distinguishable from a despotism. It will thus be seen that the French Revolution did not establish any government which can be taken as a model of a democratic republic. The democratic republic of 1848 was too short-lived to afford materials for a judgment on its defects or merits, and it is not until the present French Republic, founded in 1871 on the ruins of the second empire, that we reach a form of government in France which can supply profitable lessons to other countries which may desire to inaugurate a similar experiment.

Passing from these historical considerations, let us view republican government as it exists in the world at the present time. According to the authority of the "Government Year-Book" the number of republics and monarchies in the world are very nearly equal. Counting Brazil as a republic, there are twenty-four monarchies in the world, and twenty-six republics. But if we make the comparison either by population or by extent of territory, we shall find that by far the most important portions of the world are under monarchical government. Of these twenty-six republics, sixteen are in South America. Their constitution is so uncertain, and they are subject to such constant revolutions, that they do not afford us much information either on one side or the other. Their constitutions are generally formed on the model of the United States, with the exception that the president is sometimes elected for six, and sometimes for two years, and that in several cases he is incapable of re-election. After the review of these States, and of some other small republics which resemble them, we find that the only three republics which deserve serious consideration are those of America, France, and Switzerland, and in what I have to say further I shall confine myself to them.

It would take too long to examine the constitutions of these three countries in detail. The proper treatment of any one of them would demand at least an entire essay. As a republic could only be reached in this country by the abolition of the monarchy and the election of a president, I shall limit my remarks to the office of the president alone, and raise the question how, if it were desirable to set up a republic in this country, we should set about it and what type of republican government we should choose. It happens that the three republics I have mentioned present each of them a different type of president, and exhaust, I believe, all possible types of president. In America the president is elected for four years. He is capable of re-election, but it is an unwritten law of the constitution that he shall never be elected for more than a second time. An elaborate system is provided by the constitution for his election by indirect or dual voting. That is, certain electors are appointed in each State, equal in number to the whole number of senators and representatives possessed by that State. These electors come together and elect a president. It was hoped that the election of president would in this way be removed from the influence of popular turmoil and passion, that he would be chosen by the wisest men of the country, acting under a stern sense of responsibility. The pressure of party feeling has changed all this. The electors, instead of exercising their own judgment, consider themselves mere delegates for the expression of the wishes of others. No case has been known for many years of their voting in any other way than according to the instructions which they have received from their constituents. The election of president, which occurs every four years, is a purely popular election, carried on with every excitement which accompanies such occurrences, and with every device for securing victory which ingenuity unbridled by conscientiousness can suggest. With the example of America before his eyes, no lawgiver would have any confidence in elaborating a plan for choosing the head of the State by the suffrage of the wisest and best.

The president is commander-in-chief of the army and navy of the United States, and of the State militia in time of war; he has a very large power of appointment, subject in some cases to the approval of the Senate, which is not likely to be withheld; above all, he has an extensive power of veto on legislation, and Mr. Bryce tells us that a president is popular in proportion as he makes free use of this power. The president of the United States, therefore, is much more than a constitutional sovereign. He has far more power than the Queen of England. He not only reigns, but governs. The command of the forces by sea and land was found to be no mere formality in the days of President Lincoln. It was only by straining this power to the full that he was able to crush the rebellion of the South. Even if the Queen has technically the power of appointing ministers and officials, this really rests in the hands of the prime minister, who is responsible for any mistake which may be made in the use of it. The Crown still possesses the power of veto in England, but it has not been exercised since the reign of Queen Anne. Circumstances are conceivable under which it might again be used, although it is generally regarded as a dead letter; but we cannot imagine anything resembling the wholesale veto of an American president, who may set himself during his whole term of office in direct opposition to the popular will as expressed in Congress. The American ideal, as worked out in practice, is therefore a monarch of the Prussian type, invested with very great powers which he is not at all indisposed to use, and limited only by the short duration of his office. An unpopular or mischievous president must be borne with during his four years' term, unless he does anything which renders him liable to impeachment. He may not be re-elected, but if replaced in the White House, he has another four years' period, during which he may give the rein to his personal principles and predilections. The presidents of the United States have generally been strong men with well-marked characters. Were Englishmen to adopt a constitution of this kind, we should undoubtedly expect our very best statesmen —our Gladstones and Salisburys—to occupy the presidential chair. Whether we should be gainers by this arrangement, is a matter which will be discussed later on.

The president of the French republic is of a different type. He is elected for seven years by the absolute majority of the National Assembly; that is, the Senate and the Chamber of Deputies meeting together in congress. By the constitution he has very large powers, but they are limited in practice, that is, as far as in our short experience practice can be a guide. He selects his cabinet, who are, however, responsible to the chambers. He may initiate legislation, he has the right of pardon, he commands the army and the navy, and he may dissolve the Chamber of Deputies when he pleases. But in the exercise of all these duties and privileges he must act with the general advice and concurrence of his ministers, who are, jointly and severally, responsible for their acts to both chambers. The president cannot declare war without the previous consent of the Chambers.

It will thus be seen that the president of the French Republic is a constitutional monarch of the English type. During the seven years of his office he reigns, but he does not govern. He is the figure-head of the State; he represents the State to foreign powers and in public functions. It is not easy to say what part he takes in the ordinary transaction of public business. Certain it is that he is not prime minister, and that he has to appoint a large number of prime ministers of very different types, with many of whom he can be only in very limited sympathy. President Grévy, during his first term of office, between January, 1879, and December, 1885, appointed no less than nine prime ministers, and during the two years of his second term of office as many as four. It seems essential that if a president of this type be adopted he should be incapable of being removed during the seven years of his office. He must make up by stability what he lacks in actual power. Unfortunately the French have not found themselves able to abide by this principle. President Grévy was turned out of office by the fact that no ministers could be found to take office under him. He fell in consequence of the scandals attaching to the actions of his son-in-law, and it would seem that by the establishment of this evil principle, the corner-stone of the republican edifice has been shaken. It is not certain whether English republicans would look forward to having a president of the French type. It is difficult to see what would be gained by it. No statesman of the first rank would care to occupy a position so inferior in influence to that of prime minister. It would fall either to some excellent or worthy duke, who, in old days, might have been accepted as the figure-head of a coalition government, or to a statesman of mature years, who had no longer any chance of reaching the highest office. But should we gain very much if we had an elected Duke of Westminster as life president instead of a Prince of Wales?

Yet another form of republic is exhibited to us by the little country of Switzerland. Here the executive government is vested in the federal council of seven members, and the president is merely the chairman of the council, elected every year. A short time ago a Swiss president died during his term of office, and Europe woke up to the consciousness that such an official existed. Some people might imagine that this form would suit England with certain necessary alterations. They might say, Why should not your cabinet be your federal council, and your president the head of your cabinet for the time being? This might work well in ordinary times, although it is possible that Lord Salisbury would not desire to assume the burden of ceremony which must attach to the head of a great country, in addition to the two loads which he has now imposed upon himself—the offices of Prime Minister and Foreign Secretary. But how would this work in a change of ministry? Who would receive the seals of the outgoing ministers, and confer them on their new possessors? Who would select a prime minister, or conduct the delicate negociations by which the construction of a cabinet is effected? The Swiss federal council is elected once every three years by the several councils of the cantons. Ministerial crises do not occur in Switzerland, or are found there in a very mitigated form. No incongruity is felt in two members of the council, sitting next to each other, holding fundamentally different opinions on some important question of politics. The Swiss system has not been imitated elsewhere, and is, probably, only suited for a country under federal government, which has no foreign politics, and in which the stress of burning questions of policy is broken by their reference, in the first place, to the provincial assemblies, and, in the second place, by the *referendum*, to the judgment of the entire people.

Let us suppose, for sake of argument, that it had been determined to establish a republic in England with a president of the American type. Two important questions would have to be settled, how the president should be elected, and what should be the term of his office. I do not imagine that any one would wish a president to have the same tenure as a prime minister, that is to remain in office so long as he could command a majority in the House of Commons, and no longer. The duration of his office would probably be fixed either at three, four, or seven years; that is, taking the term either of triennial or septennial parliaments, or of the American presidency. Three or four years would probably be found too short a term; the country would be kept in continual agitation about new elections; seven years, the present nominal duration of parliament, would not be found excessive. But in seven years the mind of the country has plenty of time to change. Let us take two examples, one from the history of the last century, and one

from that of this. Between the general elections of
1780 and 1784 there were five changes of Ministry in
England, the Ministry of Lord North, of Lord Rockingham, of Lord Shelburne, the coalition Ministry of
Fox and North, and the Ministry of William Pitt.
During that period peace had been made with
America, and with Europe. How is it conceivable
that a single president of the American type could
have remained at the head of public affairs during
such violent changes of public feeling and such
alterations of public policy? It was possible for
George III., it might be possible for Presidents
Grévy, or Carnot, but it would not be possible for a
party leader, chosen with all the machinery of party
organization, and representing the principles of party
conviction, as well as the passions of party conflict.
Again, suppose that Mr. Gladstone had been elected
president in 1885, as he was made prime minister,
and had then revealed his project of Home Rule for
Ireland. How could he have remained in office as
president to carry out, I will not say a policy of
coercion, because that we may consider unnecessary,
but a unionist policy of any kind? Again, suppose
that Lord Salisbury had become president, instead of
prime minister, in 1886, determined to enforce a long
period of resolute government in Ireland, and to
oppose every obstacle to the policy of entrusting the
Irish with the management of their own affairs.
Not only would it have been difficult for the minority in the country to have given expression to
its convictions during his seven years of office, but it
would be scarcely reasonable to anticipate a perfectly

fair expression of public opinion, even at the termination of that office. The power wielded by a president, who, for the time being, was a monarch as well as a prime minister, would undoubtedly be used to secure the victory, for another septennial term, of the principles which the president was elected to maintain, even if they were those of a minority. Under the constitutional system of England, or even of France, the strongest passions may seeth and the most opposing interests may collide without endangering the security of the commonweal. In America, and in Switzerland, these conflicts, if they exist at all, are discounted and dissipated by spending their violence in the separate States before they attack the central Government. In England, and in France, where no highly developed local government exists, they would, under a president of the American type, either bring us within measurable distance of civil war, or would overthrow the very foundations of the constitution by forcibly abridging the term for which, by the constitution, the president was to maintain his office. Such would be the disadvantages of a septennial president. If a less term were chosen, no device of election would, I think, be found to break the violence of party struggle. It would matter little whether the president were chosen by the direct suffrage of the nation or by the Parliament which had just been elected by that means. In times of excitement the popular will would certainly make itself felt, and members would be sent to Parliament with a mandate to elect a particular president.

We must take into account another consideration

of great importance. By our present system we are able to obtain the services of our statesmen for very long periods, whether in office or in opposition, and a statesman can do almost as much good in opposition as he can in office. No statesman has left a higher reputation than Sir Robert Peel, yet the greater part of his life was spent in opposition. Mr. Gladstone has been in parliament for nearly sixty years; he was prime minister twenty-four years ago. Pitt held an unbroken premiership for seventeen years. The Duke of Wellington, having attained the position of arbiter of Europe, in 1815, afterwards held nearly every cabinet office, was prime minister at several important crises, and served the State till his death. We do not find this state of things in America. American presidents have been on the whole distinguished men and powerful personalities, but they have frequently not been heard of until they attained the position of president. The exercise of a subordinate office will often, in the case of a powerful man, raise up enmity sufficient to prevent him from occupying the headship of the State. After their eight years of service, if they have the fortune to serve eight years, they must retire into insignificance. President Lincoln and President Garfield were shot during their term of office, so that we cannot speculate as to what Lincoln would have done after his retirement, or as to what Garfield's career would have been. But President Grant, as we know, after engaging in commercial ventures which were not very successful, died in comparative poverty, forced to provide for his old age by selling his personal reminiscences at a high price. Public pensions were subscribed for Mrs. Lincoln and Mrs. Garfield. An ex-president is too great a man to serve in a subordinate capacity, just as Pitt was too powerful in himself to give any efficient support to the ministry of Addington. It is rare, even in England, for an ex-prime minister to be able to accept a subordinate office in any future Cabinet. This evil is of importance in America because two ideas with regard to office are inveterate in their political system, and are very different from those which prevail in our own. One of them is that all constituencies must be represented by local candidates; and the other, that there should be a certain round or succession of offices, and that they should not be monopolized by a single individual. But if, during the last hundred and fifty years, our foremost statesmen had been limited to eight years' exercise of supreme power, some of the most glorious pages in our annals would not have been written. It has been argued that if the monarchy were abolished, its functions might be exercised by a board of commissioners, but this board in a great country must have a head who would be virtually president.

Another matter which demands our consideration is the comparative cost of royal and presidential government. The advocates of a republic frequently complain of the cost of a monarchy, perhaps not without reason. But it is difficult to calculate the expense of government in any State. It does not depend merely on the expense of the head of the State, or on the nature of his allowances; we must

F. V. A A

take into our view the whole machinery of government, and compare the whole cost in one case with the whole cost in the other, as well as the comparative efficiency of the two systems. In America there is certainly much to be complained of. Inhabitants of American towns will tell you that the rates are extremely heavy, and yet the services which they are supposed to provide for are not performed. Streets are not paved, houses are not drained, gas and water are not properly supplied, although they are provided for five times over in the rates. The money destined for them goes into the pockets of town committees, and never comes out again. We are free from this pest in England. Again, public offices are regarded as a source of profit, and of profit alone. It is difficult to get work done without pay. Nor is this confined to America. The republican government of France has for some years past possessed the evil reputation of being a ring for the enrichment of its members. I do not say that corruption is unknown under monarchical forms of government; in Spain and in Greece, and perhaps in Italy, but it is practically unknown in England. Undoubtedly these evils would be incompatible with a high sense of duty, and public duty is generally reckoned as one of the stern virtues of republicanism. But a sense of duty amongst weak and frail mortals is largely maintained by social influences and sanctions. In a society which is based upon the fundamental principle of *noblesse oblige*, where there is a gradation of honour spreading from the crown to all ranks of society, taking multitudinous forms, some tangible, some intangible, but all contributing to the idea that unpaid service to the State is the obligation of all its members in their several spheres, and that such service brings with it a valuable reward in the recognition and appreciation of those where appreciation is most worth having, corruption is not likely to exist, paid work will be well done, and unpaid work will be abundant, and indeed incalculable. In a more advanced stage of social morality, a republic might appeal to the effort of its members more than a monarchy, but it is always dangerous to base a system of action upon a standard of morality higher than that which we have good reason to believe exists. *Quid leges sine moribus vanæ proficiunt?* Laws cannot teach morality; they must lag behind it if they are to be effective and crystallize the ordinary manifestations of the current morality into a solid custom, from which retrogression is difficult. It has not been my object in this essay to pronounce a panegyric upon monarchy or to decry republicanism. A wise and good monarch would, I think, look forward to the time when his people might be fit to do without him and to govern themselves. Those who have an enthusiasm for democracy believe that a community worse governed by itself is a more satisfactory object of contemplation than one better governed by an aristocracy. It is right that we should look with admiration upon those rare instances where prosperous and virtuous republics have been established for the good and the advantage of all, upon the Athens of Pericles and upon the Florence of Dante, upon the Geneva of Calvin, or upon the Massachusetts of the

Pilgrim Fathers. May the dreams of Milton and Algernon Sidney become realities, and may we perpetually invigorate our political principles by recurrence to the highest level of political speculation. But if we are Republicans by conviction or by sentiment, we should look facts fairly in the face, and calmly consider what a republic in England would mean, and take the best counsel we can as to the only means by which it can be brought about.

www.ingramcontent.com/pod-product-compliance
Lightning Source LLC
Chambersburg PA
CBHW032351230426
43672CB00007B/667